I0539687

PRAYER

THE BELIEVER'S SPIRITUAL UMBILACAL CORD:
CONCEPTS, PRINCIPLES AND VALUE

ONÓRIO CUTANE

PRAYER

The Believer's Spiritual Umbilical Cord
CONCEPTS, PRINCIPLES, AND VALUE

ONÓRIO CUTANE

Copyright © 2024 by Onório Cutane

All rights reserved. No part of this publication may be reproduced, distributed, or transmitted in any form or by any means, including, photocopying,recording, or other electronic or mechanical methods, without the prior written permission of the copyright owner and the publisher, except in the case of brief quotations embodied in critical reviews and certain other noncommercial uses permitted by copyright law. For permission requests, write to the publisher, addressed "Attention: Permissions Coordinator," at the address below.

ARPress
45 Dan Road Suite 5
Canton MA 02021
Hotline: 1(888) 821-0229
Fax: 1(508) 545-7580

Ordering Information:
Quantity sales. Special discounts are available on quantity purchases by corporations, associations, and others. For details, contact the publisher at the address above.

Printed in the United States of America.

ISBN-13:   Softcover   979-8-89389-670-1
                  eBook   979-8-89389-671-8

Library of Congress Control Number: 2024921846

Table of Contents

Preface

In my tenth book, "The Four Essential Habits of a New Creature in Christ," which preceded this piece, I gave a treaty on the habit of prayer. Prayer constitutes one of the most profound and essential habits of a new creature in Christ. In that work, as in a shallow flight, I touched on prayer and part of its definition almost superficially. All with the aim of injecting the reader the desire and discipline to pray - an indispensable habit for his spiritual growth and stability as a citizen of the Kingdom of Heaven. Prayer can be described as the habit of the great champions of whom we read and study in the Holy Scriptures. Jesus prayed, and the prophets and apostles of the past prayed. The patriarchs Abraham, Isaac, and Jacob were men of altars, and they all prayed.

An interesting aspect of all of them is that because of this exercise of prayer, they solved problems that seemed to have no solution, like Solomon, who asked God for knowledge. They won fierce battles as King Asa did against an enemy army of a million soldiers and chariots who were numerically superior to them. They interceded, like Abraham and Moses, to the point of changing certain drastic decisions that God had already taken against the people rebelling against his word. Some, like Moses, were transfigured and had the skin of their faces glowing with glory. Others were defeated giants, covered the mouths of bears and lions, escaped death and macabre plans, and had their dead resurrected. Still, others were even called friends of God, as in Abraham's case.

What did they all have? Close intimacy with God. If we superficially define prayer as just communication with God, we wouldn't be doing justice to this great spiritual principle. In prayer, there was more than communication; there was intimacy, trust, and surrender that enabled man's spirit to hear God's voice and not just talk to Him. Most believers today have made prayer a ritual or habit they must exercise for their spiritual growth. However, few are those who have really listened to the voice of God. Is prayer just something one-sided, where man invokes God, and He doesn't answer? Well, it was the Lord who said, "Call to me, and I will answer you and tell you great and unsearchable things you do not know" (Jeremiah 33:3 NIV). Looking at these words from God, we can notice three key things:

First: the invitation to pray. It's God who extends this invitation – he calls out to me. Many looked at prayer as crying out and shouting in the past. As the Psalmist says in Psalms 34:15 NIV, "The eyes of the Lord are on the righteous, and his ears are attentive to their cry." The reason it is described as *crying out* isn't because of the cry but because of the enthusiasm; that is, it shows that it was something that came out of the heart and not just because words were spoken through the mouth. We notice here that prayer must come out of the heart, and it's not enough to just open one's mouth and speak, assuming that one is talking to God. True prayer springs from a heart surrendered to God, trusting in Him, and depending on Him.

The mouth only verbally expresses what was already fertilized in the heart. God examines hearts and knows the intention of the spirit. That is why the apostle Peter simplified the interpretation by replacing "clamor" with "prayer." So, depending on the purpose and circumstances of the one praying - whether clamoring, speaking, or meditating - the source of prayer should be the heart. That is where God interacts with man. The scripture shows us the God who invites us to pray. Soon, we realize that we participate in the process - talking to God in prayer. But this is the level that many are at. After reaching this level, they no longer proceed to the other levels foreseen by God, who invites us to pray.

This book will provide revelations and divine principles that will raise you to this level of spiritual awareness through the work of the Holy Spirit in your life. You must ask yourself: why does God invite us to pray? Because of the second point.

Second: He wants to answer our prayers. Christianity is not a religion but a communion with God - through Christ. And in communion, we talk to God, and He talks to us. Here is one of the major differences. In many pagan religions, their adherents pray and invoke to their god or gods. Still, it's a one-way communication since they can neither speak nor respond. And if they cannot respond, why pray then? It reminds me of the prophet of God, Elijah, who made fun of the 450 or so prophets of Baal who had started praying from noon until the afternoon without any response from him. Elijah even mocked them, saying that maybe Baal was asleep, tired, or had traveled. Several sacrifices, shouts, dances, and rituals were made to invoke Baal. Still, Baal never answered because he was not God and never was. The fact that most were on the side of this idol, and he had his prophets, worshippers, and temples, didn't mean that he was God and could answer their prayers. But this is precisely what has been happening in the world: people get tired of clamoring, performing ceremonies, rituals, and prayers to a god who doesn't speak, doesn't answer and doesn't act. Even so, they don't stop to reflect, repent from this practice of idolatry, and turn to Jehovah - the Father of our Lord and Savior, Jesus Christ. It's only He (the Lord) who is God, and it's only Him that we should worship and serve.

In Elijah's time, people were living in idolatry. It was part of his mandate to bring the children's hearts back to their parents - to bring the children's faith back to God and to guide them to the straight ways of their parents in faith. Notice that Elijah just prayed, "Answer Lord, that it may be known that you are God." What happened? God answered Elijah's prayer by sending fire from heaven that consumed the stone altars and licked the surrounding water. And in the face of this deed, all the people cried out in unison, "The Lord alone is God." Without a shadow of a doubt, they all returned to their homes, knowing they were walking with and serving a God who heard and answered prayers.

Dear reader, feel the Holy Spirit's impression in your heart, His promptings inviting you to pray. When was the last time you spent time with God? Many pray but expect no answer. Why do you pray? Others answer: "Because it's a habit, it's a ritual. In my church, we were told that we must pray. So, we pray." Do you expect an answer? "Oh no, I'm just doing my duty." Many people consider prayer a ritual; when they forget to have prayed at a specific scheduled time, they feel bad, as if they have betrayed God. They carry a feeling of guilt for not having followed the ritual. But prayer is not like that. It's lubricating a relationship between God and His children. It's communion, so there must always be desire, pleasure, and willingness to talk to your heavenly Father because something good happens in our spirit when we pray. When you pray, you should expect answers. Why would God invite us to pray if He doesn't want to answer? It's more than clear that He has the desire and pleasure to answer our prayers by speaking to us and granting our petitions. This is where faith in prayer is born: we pray expectantly, waiting for answers. Whenever I pray, the Lord answers me, and I will share with you some of the principles that govern effective prayer.

Third: The Scripture says, "I will show you wonderful and mighty things." This is what also happens when we pray. Prayer increases the sensitivity of man's spirit and elevates him to hear and see things in the spirit. God wants you to pray because when you pray, you will also be able to see things you couldn't see with your carnal eyes without His illumination in your spirit.

Whenever I pray, I see in my spirit, I see in my imagination - I travel in spirit to territories and arenas higher and more glorious than the physical ones. I am shown what to do and how to do it. In prayer, I have a direction for my life, so I make choices and decisions according to God's will.

Prayer aligns the spirit of man with the will of God. So we read in Acts that when God wanted to show Peter something, He inspired him to go up on the terrace to pray. Soon he went into a trance, a trance of senses, and saw a sheet with various animals on it. After this, he heard the voice of the Holy Spirit speaking to him, giving him direction concerning the men that Cornelius - the Roman centurion who wanted to be saved - had sent.

We read an identical scenario in Revelation 4 when John saw an open door in heaven and was taken in the spirit. He saw Jesus sitting on the throne and heard a voice saying, "Come up here, and I will show you things which must take place after this."

You can know about the future without being a prophet. It is the ministry of the Holy Spirit guiding us into all truth and revealing the future to us. As Jesus said, "He will guide you into all truth and show you things to come." All this is possible through prayer. Moments of prayer are moments of revelation, spiritual elevation, and activation of the awareness of the spiritual world around us. Through Elisha's prayer, his eyes were opened, and he saw in the spirit that there were chariots and horses of fire around him. These chariots and horses of fire were there to protect God's servant. Therefore, he was not afraid.

The background is that we should pray and that prayer has many benefits for men in communion with their Creator.

This book isn't a comprehensive treaty on prayer but rather a contribution to Christian literature and the body of Christ worldwide, from the simple believer to ministers of the gospel. It seeks to answer questions concerning its concept, motivations, principles, and benefits. In other words, the reader will have answers to the questions, even if not entirely, but in terms of encouragement to study prayer in depth: what is prayer, and why should we pray? How should we pray, and what are the benefits of prayer?

I use plain language in this piece, which is simple to understand. Read it with an open heart, absorbing its revelations and applying the divine principles presented in your practical life. I hope it will be helpful to you in your spiritual journey with God.

PART I

The Concept of Prayer

Introduction

Prayer constitutes one of the fundamental and indispensable elements of our communion with God. It's a determining factor in the contact between the spiritual and the physical because of the legality and intensity of heaven's impact on earth. God's intervention in the lives of men on the earthly plane depends on it. All the great men and women of God who passed through this earth and had their names engraved in the annals of history or the chronicles of the heroes of the faith were people of prayer. Their communion with God in prayer gave them the faith and conviction with which they defeated adverse kingdoms that were numerically superior to them. This was the case of King Josaphat when three kingdoms joined together to attack the kingdom of Judah.

In this battle, they didn't have to fight. God fought for them, and they saw the corpses of the enemy armies slaughtered without human intervention. It was up to them only to gather the plunder of goods, livestock, gold, silver, and clothing, which lasted almost three days. At the end of it all, it was a story of sorrow and a threat that turned into a glorious end of passive victory. The same can be said of King Hezekiah, who prayed together with the prophet Isaiah after being threatened by King Sennacherib of Assyria. In response, God sent only one angel who exterminated about 185,000 braves of the invading Assyrian army. In this example, they won without having fought physically. Their prayer of faith was much more than a weapon of spiritual warfare; it was a spiritual missile of great impact.

The truth is that other characters described in the Holy Scriptures faced challenges and problems with almost similar harmfulness to those we face in the 21st century. Yet, they overcame them all through prayer, whether at the level of health-related challenges or the threat to peace, prosperity, and stability. What about Queen Esther, who, through prayer, saved her people from the almost irrevocable plan of extermination drawn up by Haman?

Haman was an enemy of the Jews. Yet, in the last hour, and almost to the time he was already celebrating the success of his genocidal and gruesome plan against God's people, he saw his entire lobbying row and his influence on the Assyrian government being thwarted. He finally hanged on the gallows he had prepared for Mordecai, in what in common jargon could be described as "he was caught in his own web." How did Esther manage to have an irrevocable law repealed and sealed with the ring of the law? How did she consequently annul all the royal plans and decrees already written, ratified, and published, awaiting only their execution and which, after humanly observed and analyzed, were irrevocable and unchangeable? The answer persists: it was through prayer. It seems to us that prayer is an instrument with a deeper potential than what is commonly understood and regularly done nowadays by believers, that is, Christians or in other circles of those who invoke divinities over their affairs on earth.

The concept of prayer itself is so common that it's almost seen by many as a simple and already easily understood subject that we don't need to study in depth. This is because tens of thousands of believers and followers pray daily in their homes and every religious service until prayer becomes a ritual. A ritual where everyone knows they must pray and sets a fixed time each day to pray, or the laziest do it only during services or masses in churches, mosques, and other places. Looking at prayer from this point of view is to confiscate it of its true value, its most profound meaning, and its latent power to impact, improve and change the course of events here on earth. It's easy to notice this, as many believers read in the Holy Bible about God's extraordinary deeds in answer to the prayers of his children, as recounted to us in the Scripture. But why don't we see the same results that they had and have the same or even better experiences that they had? Because there is something about the prayer they knew and practiced that gave life to their fellowship. That is, to the interaction with God that opened the heavens and put angels into action, battling on behalf of God's people. All this shows us that we must get out of the traditional view of prayer and ascend like John into lofty arenas of glory.

John was in prayer on the Lord's Day and a door opened in heaven, and a voice said, "Come up here, and I will show you what must take place after this" (Revelation 4:1 NIV). In verse 2, John recounts that he was caught up in spirit; before him was a throne set in heaven and one sitting on it. The background here is that he had experiences with the supernatural: he was taken in spirit into an immaterial world, a heavenly atmosphere, that is, into heavenly places, and two things happened to him: he saw and heard in the spirit. He was even shown what was to happen.

For the rest, you, dear reader, and we in general as God's church, can and should all have these and various experiences with God. But to do so, we must rise to "the here."

There are two planes: earthly and heavenly. Many people have lived several years and had countless experiences with the earthly "here." However, they find it very strange and even crazy when some of us, born again and Spirit-filled with an intimate fellowship with God, talk, write, preach, and talk about our experiences with the heavenly "here." This is because it's a higher dimension than this world's carnal and ordinary men. It's from here that, in interaction with God in prayer, we exert influence and literally dictate and change the course of things and events here on earth. Jesus told the religious Jews that they had the law of Moses, the letter, not the Spirit. He also said to them that they had religion without fellowship with the God they prayed to. However, they had never had experiences and stubbornly and ritually persisted in teaching about the God of whom they had never heard anything. It was for a theology without *theocommunionlogy*. I created this concept to designate a state of intimate communion with God rather than someone who scientifically or rationally studied and read about God in the seats of theological schools. Those try to define the God with whom they had never had any experience.

The truth is that the people who revolutionized the world of their time impacted it in various realms and spheres of human life. They were not those who had come out of mental absorption and apprehension of the knowledge of God through rational human investigation; instead, they were men who had experiences with God. Men who traveled to heaven in spirit, like the apostle Paul, sailed in the spirit with the spiritual navigator called the Holy Spirit and even saw things that would happen even after their contemporary time. Isaiah saw the passion of Christ and the glories that would follow (Isaiah 53:4-8); Daniel predicted the time of the antichrist. Men who escaped from the fiery furnace, like the three young men Abednego, Meshach, and Shadrach, who did not fear the wrath of the king.

On the contrary, trusting in their God, they preferred to be thrown into the fiery furnace rather than agree to worship the king's statue, which was an idol that neither spoke nor heard. Where did they get this boldness, courage, determination, and firmness? The answer is simple and obvious: from their intimate fellowship with God. They knew their God. These were the words of Daniel, their countryman, "...but the people who know their God shall be strong, and carry out great exploits" (Daniel 11:32). He himself had escaped from the den of hungry lions because he not only knew his God but also had fellowship with him.

Dear reader, I am listing several of these examples so that first, you may thirst and hunger to grow in communion with God. Second, you may have a new approach and perspective on prayer and leave behind the traditional and culturally seen ritual.

Notice that we often read about men and women of faith in the Bible and try to have faith in our own way, thinking that we just have to read the Bible, and soon we have it. But it's not like that; they didn't read the manuscripts rationally and academically as many do today. Instead, they looked at the Scriptures as the living words of God with which they order and arrange their lives. God's word was seen as a kind of constitution of God's kingdom that ruled and regulated the lives of his people. When they obeyed, they were blessed and prosperously victorious. As God said through Moses that his words were life. He himself stated that not by bread alone shall man live, but by every word that proceeded out of the mouth of God. It was the fellowship they had that strengthened their faith. They listened to the word to practice it and not use it as a garment they could change whenever it wasn't convenient, as we witness these days with many promiscuous Christians. So why are many believers today not steadfast and consequently walking around worried, frustrated, and fearful? Why are they unable to defend their faith? Because they have no convictions but say they have faith.

Now, faith, as the Scripture defines it in Hebrews 11:1, is the assurance (conviction) of things hoped for and the evidence of things not seen, and by it, the ancients' obtained testimonies. Where are the testimonies of 21st-century believers? If they were placed in the same situations or faced similar challenges as the men and women we read about in the Holy Bible, they wouldn't have the same testimonies. Many would deny Jesus and abandon their faith. That is why Paul prayed for the Ephesians, "...according to the riches of His glory, to be strengthened with might through His Spirit in the inner man, that Christ may dwell in your hearts through faith; that you, being rooted and grounded in love" (Ephesians 3:16-17 NKJV). Paul prayed that these brethren would be rooted in faith and love in Christ and for other brethren. Did you notice that it took Paul's knees in continual prayer for this church that they would come to steadfastness in the faith? Otherwise, life circumstances can cause you to abort the Christ in your heart, sinking in faith.

The average believer today (at least according to what I have observed) lacks conviction, and many need to have the fear of the Lord in their hearts. Faced with a seemingly compromising situation in their faith, they would sink. Why? Because they don't have the conviction and the joy of salvation and don't have intimate fellowship with God. In Acts 4:13, Luke recounts the incident where Peter, along with John, were confronted by the religious consortium of the then-Jewish court (the Sanhedrin). They were questioned about the miracle Peter had performed, which was healing a lame man from birth. In court, Peter and John did not cower or bite their tongues; on the contrary, they spoke with conviction and knowledge of the Jesus of whom they spoke and preached. The Scripture recounts that after seeing the boldness and conviction with which Peter and John spoke and informed that they were unlettered and untaught men, they recognized one very fundamental thing: "they had been with Jesus." Glory to God for communion with God! Glory to God for the privilege of praying.

At various times the Spirit will always put that desire and willingness in you to pray and talk to God. This represents a vital sign of your spirit. Without prayer, none of this would have happened.

Prayer, seen as the intimacy that produces the ability for you to hear God's voice in your spirit and act on it, brings forth and produces extraordinary results. Jesus told the religious Jews, "you are from here, but "I am not from here." So, dear reader, with this book, I invite you to rise to the "here" above and look at life from this dimension. This way, you will see that everything is possible and there is no unchanging situation. You will come out of any spiritual prison, as Peter was released from the maximum-security prison. All the effects of spiritual curses, covenants, and bans on your spiritual, sentimental, professional, ministerial, or academic life will be annulled.

It's time to rise to new dimensions of understanding God's word - the dimension of revelations and inspiration. It's time to rise to dimensions of glory and ministry - doing extraordinary things. It's time to *rise* to new dimensions of fellowship - developing intimacy with God, hearing his voice, and acting on it for life success and glory for God. It's time to *rise* to a life of active and practiced awareness of the spiritual world and the laws that make it work. This triggers spiritual laws with which you can influence life here on earth. It's time to *rise* to a spiritual level above the principalities, powers, and princes of the darkness of this century and intercede for the good of humanity, families, and nations. Essentially, it's time to step up and take your position as a spiritual watchman - defending and protecting lives and completing missions through intercessory prayer, stopping and neutralizing all the fiery darts of the evil one.

Finally, it's time to live on earth as if in heaven - aware of the spirit world around you. Aware of the power of your God; of the love and faithfulness of your Christ; the ministry and availability of the angels of healing, deliverance, protection, and warfare that God has predisposed to assist (help) us as heirs of salvation (Hebrews 1:14). Thus, we will fulfill Jesus' prayer model: "Your kingdom come, your will be done, on earth as it is in heaven" (Matthew 6:10 NKJV).

It's time to influence the earth and nations with the culture of the kingdom of heaven and to strengthen the fulfillment of God's will on earth - while maintaining its impact on the lives of human families.

The Holy Spirit imprinted in my heart to write this book to activate the glorious potential and miraculous power deposited by the Holy Spirit in the spirits of His children. Thus, you can find yourself in the center of God's will. You were propelled by the Spirit to be in the right place at the right time, doing the works you were meant to do here on earth: live a full and fulfilled life in every way to the honor and glory of the Lord Jesus Christ.

Prayer is one of those spiritual vectors whose treatment cannot be exhausted in a sermon or book. It's one of the greatest spiritual laws that cannot be ignored because in it lies the essence of the eternity of our communion with God. From salvation to eternity, we will always have to speak and hear from God. In this relationship of intimacy with God, a solid foundation is established on which we grow in faith. We are stimulated in our spirit; we are protected, guided, and directed in the good works of the Lord. Prayer is indeed a foundation. It's a spiritual ground upon which we stand in connection with God. It's a spiritual umbilical cord that, unlike humans, must never be cut. From it, we are fed and nourished, from glory to glory and faith to faith until we are entirely but continually transformed into the image of the glory of the God who called us out of darkness into his marvelous light.

Many books have already been written about prayer, and even more will be. Still, the essence is that we must never disconnect from this spiritual umbilical cord that connects us to God. It brings the heavens to earth and leads humans to experience heaven's glories even while on earth. Undoubtedly, prayer keeps our spirit active and aware of the spiritual world. But, without it, we are mere humans, made of flesh, blood, and bones, and limited in every way as to the possibilities of what we can do in God's image and likeness on earth. Therefore, with this book, the reader will learn and understand that the reasons to pray are many more than simple requests for the supply of our physical and material needs on earth.

Prayer is the telephone line that establishes the communication system between heaven and earth and every day (day and night), as Paul would say, "pray without ceasing." This line must always be kept open and active with the network provided by the Holy Spirit. The antennas of our human spirits link and connect us with God. Thus, they keep us alive and able to bring all the good environments to life and circumstances around us. This way, we will always have this ball of light surrounding us and protecting us every day from the present to eternity.

This is what happened to Moses, who found himself staying for forty days on Mount Horeb, talking to God and hearing from God until he lost sensitivity to biological needs (water, food, marital intimacy, among other things). The skin of his face was transformed; it was filled with a glory that even needed a veil to cover it from normal humans. He looked like an agent or a being that came from heaven. This caused God to transfer Enoch to die and not stay on earth for a long time because he had experienced a dimension of intimacy with God that could no longer be counted among ordinary human beings. He was already one of the beings that deserved a world bigger and better than this world full of sin and violence.

One thing is certain: no matter your spiritual level or knowledge of the Scriptures, how God has used you, or what kind of blessings you already have, you will always need to pray. The more you pray, you will notice that you need to pray more, and at the end of your journey on earth, you will feel that you wish you had prayed more than you have so far. This will show you that there are levels in prayer and stairs that you climb in your spirit to eternity. Each time you climb, the spirit completely controls the flesh and embraces us.

Dear reader, I pray that the Holy Spirit will make you want to pray and pray more. Praying is like being pulled by a love rope - but a spiritual umbilical cord. Born in the spirit with your body on earth, you become a unification of two worlds - heaven and earth in your body. So, the more you pray, the more God's Spirit will pull you closer and closer to Himself. To the lofty arenas of His glory, the profound revelation of His eternal love, attributes, and His will. You will be transformed.

Prayer makes us realize that there is no life independent of God; always and forever, we need and will need him. So, we pray when we are well or faced with challenges; we pray when we are blessed and prosperous or when we need them. We pray if we want to be saved and set free or when we already are. We pray before the journey, during it, and even having reached the glorious destination given to each of us here on earth. But the truth is that we will always have to pray.

Dear reader, if you notice that you no longer feel like praying, you must know something is wrong with you. So fast, and make a request: "Father, give me back my thirst for prayer." Pray that you may pray. Then, as Habakkuk said, "Revive me, Lord," you too will do the same thing.

This book doesn't attempt to exhaust everything on the subject of "prayer." Still, I hope it will contribute to Christian literature and the lives of believers worldwide. Know this: the health of your fellowship with God determines your spiritual health, and your spiritual health determines your mental, physical, emotional, sentimental, professional, and financial health, and well-being. Therefore, the text in 3 John 2 NKJV postulates, "Beloved, I pray that you may prosper in all things and be in health, just as your soul prospers." Prayer is indeed an investment we make in our spirit that has an immeasurable, unimaginable, and determining weight of glory for our good here on earth and for eternity.

Chapter I
Why should we pray?

The answer to this question takes us back to the beginning of all things. From the beginning, God always wanted communion with the man He had created. The very design of the creation of the universe and the order in which all things on earth were made was already a foreshadowing of God the Father's deepest desire to have communion with man. Therefore, man was the last to be created and consequently became the crown of creation, a masterpiece of the all-powerful God. We see God's satisfaction in that after he created man, he rested from the work of creation. He didn't rest because he was tired but because he had already finished his project, the work of creation. There was already an administrator, a king on earth - man. The Scripture says, "What is man that You are mindful of him, or the son of man that You take care of him? You have made him a little lower than the angels; You have crowned him with glory and honor, and set him over the works of Your hands" (Hebrews 2:6-7 NKJV).

We understand from this text that man in his creation was crowned with glory and honor by God. Moreover, God put all things on earth under his feet. What was so special about the man that he deserved so much care, investment, and dominion? Well, let's look at the text from Genesis 1:26 NKJV, "Then God said, "Let Us make man in Our image, according to Our likeness; let them have dominion over the fish of the sea, over the birds of the air, and over the cattle, over all the earth and over every creeping thing that creeps on the earth." This is where man's authority over the earth lies and why prayer by man is indispensable for God to intervene on earth legally.

God has invested his image and likeness in man. Image in this context refers to character and *likeness* to God's *modus operandi*. God created the universe through words and gave man the power to create through words of faith. But these words will only be effective and efficient when he is in intimate communion with God - his Creator.

Moreover, God injected His Spirit into man when He breathed into his nostrils, and he became a living soul.

We understand in this context that the earth was given to the man with a physical body. But, did you notice that two things happened in verse 26 of Genesis chapter 1 that we have just read? Let's see:

1. God said in his divinity conference: let us make man in our image and likeness.

It means that only man was created as a projection of God on earth. He came from God, which is why God is called the Father of spirits. The man was created in spirit long before he had a physical body. In this dimension, he is a spirit, made and composed of the same substance as God. This is why, in the book of Psalms 82:6-7 NKJV, God Himself says: "I said, "You are gods, And all of you are children of the Most High. But you shall die like men, And fall like one of the princes." There have been several attempts to misinterpret this text because its explanation, understanding, and realization go beyond human logic since it naturally implies conceiving the idea that man is a kind of a god or even God in miniature. Although many preachers and theologians try to dodge the explanation of the obvious, it's clairvoyant that man carries elements of a divine nature because he was made in the image and likeness of God.

But can you imagine, kind reader, if when you were born again as a citizen of God's kingdom, you had the awareness that you are a god - created in the image and likeness of your Father God - the Creator of the universe? This *epiphanic* realization would lead you to a question, "How does God operate? How can I imitate Him?" Well, notice that when He created man, He then rested. Why was He finished with man and then delegated all authority over the earth to him? The answer is simple: because man bears the image of God. Since he was made in His likeness, he must function, act and operate like God. To operate like God, you must first have His nature, that is, His image.

God is holy, and He hates sin. Therefore, you must be born again by faith in Jesus Christ and by the regeneration of the Holy Spirit. The assistance given to man by the power of the Holy Spirit enlightens his spirit and makes his new birth possible. Thus, man becomes a new creature - recreated in Christ for the works God had already prepared for him. Unfortunately, because of sin, man disconnected from God finds himself in a lower position than God had actually placed him. He has lost the dominion that God had given him. This is why the text in Hebrews 2:8-10 NIV says, "In putting everything under them, God left nothing that is not subject to them. Yet at present, we don't see everything subject to them. But we do see Jesus, who was made lower than the angels for a little while, now crowned with glory and honor because he suffered death, so that by the grace of God he might taste death for everyone. In bringing many sons and daughters to glory, it was fitting that God, for whom and through whom everything exists, should make the pioneer of their salvation perfect through what he suffered."

We notice in this text that man fell from glory, lost the image of God, and consequently lost dominion over the earth to the devil and his tormentors of the kingdom of darkness. It was, therefore, pleasing to God to send his Son, Jesus Christ, to restore God's original design for the earth and man. To give man back the dominion over the earth that the devil had stolen due to the sin of disobedience. This is why God will create a new heaven and earth, even at the end of everything. Why new earth? Because God's plan was never for man to live eternally in heaven but instead on earth - managing and administering it, as we will see in point two.

Dear reader, realize this: man's life is bound up with the earth, and that plan has not and will not change. Indeed, this earth will pass away because of condemnation, and the devil and all the wicked will be cast into the lake of fire. After that, however, there will be a new earth and a new heavenly Jerusalem that will descend from heaven to earth. God's saints - those who have been washed by the blood of God's lamb that takes away the world's sin, will dwell forever by their faith surrendered to Jesus Christ as Lord and Savior. This is why Jesus is fundamental in this project to rescue man and restore him to his fellowship, image, and likeness. The action of the Holy Spirit removes the corruption from man's heart and regenerates him to be a new creature. Once restored to

God's image, it's time to begin to demonstrate his likeness, that is, to operate like God.

How does God operate? He operates through his word and his Spirit. God speaks, and the Spirit creates. Therefore, every time he speaks, realities are created. This is how the whole universe was created. As a man, you were and have the power of the word - with your tongue, you can call things into existence. First, however, and for that purpose, you need to have faith in God. As Jesus said in Mark 11:22-23 NIV, "Have faith in God." Jesus answered. "Truly I tell you, if anyone says to this mountain, 'Go, throw yourself into the sea,' and does not doubt in their heart but believes that what they say will happen, it will be done for them." Oh, glory! Can you imagine reaching this stage, where whatever you want to conceive in your heart, just by believing and saying, soon comes to pass? But this is what caused God to rest from the work of creation. The Lord had already made a man like Him. Someone who could do on earth the same things that God did from heaven - not all of them because God is omnipotent, omnipresent, and omniscient, but he could speak, and miracles would happen. This faculty is available to you today; therefore, you must have fellowship with God.

The text from Proverbs 18:21 NKJV says, "Death and life are in the power of the tongue, and those who love it will eat its fruit." Have you ever wondered what you could do with your tongue? If the trees, vegetation, fish, seas, and birds were created through a creative command word from God, and this same God gave you authority also to speak, and things happen? We call these miracles because they have no scientific or logical-rational explanation. Nevertheless, it should be normal for us daily because we are made in the image and likeness of God.

Jesus cursed a fig tree, and it withered. Then, with a command word, he calmed the winds and waves, and there was a bonanza. You, too, can exercise this kind of authority and dominion over the earth - but to do so, you must have and be in communion with God.

In summary, we understand in this case that God has invested his image and likeness in man. God is Spirit, and man is also spirit. Spirits are not like matter that decomposes and disappears definitively or forms itself into other states. On the contrary, man's spirit is eternal. He will live eternally in the new heavenly Jerusalem here on earth if he has accepted the lordship of Jesus and repented of his sins. Otherwise, he will live in eternal punishment in the lake of fire with the devil, beast, and false prophet. That is, if he has not been born again, as the Scriptures postulate (Revelation 20:11-15). Now, regardless of whether man was created in the image and likeness of God, he was given something else by God.

2. God gave him dominion over all the earth and everything in it.

Note this text again: "...let them have dominion over the fish of the sea, over the birds of the air, and over the cattle, over all the earth and over every creeping thing that creeps on the earth." Because God is a King with his throne installed in heaven, he equally extended his kingdom on earth through the man he had created - created spirit-like with God and in his image. This is where we have the secret of it all: man, created in the spirit and with dominion over the earth, only had to exercise this governmental and royal authority on earth under one condition - he had to have a physical body. Thus, the body gave man legality over the earth. Without the physical body, no spirit has legitimacy on earth. To understand the implication of this decree of God, He Himself had to submit to this principle that He had established. This is why Jesus became incarnate and a man with a physical body. Only this way could He save man by dying for us on the cross and shedding His precious blood for the remission and atonement of our sins. Only as a man could his death and sacrifice be accepted on our behalf - but a man without sin made sin for our sake. The Scripture in Genesis 2:7 states that God created man from the dust of the ground and breathed into his nostrils the breath of life, and man became a living soul. In this state, man could already exercise dominion over the whole earth in communion with God, his Creator hence why the Scripture says that the heavens belong to the Lord. Still, He has given the earth to the children of men.

Because the earth has been given to the man with a physical body, prayer becomes necessary to have dominion over it. For this reason, we must pray, for prayer establishes contact between heaven and earth so that God's will is done on earth as it is in heaven. God's plan is for heaven to colonize earth with its will, culture, and purposes so that men on earth can access the peace, health, life, and joy in heaven's kingdom. It's through prayer that man has access to the blessings and glory that are in heaven. Heaven will not invade the earth and force its will upon it without someone praying. The Scripture says, "Now because of this King Hezekiah and the prophet Isaiah, the son of Amoz, prayed and cried out to heaven" (2 Chronicles 32:20 NKJV). They were receiving threats from the king of Assyria - Sennacherib, but when they cried out to heaven - God sent an angel who wiped out 185,000 and delivered Hezekiah and the residents of Jerusalem from the hand of Sennacherib. Did you notice that the Scripture doesn't say they cried out to the "heavens," but to "heaven"? Why? Because that is where God's throne is. Now, we can access all the blessings and glory through prayer. An angel was sent from heaven to solve a problem that God's people were facing on earth. However, this angelic intervention was the result of the prayer of two men who were on earth. This leads us to consider some definitions of prayer.

Chapter II
What is prayer?

The concept of prayer is extensive, encompassing several interconnected definitions, but which have as a common element the communication between God and man. So now, let's look at some of the definitions of prayer.

Prayer is the legality that man gives to God for Him to intervene in the affairs of the earth.

Someone may ask, "On what basis can a man give God the legal right for Him to intervene in the affairs of the earth?" Well, the answer lies in the text of Genesis 1:26 NKJV: "Let Us make man in Our image, according to Our likeness; let them have dominion over the fish of the sea, over the birds of the air, and over the cattle, over all the earth and over every creeping thing that creeps on the earth." This is more than a wish on God's part. It is a mandate given to man over the entire earth. This means that the earth was given to man, not angels or the devil. In fact, God's plan for man is intrinsically linked to the earth. This is one of the reasons why God will make a new heaven and earth. As I mentioned in the previous lines, the man was created to be a god on earth. The earth is a physical extension of God's spiritual realm. This is why we read, "In the beginning, God created the heavens and the earth." These two territories were created to be intrinsically interconnected.

The earth depends on heaven for peace, health, and joy. The misfortune on earth today is the result of man's rebellion by his disconnection from his source of life - God. The earth would therefore be a physical territory administered by human spirits clothed in a physical-human body that gave them legality over it. On the other hand, heaven would be a spiritual territory where the throne of God was, with beings with a body, not a physical body, but celestial bodies. In this sense, the management of the whole earth had been completely given to man by God. No spiritual or heavenly being had a legal right to intervene or interfere on earth without man's permission. Thus God established a principle: no spirit is legal on earth without man's permission.

Four landmark moments in history

Let's look at four defining moments in the earth's history:

1. The earth is under the dominion of Adam and his descendants.

As long as Adam had fellowship with God and was obedient to God's voice that visited him at the end of the day, everything went well for him - spirit, soul, and body. He experienced on earth the same glories that exist in heaven. Furthermore, God's will was done on earth as it is in heaven. There was no sickness, curses, misery, or poverty. This is why the Scripture says, "And God saw that all was good." Man didn't know what evil was. Note that even Satan already existed and he obviously watched/heard of the creation of man - a man who was to have dominion over the earth and everything that moves or moves upon it. The devil's curses and oppression were not possible on Adam and Eve. They were not to be for their descendants either, which includes you, dear reader, and me as well. We were not supposed to live in a world of crime, fear, and terror to which humankind is subjected today. Man's oppressor, the devil, was just as real as he is today and just as evil and hateful of man as he is today. He wanted to harm man just as he still does today. The difference is that there was a fence in those days - he had no legal permission over man. He wanted to harm him, but he couldn't. There was a wide separation between the devil's will and his power over man. Man's fellowship with God was the shield of protection he had against the devil. He received from God the glories of heaven with which he impacted the earth.

2. The earth is under the devil's domination - the devil's interference.

The Scripture refers to the devil as the god of this age, that is, of this world. Jesus said, "I will no longer talk much with you, for the ruler of this world is coming, and he has nothing in Me" (John 14:30 NKJV). The word "world" employed here comes from the Greek "*kosmos*" and literally means "arrangement, set up." By extension, it means systems or how the world is organized and functions. Ever since man rebelled against God, Satan has usurped from him the authority - the legal right - that he had over the earth. After the sin of Adam and Eve, by which they were expelled from the garden of Eden, satan has become the prince of this world. In a laconic way, many preachers use the expression "fall of man" or "fall of Adam" in their preaching. But have you ever stopped to think: where did he fall from, if he was on earth when he sinned? After their sin of disobeying God's commandment not to eat the fruit of the tree of the knowledge of good and evil, Adam and Eve hid themselves among the trees of the garden dressed in fig leaves. "Adam, where are you?"

This is how the voice that came to visit the man and have communion with him echoed. The answer was, "I heard your voice walking in the garden, and I hid myself because I am naked." Did you notice that he did not fall from heaven to earth like lightning or a star? Where did the "fall of man" come from? Well, he fell from a position - a position of influence and dominion. He lost dominion over the earth and thus lost the privileges he enjoyed with God's mandate, "Let him have dominion over all the earth." He fell from the dominion, from the power he had over the earth. Since then, he became alienated from the very earth on which he was to live and dominate.

Remember the words of the psalmist: "What is man that You are mindful of him? You have crowned him with glory and honor. You have made him to have dominion over the works of Your hands." The writer of Hebrews stresses, "God left nothing that is not subject to them. Yet at present, we do not see everything subject to them. But we do see Jesus, who was made lower than the angels for a little while, now crowned with glory and honor because he suffered death, so that by the grace of God he might taste death for everyone" (Hebrews 2:8-9 NIV). Man has completely lost dominion over the earth and has relegated this dominion to the devil. Remember the devil's words when he was tempting Jesus in the wilderness? Notice this Scripture: "Again, the devil took Him up on an exceedingly high mountain, and showed Him all the kingdoms of the world and their glory" (Matthew 4:8 NKJV).

We understand two things here:

1. Jesus is in Jerusalem, the capital of Israel, the then city of King David. Israel is God's chosen nation. That is why it is called the "holy land." The word holy means "set apart."

When God brought the people of Israel out of Egypt, He never wanted them to be governed by the laws of this world or by other nations, following the model of the systems of this world. That's because they were all given to the devil's influence due to man's fall. That is why the only constitution God gave them to govern this holy nation were His ten commandments and other civil and ceremonial laws that Moses had brought from God to the people. God was their King, who walked with them day and night, protected them, healed them, and kept them all the days of old (Isaiah 63:7-9). But they grieved their Holy Spirit and asked to be given a king in the likeness of the other kingdoms over which the devil had influence, as we shall see in the following lines. This is where God gave them Saul, King David, and many others. But even so, Israel was still a monotheistic nation - worshipping one God as the prophets appealed. However, from time to time, God's people rebelled against Him, worshipping other gods and being punished with captivity in Babylon until the Roman Empire.

Jesus was born at a time when Israel was a colony of the Roman Empire. Nevertheless, the life of the people of Israel in terms of their social, cultural, and governmental organization was not disconnected from God. They were to be governed by employing God's commandments. There was not to be a dissociation between social, political, and economic life from the influence of the Torah - from God's commandments.

Today is different. Religion has no interference with the world's and nation's economic, social, and political life. At that time, Judaism was not something practiced but a way of life. Our Christianity should not be something disassociated from every aspect of our lives. Unfortunately, for many, their fellowship with God ends when they leave the church service. They live for the world, pleasing the devil, from Monday to Friday and only remember God on Saturdays and Sundays. This is why there is so much hypocrisy and hysteria within many Christian communities. Israel was the door through which the

Messiah came to earth to save humankind. Therefore, Israel remains set apart from the world for God - as a previously chosen people. This is why Jesus told the Samaritan woman that salvation comes from the Jews (John 4).

The point I want you to understand here is that despite being under the rule of the Roman empire at that time, Israel is still God's nation - the chosen people. From Abraham's perspective, they are the physical-biological descendants. And to Abraham, God had promised a seed that would save the world - a seed with which all the world nations would be blessed. So, understand that even though they were under the rule of the Roman Empire, they were not subject to the devil like the rest of the nations; they were the holy nation. Holy in the sense of having been set apart for and by God for his purposes of blessing and saving the world's nations. Don't forget that the first 12 apostles of Jesus Christ were Jews, including Paul and Barnabas. Paul was the apostle to the Gentiles - to us who are not biological descendants of Abraham but are his children by faith in Christ Jesus (Galatians 3:27-28). We have been grafted into him like wild olive trees to benefit from his saving grace (Titus 2:14-15). Therefore, the Savior of humankind - Jesus Christ - would be, from the natural point of view, a descendant of Abraham and son of King David.

2. Verse 8b of Matthew 4 says, "...And showed him all the kingdoms of the world and their splendor." Notice the use of the word "All." "All" what? The answer is obvious: "the kingdoms." Kingdoms here refer to governments - to territories inhabited by human beings whose system of governance had nothing to do with the Creator God of heaven and earth. Again, note Matthew's description: "kingdoms of the world."

It doesn't say of the earth, but of the world. Remember that Satan was described as the prince of this world- this *kosmos* - of systems that seek to remove God from the social, political, cultural, and economic life of human beings. In this case, all nations, except for Israel, had been given to the devil. He himself stated this, and Jesus did not dispute it, for, in John 14:30, he stated that satan was the prince of this world. Have you ever stopped to notice that the world is heading in a direction where family values and the freedom to worship God are increasingly being restricted? Laws and decrees are made to restrict the preaching of the gospel in many parts of the world. This isn't new.

Paul was already saying to the brethren of the Church in Thessalonica, "Pray for us, that the word of the Lord may run swiftly and be glorified, just as it is with you, and that we may be delivered from unreasonable and wicked men; for not all have faith" (2 Thessalonians 3:1-2 NKJV). Many wish that the church no longer existed and that there were no services. Many who are driven by the devil have hatred and envy. They want to see dozens, hundreds, and even thousands of believers gathered together to hear the word of God and will do everything to stop the progress of the church. But thanks to God, the gates of hell will not prevail against the church. Therefore, as children of God, we must pray and pray always. Thousands of people can gather to watch a live soccer match, basketball match, or even athletes running on big tracks in the world's biggest stadiums - this is commendable. However, when the matter involves people gathering to hear God's word, pray and worship God, it's seen as an offense and a scandal to those who have no faith in God. A witch can practice his superstition in a hut, and many people visit it, but churches are seen as a threat. But what threat, if it's the church that, due to the prayers of the saints, protects the earth and humankind from being completely eradicated by the devil? The reason is simple: Satan is the god of this century - of this world. Matthew narrates that satan showed Jesus not only all the kingdoms of the world but also its glories. Have you noticed why someone can make a pact with the devil to enrich himself to the point of sacrificing his children or brothers for the sake of greed? The devil apparently gives these mirage riches but then charges them with another hand - tormenting and afflicting these people and their generations with various kinds of evils, diseases, bad luck, and blockages in sentimental life and other areas.

Dear reader, I want you to understand that Satan has been given all the nations of the world except for Israel. Notice the devil's words: "All this I will give you if you will fall down and worship me." He always wanted to be worshiped. So he incited King Nebuchadnezzar to have a golden statue erected to be worshiped. Thank God, Abednego, Meshach, and Shadrach, who knew their true God, didn't bend their knees before the statue. The God of Israel delivered them from the burning furnace because of their faithfulness, obedience, and faith in Him.

Satan promised Jesus that he would give him everything (the kingdoms of the world and its glories). You can only give that which is under your control. A preacher once said, "The devil was lying to Jesus that he would give him everything because he has nothing." Well, this reveals ignorance regarding the knowledge and interpretation of Scripture. By the way, Jesus didn't even say in this context that the devil was lying. See how Luke narrates the same scenario by quoting the words of the devil: "All this authority I will give You, and their glory; for this has been delivered to me, and I give it to whomever I wish" (Luke 4:6 NKJV).

The question is, who gave the devil all this power and glory? Well, before answering this question, we must ask a counter question: whose was this power and authority and glory over the kingdoms of the world?" We already read the answer in Hebrews 2:7-8 NKJV, "You have made him a little lower than the angels; you have crowned him with glory and honor, and set him over the works of Your hands." All this belonged to Adam - to man.

Now, let's answer the first question: who gave the devil all this power and glory? Man - Adam. When? When he sinned against God. That's why we talk about the fall of man. If he fell, then someone else took his place on earth. That is why the writer of Hebrews retorts, "He put all in subjection under him" (Hebrews 2:8 NKJV). Why? Because he relegated this authority to the devil.

Jesus' apostles had this understanding. Hence, Paul also referred to the devil as "the god of this age, the prince of the powers of the air." He rules over people disconnected from God and influences the minds of human beings from the sky. This is why Paul stated that we are at war against the princes of the darkness of this age, against the spiritual hosts of wickedness. They are the ones who have taken control of the world and afflict it with wars, accidents, miseries, and all kinds of evils. He has blinded the unbelievers' minds so they cannot see the light of the glory of the gospel of Christ. That is why we must always pray. Because prayer is work - pray without ceasing.

Prayers must go up to God every second. If a man doesn't repent and return to God through faith in Christ, he will never experience true peace and joy here on earth. Even today, the devil negatively interferes in the lives of human beings - in their homes, marriages, jobs, businesses, families, and health. What he wants primarily is: to steal, destroy, and kill. And ultimately, to lead man to perdition and eternal fire through fraudulent pleasures and deceit.

Dear reader, be sure to pray for your country, nation, and family. Break the devil's influence under the decision-making spheres at all levels of human social life.

3. The earth under Christ's authority: God's intervention on earth.

Dear reader, up to this point, we have been talking about the authority given to man on earth. We have seen how the devil stole this authority from him and how he set up his kingdom of darkness, controlling or influencing the governments and people of the nations of the world. Adam didn't keep an eye on him and, therefore, lost his authority to the devil - man's enemy. Once the earth was given to man, we see that the devil obeyed the principle we read earlier, "no spirit has legality/right on earth without the permission of a physical body inherent in the earth." Therefore, he needed to enter a serpent in order to have a legal basis to interact with Eve and seduce her into leading her husband into disobedience of God's word. The authority with which the devil has been comfortable in his forays against humankind on earth, he has stolen from man, usurping it because of sin.

In light of the above, we can also see that even God Himself, the Creator of the universe, decided to follow the principle He had established. He is sovereign - in the sense that he acts of his own free will and dominates without being coerced by man. However, His sovereignty is linked to His word. He cannot violate His word. In the Psalms, we read that He exalted His word above His name. In this context, *name* means "character." This is why Jesus became incarnate to redeem man. He obeyed this principle to come into the world. He had no biological father, for Mary conceived of the Holy Spirit. "Therefore, also, that Holy One who is to be born will be called the Son of God" (Luke 1:35 NKJV). The Scripture states, "Who is he who overcomes the world, but he who believes that Jesus is the Son of God? This is He who came by water and blood—Jesus Christ; not only by water, but by water and blood. And it is the Spirit who bears witness, because the Spirit is truth" (1 John 5:5-6 NKJV). Elsewhere, John had already argued, "By this you know the Spirit of God: Every spirit that confesses that Jesus Christ has come in the flesh is of God" (1 John 4:2 NKJV).

What can be denoted here? First, Jesus became incarnate so that he could die on the cross for us. He died as a man - in the place of all men - so that through his sacrifice, we might be saved and restored to fellowship with God the Father and thus gain back our lost authority.

"For the Son of Man has come to seek and to save that which was lost" (Luke 19:10 NKJV). Did you notice that it doesn't say "who had been lost," but "what had been lost?" This refers to authority. What authority? The authority that Satan had usurped from man when Adam sinned. It's a fact that Jesus came to save the lost man. But it's also important to note that He came to restore him to a position of authority so that he has dominion over the earth and the circumstances of this world. To that end, Jesus had to, by his death, annihilate the one who had the empire of death, that is, the devil, and deliver all those who, for fear of death, were subject to the devil for life (Hebrews 4:12-16). He didn't take the seed of angels, that is, He didn't come in spirit form, but took the nature of Abraham's children - "flesh and blood" nature - spirit with a human form. So that when He died on the cross, it was as if we all died too. This is what water baptism represents: "death, burial and resurrection with Jesus" (Romans 6:1-4; Colossians 2:15). It's easy to understand this by observing the following scripture: "And the Word became flesh and dwelt among us, and we beheld His glory, the glory as of the only begotten of the Father, full of grace and truth" (John 1:14 NKJV).

By His death on the cross, Jesus eternally defeated the devil, paralyzed him, and restored authority to us who believe in Him - His church. The Scripture states, "And having disarmed the powers and authorities, he made a public spectacle of them, triumphing over them by the cross" (Colossians 2:15 NIV). Jesus disarmed the devil and entirely and eternally neutralized him. Therefore, there was joy in heaven when He presented His blood in the eternal sanctuary of God the Father. He paid the full price so that all humankind would be free from sin, death, sickness, and misery - provided they believe in Him and accept Him as Lord and Savior. That's why the Scripture says, "If you confess with your mouth the Lord Jesus and believe in your heart that God has raised Him from the dead, you will be saved" (Romans 10:9 NKJV). The law - Jesus broke the devil's legality on earth, and the victory was given to believers by the blood of Christ. "And they overcame him by the blood of the Lamb and by the word of their testimony, and they did not love their lives to the death" (Revelation 12:11 NKJV).

Dear reader, understand that all that Jesus did as miracles and extraordinary works, he didn't do as God, but as a Man dependent on the Holy Spirit.

He was one hundred percent God and one hundred percent Man. Paul says that Jesus laid aside His glory with the Father, emptied Himself, and found Himself as a man. "He humbled Himself and became obedient to the point of death, even the death of the cross. Therefore God also has highly exalted Him and given Him the name which is above every name, that at the name of Jesus, every knee should bow, of those in heaven, and of those on earth, and of those under the earth, and that every tongue should confess that Jesus Christ is Lord, to the glory of God the Father" (Philippians 2:8-11 NKJV). Jesus Christ is Lord.

4. Authority over land returned to man: the church era.

In the text from Matthew 16:18-19 NKJV, Jesus declares to Simon (Peter), "I also say to you that you are Peter, and on this rock I will build My church, and the gates of Hades shall not prevail against it. And I will give you the keys of the kingdom of heaven, and whatever you bind on earth will be bound in heaven, and whatever you loose on earth will be loosed in heaven."

Jesus delegated all His authority to the church, you and me, who believe in Him. Before the rapture, the devil cannot walk his class because we have the power to neutralize him. Why? Because we have authority restored to us. This is something euphoric and glorious for us. The gates of hell will not prevail against the church of Christ. It's a Spirit-filled, empowered church and manifests the character of the Spirit of God on earth, making the will of God prevail in the spheres of men.

Notice the text in Matthew 28:18 NKJV: "All authority has been given to Me in heaven and on earth." Glory to God in the highest realm for Jesus Christ! He has won the victory for us. The word "Power" comes from the Greek "*Exousia*" and means to rule - to reign in heaven and on earth. The devil has zero power, and Jesus has conquered all power. What did He do with that power? He gave it to the church. Verses 19 and 20 attest to this fact: "Go therefore and make disciples of all the nations, baptizing them in the name of the Father and of the Son and of the Holy Spirit, teaching them to observe all things that I have commanded you; and lo, I am with you always, even to the end of the age."

Dear reader, what will you do with this power? Receive the power now and start exercising it consciously. Thus, you should pray.

Let's go back to the beginning. The earth was given to a man with a physical body, and no spirit has legality on earth without a physical body. Do you understand now? To pray is to give God the legal right to intervene in the affairs of the earth.

Many people commonly say, "If God is love and exists, why is there so much evil on earth? Why doesn't He do anything to change the evil on earth today?" Of course, this is an ignorant question. But well, the answer is simple: because He gave the earth to man, and if he doesn't pray, nothing will change, and nothing will happen.

You have authority. Pray with authority.

God can see the evil about to happen in the land, neighborhood, city, or country where you live, dear reader. However, He cannot do anything until someone on earth prays. We have two typical examples in the New Testament:

In Acts 5:17-21, the apostles are arrested for preaching the gospel and healing the sick. They are imprisoned in a public prison. Since the church was still a baby then, they didn't pray. Nevertheless, God sent an angel who, opening the prison doors, brought them out unharmed. They continued to rest on their laurels - doing nothing - thinking that God would always do this way.

In Acts 12:1, James is arrested at the behest of King Herod and is executed by the edge of the sword. Herod went ahead and had Peter arrested, wanting to do the same thing to him. However, the church had already awakened to its responsibility to pray this time. Verse 5 says the church continually prayed to God for Peter until the Lord sent an angel who delivered him from prison and Herod's evil plans. Why didn't the angel of the Lord come to James' rescue but instead let him die? Because the Church didn't pray. And why did the same angel come down and deliver Peter? Simple: because they prayed.

Understand this, dear reader: when we pray to God, we give Him permission to stop accidents, stop wars, cancel evil, and reverse all the devil's evil plans against us.

I am writing this chapter aboard the TAP Portugal plane, leaving Lisbon, Portugal, for Maputo, Mozambique, after the missions we did in that Lusophone country at the Superbock Arena. The flight took off at 7:50 pm. When it was about 9:30 pm, we passed through a long, turbulent zone where the flight attendants had to stop serving meals due to the plane's uncomfortable movements. Cutlery and plates started falling to the ground, like a car going at high speed over large bumps. Most people were so frightened that they didn't know what to do but obey the instructions of the cabin chief who, in a voice of comfort, told everyone to fasten their seat belts and not move from their seats. I was writing this chapter and praising God in my spirit. I had to hold my MacBook tightly so it wouldn't fall.

Suddenly, the Holy Spirit palpitated in my heart, "This isn't normal turbulence, you have just returned from a big mission, and the devil is angry. But there are no problems because you have authority. Everyone on this flight is protected because you, my son, are here. You have the authority to order this turbulence to stop. Pray from your heart." So I did. In a calm voice, amidst the astonishment and despair of many, I began to pray from the bottom of my heart, "Father, protect everyone on this plane, and don't let anything bad happen in the name of Jesus."

Then I commanded, "Satan, in the name of Jesus, take your hands off this plane now, in the name of Jesus." Right after that, the situation settled down, and everything returned to normal. Now, we have a great trip ahead, and I am here watching in prayer, with faith in Jesus, and resting in my spirit. Jesus Christ is the same, yesterday and today and forever. It's 00:34 now, as my cell phone clock registers, and everything is under control.

Dear reader, I don't know what kind of zone of turbulence you are going through right now. Whether in your marriage, sentimental life, professional life, health, academic life, business, studies, or if you are in debt, which is robbing you of sleep. But you can pray now with faith and authority, and this storm will pass. Receive light and victory in the name of Jesus. I speak peace to your heart now: receive peace.

Take about five minutes now and begin to pray as you prepare to read the next chapter.

Chapter III
How to pray correctly

During his three years of itinerant ministry in the land of Israel, Jesus worked many miracles of healing and deliverance. He demonstrated he had complete authority over the spiritual forces of darkness and the forces of nature. He cast many demons out of many people, raised the dead, healed the sick of various diseases, and calmed storms and waves. His disciples observed this closely and experienced several glorious moments when the supernatural dominated and controlled the natural, causing miracles, that is, phenomena without logical-rational explanation. They experienced moments where destinies were changed, and situations thought impossible became possible before the power that Jesus demonstrated. It's evident that, as Jesus' disciples, most gospel ministers and current believers would ask Jesus to teach them to heal the sick and cast out demons, just as the Master did. However, this was not what impressed the disciples, although they were fascinated by miracles. Instead, it was the source of this power that seemed to interest them.

They watched as Jesus woke up in the early morning, went to a deserted place, and prayed (Mark 1:35). Then, coming out of that place of prayer, he went to minister with such ease. With a simple word, He commanded the unclean spirits to come out, and they obeyed. With a simple touch, he cleansed the leper. Of course, they had seen Him go up on the mountain at night to pray while they were rowing the boat across to the other side of the lake. Suddenly, He appears walking on water naturally, as if He were stepping on dry land. Again and surprisingly, they see Him talking to the wind and the waves, and they obey Him. Indeed they were interested in one thing: the way He prayed. So they asked him for only one thing: "Teacher, teach us to pray, as John taught his disciples to pray." Some of them had been John's disciples and knew that he prayed, and the Pharisees prayed. Still, there was one big difference - Jesus' prayers had immediate, visible, concrete, tangible results. They also wanted to see this happen in their lives, so they asked him to teach them how to pray.

Often, the concept of prayer has not received much attention. Although there are several preachings on it, it still seems to be an inexhaustible topic. This is because we are born listening to people praying for a few hours and others long hours without any tangible result. In this chapter, I will teach you how to pray and receive answers from God. Jesus' disciples learned to pray; from prayer, they became champions and performed feats. At the ninth hour, which is the hour of prayer, when Peter and John went to the temple, Jesus worked his first greatest miracle after Christ was lifted up on high. "Silver and gold I do not have, but what I do have I give you: In the name of Jesus Christ of Nazareth, rise up and walk" (Acts 3:6 NKJV). With these words and taking the man (who had been lame for forty years) by the right hand, he lifted him up, and the power of God entered him, and he leaped up at once and began to walk normally.

There is power in prayer, for it is how we are spiritually supplied with heavenly fuel, with divine power - the anointing. People often wonder why Jesus prayed, being God in human form. The answer is simple: prayer is how man gives God legal permission to intervene in earthly affairs. God will not move on behalf of humans on earth if there is no one to pray to. Prayer is irreplaceable.

Peter recognized this when the angel of God released him from the maximum security prison where he had been put after being sentenced to death. The church discovered the power of prayer, interceding intensely and unceasingly on his behalf (Acts 12:5). Paul understood the power of prayer so much that, in several moments in his epistles, he asked: "Pray for us that the message of the Lord may spread rapidly and be honored, just as it was with you. And pray that we may be delivered from wicked and evil people, for not everyone has faith" (2 Thessalonians 3:1-2 NIV). Prayer is indispensable for the believer, so the disciples asked, "Teach us to pray." They wanted the formula for this master key.

The Lord's true prayer

In the text of Matthew 6:9 NKJV, we read, "In this manner, therefore, pray..." Looking at this statement of the Master, we can understand that He was giving a formula, a principle of how to pray, and not necessarily the words of the prayer. Depending on the context and the situation, the believer will have to make the type of prayer corresponding to the issue or situation he wants to deal with. Over several years, I have always heard in Christian forums at the end of services the minister saying: "Let's pray the Lord's prayer: Our Father in heaven, hallowed be your name...". It seems that this concept of dealing with the Lord's prayer has been accepted in a laconic way for several centuries because many have never bothered to study the Holy Bible. Therefore, they repeat religious notions and verses without life or power.

Dear reader, understand this: Matthew 6:9-13 is not the Lord's prayer, but the model of prayer. In this text, the Lord Jesus didn't pray at all. The Lord's true prayer is recorded in the text from John, chapter 17.

The Scripture states, "Jesus spoke these words, lifted up His eyes to heaven, and said: "Father, the hour has come. Glorify Your Son, that Your Son also may glorify You, as You have given Him authority over all flesh, that He should give eternal life to as many as You have given Him. And this is eternal life, that they may know You, the only true God, and Jesus Christ whom You have sent...". In this prayer of Jesus to the heavenly Father, we find several types and models of prayer that we will study in detail in the next chapters. First, Jesus exalts and glorifies the Father. Next, he intercedes for his 12 disciples in particular. Then he intercedes for all of us, his disciples, who would believe in the message of his first disciples. This is a truly inclusive prayer because He even prayed for you and me. "I pray for them. I do not pray for the world but for those whom You have given Me, for they are Yours" (verse 9).

What a prayer! What words! Jesus prayed that we would be protected from evil on earth, notice his words: "I do not pray that You should take them out of the world, but that You should keep them from the evil one" (verse 15). And, in a gesture of love, Jesus includes you and me in a prayer made two thousand years ago: "I do not pray for these alone (the twelve, in this case), but also for those who will believe in Me through their word; that they all may be one, as You, Father, are in Me, and I in You; that they also (the twelve, you and I, that is, the entire church) may be one in Us, that the world may believe that You sent Me" (verses 20-21). This was an intercessory prayer on behalf of believers, the church whose validity extends to this day and serves as an insurance policy against all kinds of evils on earth, in defense and protection of the church. Isn't it wonderful to know that Jesus prayed for us two millennia ago? Of course it is! He begins with the tone of one who has intimate communion with the Father: "And now, O Father, glorify Me together with Yourself, with the glory which I had with You before the world was" (verse 5).

Jesus reveals to us here that prayer is intimacy and communion with God. He has always been with the Father. He who became flesh and dwelt among humans to save them from sin and eternal death and to give us eternal life. He has always shared intimacy and communion with the Father. But now, in human form on earth, He had to pray to the Father in heaven, teaching that we also need to establish and keep alive this flame of intimacy with the Father. He was so full of the Holy Spirit that he no longer needed to close his eyes when praying. Even with his human eyes open, he saw the spiritual world with the eyes of the spirit. So he lifted his eyes to the heavens and saw the glory of the Father just as Stephen saw it in Acts 7:55. Stephen also needed to be filled with the Holy Spirit. When you spend time with the Father in prayer, you will always be filled with the Holy Spirit. Praying is a way to maintain a constant divine consciousness and establish permanent contact with heaven.

In summary, John chapter 17 is where we find the longest and greatest prayer of Jesus, and this is the Lord's true prayer. So don't pray the "Our Father..." prayer anymore with the idea that you are praying the Lord's prayer because you are not. This is just a model that he has given us.

It's easy to understand this by carefully observing the Lord's words, "In this manner, therefore, pray." Did you notice the use of the term "Therefore?" This reveals a way, a form, and consequently a formula, not precisely what is to be said. Jesus wants prayer to come out of your heart, not your head because you have memorized some verses. Don't forget that prayer is communion - and for it to be intimate, it must come out of the heart. Therefore, prayer's power is not in how many hours a person takes to pray. It is in the contact that is established between the spirit of man and the Spirit of God, allowing the heavens to intervene in the affairs of the earth.

Prayer should be personal, intimate, genuine, and coming from the heart, not from a piece of paper. We shouldn't read prayers but "speak" prayers. We shouldn't make recitations but make prayers. We should connect our soul and our being - our spirit - in surrendering total dependence and trust in God. This is how Jesus prayed, as the Scriptures reveal to us. Notice these words in Hebrews 5:7 NKJV: "Who, in the days of His flesh, when He had offered up prayers and supplications, with vehement cries and tears to Him who was able to save Him from death, and was heard because of His godly fear." These prayers come out of the spirit. Once, Jesus prayed until his sweat came out in the form of blood. Prayer keeps man's heart connected to the throne of God in heaven. A person who has intimacy with God is undefeatable.

Chapter IV
Prayer model

Matthew 6:9 should be seen as the first model of prayer. And note that Jesus gave this model to His disciples who were still under the Old Testament. There was no New Testament, for He had not yet died and risen, nor had the Holy Spirit descended upon the disciples. Therefore, none of Jesus' disciples had been born again yet. They were carnal men, but only with faith. This is the reason why they couldn't pray for an hour. They always slept, and their eyes were heavy with sleep. Let's look at the model:

1. We pray to the Father. "Our Father who in heaven."

Jesus introduces a notion of prayer that wasn't common to the Jews or the clerical class of that time. For them, it was inconceivable to call God "Father." Other terms could be used, "*Hashem*" - the name, "*Adonai*" - The Lord, but not "Father." So he said to them, "<u>You</u>, pray like this." And praying like this distinguished Jesus' disciples from those of Moses and John. The entity to whom we pray is powerful, majestic, glorious, miraculous, holy, a consuming fire, and the Creator of the universe. Yet, despite all these qualities and attributes, he is our Father. And being our Father, He wants to establish intimacy and deal with us personally, directly, and as children, not as religious. Jesus brings a notion of closeness between God and men. He removes the gap that the Jewish religion had established of even forbidding to call him by his name "*Yahweh*" - the Eternal, the uncreated Creator, the LORD.

Therefore, Jesus' disciples would be intimate with the Father to call him "ABBA, Father." Jesus establishes a notion of fatherhood that was previously inconceivable: "Children of God" by using the term "Our Father in heaven." In addition to our biological or human parents, we should know that when we are born again, we have a Father in heaven. The heavenly Father who cares for us and watches over us. With this model, the sense of fear that one had of God disappears; distance is shortened, and prayer connects heaven to earth whenever man on earth communicates with God the Father in heaven. There is a notion of love and closeness that this new model introduced by Jesus establishes.

2. "Hallowed be Your name."

The principle established here is reverence, respect, praise, and worship toward the Lord's name and personality. We can state that when we pray, we should begin with praise and worship and not with requests. This is called *praise prayer*, as we will see later in the following lines. Dear reader, when praying, begin by thanking God for all that he has done to and for you. Consider the good things the Lord has done for you and how much He has delivered you from various diabolical snares. The Psalmist said, "Bless the Lord, O my soul; And all that is within me, bless His holy name! Bless the Lord, O my soul, And forget not all His benefits: Who forgives all your iniquities, Who heals all your diseases, Who redeems your life from destruction, Who crowns you with lovingkindness and tender mercies, Who satisfies your mouth with good things, So that your youth is renewed like the eagle's" (Psalms 103:1-5 NKJV).

The background here is that as you begin to pray, you should praise Him, worship Him, and give Him thanks. Many believers start with endless requests whenever they want to pray, "Father, I ask for a job, a house, and money in the name of Jesus." It is not wrong to ask because He is the one who said, "Ask, and it will be given to you..." (Matthew 7:7 NKJV). But you must recognize Him first and before you ask for something new, be thankful for what He has already done. For example, how would you feel as a parent if your child always just came to ask and never thanked you? Of course you would keep giving, but you would feel more motivated if he acknowledged what you have already given him or done for him.

3. "Your kingdom come. Your will be done, here on earth as it is in heaven."

This is called *intercessory prayer*. In it, we pray to strengthen God's will here on earth so His peace, joy, and light will be made on earth.

Looking at the world around you, you will see much misery and destruction. Opening newspapers or turning on the television to watch the news, you will hear of wars and robberies, violence and rape, famine and pestilence, disease, and natural calamities. All these ravages plague humans and put them in a state of misery. And we know who is behind all this - Satan, man's enemy. The only entity on earth that can stop him is the church. So we must pray for our neighbors, our unsaved family members, that the light of Christ's gospel will shine in their hearts so they will be saved.

We should pray that our rulers rule with justice and the fear of God; that they will have divine wisdom to solve problems and bring development and welfare to their fellow citizens. We should pray for the peace of Jerusalem and peace in the hearts of men worldwide. To pray this kind of prayer, you must be moved by intimate compassion and love for your neighbor and not be selfish. The final solution to everything is the kingdom of God installed in the hearts of humans. Therefore, we must pray for the kingdom to be installed. Not for it to come because the kingdom has already come and is in us. Now we pray for its expansion.

4. "Give us this day our daily bread."

This is the prayer of petition. Here you can ask for whatever you want, particularly the Lord's provision. As the Psalmist David said, he is the God of provision: "The Lord is my shepherd; I shall not want. He makes me to lie down in green pastures; He leads me beside the still waters. He restores my soul; He leads me in the paths of righteousness For His name's sake" (Psalms 23:1-3 NKJV). Paul said, "And my God shall supply all your need according to His riches in glory by Christ Jesus" (Philippians 4:19 NKJV).

5. "And forgive us our debts, as we forgive our debtors."

This model contains a confession of sins, but it's conditional. This model was before Christ died on the cross and washed us of our sins. Furthermore, He does not forgive us our debts because we forgive those who owe us but because He loves us. The Scripture says in Revelation,

"To Him who loved us and washed us from our sins in His own blood, and has made us kings and priests to His God and Father, to Him be glory and dominion forever and ever. Amen" (Revelation 1:5-6 NKJV).

We have already been washed of sins and made kings and priests. As kings, we declare what we want with our words, following God's will, and things happen. We are not poor, begging for our daily bread, for we have already sought the kingdom of God, and all these things of eating, drinking, and dressing have already been given to us. We have already arrived at the place of provision "in Christ," where all needs are supplied. What to do, then? Recognize the Lord's provision and give thanks for bread, clothing, and shelter even before we physically have them, and you will see their manifestation. We forgive those who offend us because we have also been undeservingly loved and forgiven by Christ on the cross.

6. "And do not lead us into temptation, but deliver us from the evil one."

This model represents the *request for protection*. The idea was to ask God the Father to keep us from stumbling. To keep us pure and clean until Christ comes. Also, while we are on earth, He preserves and delivers us from all evil. You can also make this kind of prayer, and God will extend His arm of power to deliver you from evil. So Judas, not Iscariot (traitor), prayed for the brethren when he said, "Now To him who is able to keep you from stumbling and to present you before his glorious presence without fault and with great joy—to the only God our Savior be glory, majesty, power and authority, through Jesus Christ our Lord, before all ages, now and forevermore! Amen" (Jude 24-25 NKJV).

God can deliver and keep those who yield to Him in spirit, body, and soul. God doesn't lead us into temptation, nor does He tempt anyone, as James said: "When tempted, no one should say, "God is tempting me." For God cannot be tempted by evil, nor does he tempt anyone; but each person is tempted when they are dragged away by their own evil desire and enticed" (James 1:13-14 NKJV).

7. "For yours is the kingdom and the power and the glory forever. Amen."

With this model, there is a recognition of God's greatness, sovereignty, and power. Everything begins and ends with Him. To Him belongs all the kingdom, power, and glory. So the background here is that you acknowledge God's greatness as you finish praying. End the prayer by thanking and praising Him in recognition of His majesty.

PART II
The importance of prayer

Introduction
The importance of prayer

In the book of Luke chapter 18, Jesus gave a parable about the duty to pray always and never faint. He tells of a widowed woman who persistently asked the unjust judge of a specific city to do justice for her. At first, he ignored her, but because of her insistence, he brought justice to her case so that she would not bother him again. With these words, Jesus wanted to make his disciples realize the importance of patience, persistence, and perseverance in prayer. He also encouraged us that God hears our prayers and will quickly bring justice. It's very common that, as a believer, many brethren pray to God about a persistent issue that seems to be resisting change. And because of this, some brethren may faint in prayer, thinking that God is not listening or that the situation will not be answered.

As a consequence, they lose confidence in prayer and end up thinking that prayer is no longer important. This is why Jesus asked, "Nevertheless, when the Son of Man comes, will He really find faith on the earth?" (Luke 18:8 NKJV). Faith is essential for prayer to work. This is why James said, "And the prayer of faith will save the sick, and the Lord will raise him up. And if he has committed sins, he will be forgiven" (James 5:15 NKJV).

Prayer is so important that without it, the earth would be entirely desolated by the devil. It's the continuous prayers of the saints that stop evil on earth. I am reminded of the words of the Lord Jesus when He said to me in 2013, "Prayers must come up to me daily for the sake of mankind." With these words, the Lord wants us to look at prayer as an indispensable part of our fellowship with God and as a job - the job of praying. Paul told the Christians who were in Rome, "Now I beg you, brethren, through the Lord Jesus Christ, and through the love of the Spirit, that you strive together with me in prayers to God for me, that I may be delivered from those in Judea who do not believe, and that my service for Jerusalem may be acceptable to the saints" (Romans

15:30-31 NKJV). Paul was a man full of the Holy Spirit and anointing. Even his handkerchiefs and aprons worked the miracles of healing and deliverance to those oppressed by the devil. However, he placed a lot of emphasis on prayer. He looked at prayer as a combat - a battle. In fact, we fight through prayer in spiritual battles. This reveals that prayer is multifunctional, establishing and strengthening our fellowship with God. However, it's also an indispensable tool in spiritual battles against the forces of evil. It's in prayer where champions are born, where spiritual giants are awakened, activated, and raised. Both Jesus and the apostles put a lot of emphasis on prayer. And they did it not only with words but also with actions, for as we read in the previous chapters, they were men of prayer.

Speaking of Jesus, the Scripture says that during his years of ministry on earth, he offered up prayers and supplications to his father with great crying and tears that could deliver him from death (Hebrews 5:7). Jesus, as a man, prayed in his humanity. As a God, he didn't have to, but at that moment, he had come in human form. He had become incarnate to die on the cross, shed his blood, and save humanity from eternal damnation. Being in human form like us, he prayed and prayed every day. He would wake up at dawn, go to a deserted place, and pray there. At night he would go out to a mountain and pray too. The disciples spent most of the time sleeping because sleep weighed them down. One of the enemies of prayer is the flesh. It doesn't want you to pray because you are tired from working during the day. So, you take a bath, have dinner and then go straight to bed to rest. Then, in the morning, you wake up in such a hurry to leave the house for school, work, or a place of business, that you don't seem to have time with God or for God. Thus, your spirit cools down, and you gradually lose your spiritual fire until you're easy prey for the devil. This is because you haven't practiced the discipline of praying. Prayer is discipline; you must discipline the flesh to pray even when you don't feel like praying or when you feel tired. Don't give in to the weaknesses of the flesh. Jesus said, "The spirit indeed is willing, but the flesh is weak" (Matthew 26:41 NKJV).

The flesh is never ready. That is why it must be disciplined to obey the spirit whenever the spirit wants. This exercise is not easy at first, but the flesh will conform to the Spirit's command over time. This is why, by God's inspiration, I wrote the book: The Four Essential Habits of a New Creation in Christ: CUTANE. Onório, 2022. I recommend that you purchase and read it. Speaking of the flesh, the apostle Paul said, "But I discipline my body and bring it into subjection, lest, when I have preached to others, I myself should become disqualified" (1 Corinthians 9:27 NKJV). You must subdue the flesh - you must master it - how? Investing in your spirit through reading, studying the word, and prayer and meditation, accompanied by an attitude. Whenever the spirit feels like doing something in reaction to God's word, do it even when the flesh doesn't feel like it. Have discipline and dominion over the flesh, for only then will you have a stable and growing prayer life without interference from the weakness of the flesh.

The Scripture tells us that Jesus was in the habit of waking up early in the morning while it was still dark. Then, he would go to a deserted place and pray (Mark 1:35).

It's fascinating to study the prayer life of Jesus Christ. The Holy Bible says that although He was a Son, He learned obedience through the sacrifice He went through. During his time on earth, He prayed to God, crying out with supplications before the One who could deliver him from death. Prayer for Jesus was part of his discipline and ministry ethic. What do you think He asked for in those moments of prayer? It's evident that He didn't ask for a wife, job, house, money, or promotion. Likewise, he didn't ask for peace in his home, restoration of his marriage, or for God to cancel some debts he had. These were not Jesus' prayer points. There was something bigger than that - fulfilling his purpose on earth. He was so focused on his mission that he told his disciples, "My food is to do the will of Him who sent Me, and to finish His work" (John 4:34 NKJV). "But He couldn't ask for all this because He was God," - someone might think. Well, I have already explained that Jesus didn't come as God, didn't live or minister as God. He came as a man, lived and ministered as a human being, but dependent on the Holy Spirit and without any sin in Him. It's this dependence on the Holy Spirit that made him pray. He wanted to be one hundred percent connected to heaven and sensitive to the voice of the heavenly Father. Therefore, he spent most of his time with his Father in prayer. He understood the importance of prayer. As God, he couldn't and shouldn't pray, but as a Man dependent on God - he should.

It's funny that the motives that move many believers to pray are more carnal than divine. They have to do with meeting man's biological and transient needs: food, drink, and clothing. Clothing, by extension, would include shelter and housing. These things roughly drive a man to study, work, wake up early, or even live with insomnia, thinking about what he will eat or feed his children. And for those who have this, insecurity and fear take over, which leads them to hire armed security. Even then, they live distrustful of everyone, including their own shadow and family, because they have no protection. As happened to the rich man without God: "What you have gathered, who will begin? With whom will it remain?" Jesus saw these worries in his disciples' hearts and didn't want them to be carried away by the same waves of apprehension that the rest of the people were subjected to. So he gave them a secret: "But seek first the kingdom of God and His righteousness, and all these things shall be added to you" (Matthew 6:33 NKJV). They understood this later and surrendered to his will - and the Lord supplied all their needs.

As Paul rightly stated, "And my God shall supply all your need according to His riches in glory by Christ Jesus" (Philippians 4:19 NKJV). He enforced and echoed the words of King David, who poetically stated, "I have been young, and now am old; yet I have not seen the righteous forsaken, nor his descendants begging bread" (Psalms 37:25 NKJV). What did they all have in common? They had surrendered to the Lord God, to live for Him and depend on Him in everything. This is why, in David's case, his prayers included seeking the presence of God and staying in His temple in worship and praise. He would wake up at midnight and sometimes at dawn just to praise the Lord. No wonder he said, "The Lord is my shepherd; I shall not want. He makes me to lie down in green pastures; He leads me beside the still waters" (Psalms 23:1-2 NKJV).

On the other hand, Paul looked for quiet places to pray, even to the point of going with Silas and Luke near a river where he thought there was a place to pray. They certainly didn't have so many carnal and selfish requests that many believers have today. God had taken control of their lives, and they lacked nothing. But why did they pray then? Well, they understood something about prayer that many don't understand today - an indispensable aspect of the importance of prayer. That's what I'm going to show you next. When you reach this level, you will lack nothing, and whenever you pray, you will be filled with the glory of God.

The importance of prayer lies not so much in the answer God gives us but in what happens in our spirit when we pray.

Chapter I
The impact of prayer on man's spirit

The Benefits of Prayer go beyond God giving us things; it's what He does in us. The reason God asks us to pray is that when we pray, He begins to work. God does not act when there is no prayer; He always acts in response to prayer. Just as your body has pores through which it breathes, so does your spirit.

Why do we often fast when we have a serious matter? The purpose of fasting is not to move God to answer prayer. Otherwise, He would be a bad Father who starves us whenever we want to ask for something. So why do I have to go without food for my Father to hear me if He is my Father?

The purpose of fasting is to weaken your flesh, give power, give wings, and give strength to your spirit.

When your spirit is full of God and glory, it pierces your skin and begins to contain your body; it is no longer your body containing your spirit. Remember what Paul said in 1 Corinthians 6:19-20: it means that the Holy Spirit dwells in us, but there is a level at which we come to dwell in Him because, in Him, we live, exist, and move.

When your spirit is activated, empowered, and awake, it pierces your skin, stands on the outside of your skin, and protects your body against the attacks that come against you. Imagine that I'm writing a resume to apply for a job. I will use my physical hand to write; if that physical hand is not subject to God but to the passions of the flesh, my flesh will write the resume. So, nothing may happen when I submit my resume asking for a job. However, when I pray and that glory comes over me and envelops my body, my spirit is activated and pierces my body. Then, as I pick up the computer to write, it will be my God-filled spirit writing the resume and no longer my flesh. Each thing written and the anointing on my spirit stays there on that paper, in those words, in that text. When I take that resume and submit it anywhere, I will not be submitting a simple piece of paper. It will be a document full of anointing, and there is no way it can be rejected.

This is the reason why you will always have a successful life, from glory to glory and from faith to faith. This is why Abraham's servant prayed when he wanted to get a wife for Isaac. After he had prayed, the Spirit drew the right woman from those who were going to shepherd the sheep; others were not there that day, but Rebekah was there. So the Spirit of God repelled the wrong women and drew the right one because that servant had prayed (Genesis 24:42-46).

Regardless of your trade: construction worker, mechanic, carpenter, engineer, or any other profession, when you pray, you activate your spirit and go to work. When you look at the work, the boss will be able to appreciate and approve it. And you may sign several employment or service contracts because of a single job you did that was appreciated and spread by word of mouth. Did you know that some people work hard and do their job well, but their superiors or bosses don't appreciate it? The glory you activate or receive in moments of prayer can solve this.

For example, housewives can also experience a dimension of favor and glory. When a woman's spirit is activated and cooks under the anointing, the food can taste so good to her spouse's palate as if she had put ingredients in there that she didn't actually use. But unfortunately, many husbands don't appreciate the food their wives make because it's made in the flesh.

Another typical case was that of Jesus. On one occasion, He was with about five thousand men, not counting the women and children who made up a larger number. They had eaten nothing for three days with Him and were already hungry. However, there were only five loaves and two fish, which were the boys' snacks. Jesus took the five loaves and the two fish, gave thanks, blessed them, and when He handed them back to them for distribution, a miracle happened. The loaves and the fishes multiplied until all the world was filled, and twelve bread baskets were left over. What happened in the spirit world? Well, when Jesus took the few loaves and fishes, the glory in Him passed on to the bread and fish, so they didn't run out until everyone had eaten.

Dear reader, it's essential to stay several hours in prayer in God's presence because when you pray, something happens in your spirit that you don't see. And that's what you need to enter where others won't, do what others can't, and live with victory in this world.

For example, you can spend time with God in prayer and then go to the place where you do your business, and as you begin to pick up or put away your products, the anointing can pass on to them. So people, as they pass by, even if they had no plans to buy, end up coming in and buying in large quantities. The understanding of this dimension of glory made the Apostle Paul write to the Colossians: "And whatever you do, whether in word or deed, do it all in the name of the Lord Jesus, giving thanks to God the Father through him" (Colossians 3:17 NIV).

Why must you do everything in the name of the Lord Jesus? Because you have been born again and are a citizen of the kingdom of heaven, the word of your King, Jesus. You must carry weight in your life, influencing you in everything you do and giving direction to the paths you must walk that please the Lord. Even marriage must be holy and consecrated to God. Otherwise, demons in the form of a spiritual husband or wife can come into the midst of the couple to interfere with the relationship negatively. The bottom line is that you must develop an awareness of Christ's presence so that everything you do, in word or deed, you do it in the name of the Lord Jesus. For example, cook in the name of Jesus, drive your car in the name of Jesus, and there will be no accident.

I remember when I was teaching at the University, I was a reader and had my tutor, the regent, with a lot of experience in teaching and a pedagogical career. He would explain, but the students didn't understand anything. When I would come and explain, they would say that it was me they preferred the most. How so, since he had a much higher academic level and teaching experience than me? Well, God's grace and glory make the difference. There is something about us and in us - God's grace. That's why God said to Paul, "My grace is sufficient for you, for My strength is made perfect in weakness" (2 Corinthians 12:9 NKJV).

Why is it that in the book of Mark 16:17-18 NKJV, Jesus stated the following? "And these signs will follow those who believe: In My name they will cast out demons; they will speak with new tongues; they will take up serpents; and if they drink anything deadly, it will by no means hurt them; they will lay hands on the sick, and they will recover." It's because of the anointing and glory that believers would possess by virtue of their new birth in Christ and the empowerment of the Holy Spirit. It's important to note that in this verse, Jesus was not referring to the apostles but to all believers in general - to those who believed the message the apostles preached.

Why are there believers who have demons when they are the ones who should cast them out in the name of Jesus? Because they don't know who they are in Christ, and many have never developed their fellowship with God. Jesus said that if believers eat or drink something poisonous that kills, it could kill other normal human beings. Still, if believers consumed it because of the glory activated in their spirit and passed on to their flesh, no harm would come to them. Even if they were injected or drank it by mouth, or even if a snake bit them, no harm would come to them. These signs and credentials are not for the religious but for those who believe in Christ, have surrendered to Him as their Lord and Savior, and are in living and intimate fellowship with Him.

This doesn't mean that you have to go and take some poison on purpose because then you would be tempting God. However, nothing bad will happen if someone uses poison to harm you. The biggest problem is that many brethren don't believe in the power of God, so they are terrified of the devil and the rumors outside. They are shaken by all kinds of winds and live without peace, quiet, or joy. Jesus said, "Peace I leave with you, My peace I give to you; not as the world gives do I give to you. Let not your heart be troubled, neither let it be afraid" (John 14:27 NKJV).

Dear reader, it's time to believe in God's power and abilities. It's time to believe in God's faithfulness and the integrity of his word. It's time to believe in God's promises and love for us. It's time to believe in miracles - in the God who works miracles and makes the impossible possible. All this is possible when we spend quality time with the Lord in prayer and meditation on his word.

I recall a story. A young Christian man learning mechanics in the auto repair business was thirsty. He mistakenly took the battery solution (liquid), thinking it was water. Upon realizing this, his master became desperate because he knew the effect would be fatal. However, the young man remembered the words of Jesus and the signs that would follow believers and, by faith, confessed that he had drunk mineral water and not battery solution. Upon saying this, the solution immediately didn't affect his body. The next day, his master went to the young man's home, thinking that some harm had come to him, but to his amazement, he found the young man doing homework, healthy, and in good spirits. What happened? The young man believed in the promises of Jesus and stood on them.

Dear reader, the times we live in will select the believers from the religious. It is not only the one who confesses that he is a believer who will be saved, but the present circumstances will judge who is and who is not. We can all pray and celebrate, but when the calamities come, the balance of those who will stand will be determined by how much glory each of us has in our spirit. How much of God we have absorbed in our spirit in communion with Him.

This is the time to confess God's word over your life. Although Satan throws diseases with their various forms of manifestation or degrees of severity, you must keep the confessions of faith.

Jesus once slept in the boat and tested his disciples by allowing a windstorm to come. The waves entered the boat, and the disciples were worried and afraid because of the storm, even though they were with Jesus. Why? Because they didn't know with whom they were walking, the life they had been given, and even less the authority they had.

Chapter II
Prayer – spiritual recharging process

Understand this: whenever you pray, there is something that God passes on to you, and that which He passes on to you is much more important than the things He can give you. This is because what God passes on to you is His nature. Every time you pray, you are being armored to be like Him. God has given us new languages so that by praying, we overcome the barriers imposed by our minds. So that the spirit prays well, without limitations, to say everything we want without mind-barring.

For example, I may wake up in the morning and immediately go to lay hands on someone. But on another day, I wake up early, pray (spend time with God as Jesus did), and then lay hands on someone; there will be a difference. If I lay my hands on the person without spending time with God, I will need faith to declare words over that person. Whereas, if I have prayed before, I just have to touch the person without saying anything and pass something on. I transfer the blessing, the healing, and the anointing. As Jesus said, "... they will lay hands on the sick, and they will recover." (Mark 16:18 NKJV).

Why are many believers laying hands, and nothing happens? Because they have nothing in their spirit to transfer but empty hands that are being laid on people's heads who have not absorbed the glories of God in prayer. This is why Paul boldly told the Romans, "For I long to see you, that I may impart to you some spiritual gift..." (Romans 1:11 NKJV). He was aware of what he had and could boldly pass it on, that is, consciously transfer it to other people.

Dear reader, did you know that you can pray so much that just walking down the street, someone might come up to you and praise you or acknowledge the good things in you? I remember back in my college days, in 2010, I overheard my classmates saying that the cream I applied cost too much money because my face glowed abnormally.

Likewise, I once bought a simple backpack at a meager price. Still, my classmates commented that I had a very expensive backpack. Why? The answer is simple: glory was passed from me to a cheap backpack and made it expensive. This happened because glory has the potential to beautify in the eyes of others, including things that are simple and not very beautiful to you.

That's why I'm emphasizing this: the value of prayer cannot be measured only by the answers in terms of what God will or can give you but by the results of it in your spirit. In other words, its impact on your spirit empowers and enables you to function as a god on earth with supernatural abilities. This is because prayer is the only time the Holy Spirit and man's spirit enter into spiritual romance. In this process, the glories of God are transferred from God by the Holy Spirit to man's spirit, to his inner man. This is where boldness, courage, wisdom, spiritual intelligence, fortitude, and enlightenment arise. Your spirit is so enlightened that it becomes like a recharged battery, full of spiritual electricity to impact the physical world. Everything you touch receives the blessing. As a result, you receive direction and guidance on what to do in life and your choices. This is why Moses received glory that even he didn't realize after spending forty days and forty nights on the mount with God, hearing His voice and talking to Him. It caused those under the mountain to notice that his skin shone with God's glory to such an extent that they had to get a veil to cover him every time he went out of the tent of meeting.

People who only pray when they have problems, and God solves them, will always have other unsolved problems. They will never have a completely solved life; they haven't reached this spiritual stage. This is why David summed it up by saying, "In Your presence is fullness of joy; at Your right hand are pleasures forevermore" (Psalms 16:11 NKJV).

If you want delights and joy, always activate the presence of God in your life through prayer.

In the text from Mark 1:32-35, we see a typical example of Jesus' daily life: He would wake up early to spend time with the Father in prayer, and throughout the day, he would minister the good news, healing and setting captives free. With a simple word or a quietly spoken command, he would command the demons to leave in the blink of an eye. He would touch the sick, and the diseases and infirmities would disappear in a fraction of a second. Can you see all that glory? It was taken from Him to give to the people. What did He have? Joy, life, and peace. Only when He took away, He had to refill Himself afterward. That is why even I have to refill myself after ministering because when I minister, I unload something. Therefore, I need to replenish myself in prayer - spending qualitative time with the heavenly Father.

This explains why the anointing of many men of God doesn't manifest itself in the same way in every service. There are times when the anointing is strong and at other times weak. Many don't understand why in a given service, the power of God was strongly manifested with healings and wonders. Yet, everything is lukewarm, dead, and extinguished in another service. Moreover, they don't know what to do to keep the rhythm and flow of God's power constantly at any time and place, with regularity and consistency.

I, for one, know what to do to activate the anointing. Again and again, it manifests and works without fail. It's essential to refill before distributing what we have received from God. For example, when I put my hand on someone's head in ministering or when speaking in teaching or prophesying, I am taking something from myself. From the depths of my spirit - from my spiritual reservoir. Then, I have to replenish myself again. Jesus had moments of intimacy with the Father at dawn, morning, and evening to replenish himself.

Understand this: prayer is a process of spiritual replenishment. In the spiritual arena, you are like a car where you have to fill the fuel tank. When you drive, the gasoline or diesel runs out due to the combustion process that makes the engine work by moving the vehicle. You must refill the tank for another trip, meaning you must pray all the time. Soon, after you have what you have asked for in prayer, pray more now that you have received the things than before so that no more attacks will come above what you have received. For example, there is a prayer that you pray to have or achieve success in any area of your life. Once you have achieved it, you have to say another prayer to protect and maintain it. Many only pray to have, but because they don't pray to protect, they end up being attacked and losing what they asked.

This principle is valid for various areas or spheres of life. Many couples, for example, are happy at the beginning of their relationship but later live in constant quarrels. Why is this? One of the reasons is that they had lost the intensity with which they prayed before and their motivation to pray. They think they already have what they want but leave the conquests unprotected for lack of prayer. Victory is conquered, and conquered victory is protected because the enemies you defeated were left behind. However, to climb other steps in life, you will have to face other enemies - conquering new territories. If you go up some steps and relax in prayer, you will not go up any further; the tendency will be to go backward. This is why Scripture encourages us to pray without ceasing.

For this cause, many people attend church and receive deliverance, healing, and even material blessings. Then, when their life begins to go well, they leave the church, and the worst happens to them. They start saying that what they received wasn't real. Yes, it was real; they just didn't know how to protect it.

You have to learn to protect even the people you work with. For example, let's assume you work in a company and have a boss. Pray for him because if the devil can't touch you, he may want to touch him, and by using you or influencing you, he may cause you to lose your job or attack the company to go bankrupt. This way, you lose your job. If you do business, pray for your customers because the devil can influence them not to buy the things you sell. Pray for your husband or wife that you will not be the gateway for the devil to ruin or destabilize your family. Also, pray for those under your authority if you are a leader, boss, or employer.

When the devil can't attack you, he will want to attack the people you love to hurt your heart. He knows he can't hurt you, but he will try to do it indirectly by proxy or by attacking the people around you. It's like proxy warfare, where two countries fight against each other without direct confrontation. The devil can make you suffer without necessarily touching you directly. He can make someone sick or behave abnormally at home or in your circles of people you care about.

Imagine you are getting on a bus to commute to your workplace; the devil may touch the bus driver or even cause the car to break down so that you will be late and get kicked out. Hence, you must also pray for the driver who drives you and the car you get on. Pray for the pilot of the plane and the plane. Pray for everything and everyone around you in your orbit.

Pray even for your teacher at school because you may have studied and done the semester successfully. Then, suddenly, the teacher gets sick and dies without having posted the grades. You may have to retake the exams you had already passed because the teacher died and the grades were lost. And you had good grades, but now you have to retake the exams and answer questions you have forgotten, even about the subject you answered correctly. Thus, you will have to start from scratch due to not having covered your teachers in prayer. You should also pray for the president of your country, the prime minister, or the government that runs your country's physical and social destinies. In fact, you should pray for your country. And don't forget to pray for your spiritual leaders in the church. Pray for me too, and for my family.

We have a lot to pray for. Therefore, no one can say they have nothing to put as a prayer point or have no words to say to God. Therefore, I recommend you study page 45 of the book "The Four Essential Habits of a New Creation in Christ," which discusses the Diary of Jesus.

Chapter III
The latent benefits of prayer

Looking at all the spiritual giants described in the pages of the Holy Scriptures, we can notice that they were men of prayer with deep intimacy with God. Their boldness, authority, and victory come from this communion. Moreover, God backed up their words whenever they publicly spoke in His name. Why is prayer so important? Well, I list below some reasons why it is so essential. However, know beforehand that this importance is linked to the effectiveness of prayer: what it can do or make, what it can stop and prevent from happening. In other words, everything that happens on earth will be decided by the practice of prayer or the lack of it.

Subchapter I

1. Prayer strengthens our communion with God.

It's important to know that the basis of prayer is communion between man and God and vice versa. The apostle John said, "...and truly our fellowship is with the Father and with His Son Jesus Christ" (1 John 1:3b NKJV). Indeed, we have been called to fellowship with God. This fellowship is established through prayer, and God is faithful to protect, direct, bless and keep his children based on the parameters established by this fellowship. As the apostle Paul said, "God is faithful, by whom you were called into the fellowship of His Son, Jesus Christ our Lord" (1 Corinthians 1:9 NKJV). Prayer is a life of fellowship, communication, and intimacy with God.

For example, how can a couple strengthen their fellowship with each other? Through communication - they must dialogue; they must talk. When the dialogue ends, the problems begin. Following the same diapason, we can deduce that God always wants us to talk to

Him. We talk to the Lord in prayer, and He talks to us through His word. When He speaks, we are filled with His glory, transformed, and made better; our fellowship is strengthened when we speak to him. So in prayer, you talk to God. Note the words of Daniel: "Now while I was speaking, praying, and confessing my sin and the sin of my people Israel, and presenting my supplication before the Lord my God for the holy mountain of my God, yes, while I was speaking in prayer, the man Gabriel, whom I had seen in the vision at the beginning, being caused to fly swiftly, reached me about the time of the evening offering. And he informed me, and talked with me, and said, "O Daniel, I have now come forth to give you skill to understand" (Daniel 9:20-22 NKJV).

Notice that the angel Gabriel came while Daniel was talking in prayer. This means that Daniel was conscious that he was talking, speaking with Him with faith that God heard him. Many believers start and pray without having a spirit of communication and communicability. They talk as if no one on the other side can hear the prayer.

Dear reader, have you ever stopped to think that when you pray, you are talking to God, just as you would be talking to your father or mother? How would you address someone you are talking to? You would use words expressed in sentences, with punctuation and everything else that should come in a sentence. That is, you would speak, but you would be speaking in prayer - speaking to God. So we can say that prayer is how we talk to God. It isn't necessarily the words we say but how they are conveyed to God, how we express ourselves and communicate with God.

Prayer is like a telephone line; the telephone line itself doesn't speak - we use it to convey our words, establishing contact and communication between the sender and receiver and vice versa. Therefore, prayer is a channel. Through this channel, we talk to God, our heavenly Father. It's even possible to pray without the words coming out audibly from the mouth. Hannah did this in the temple at Silo, and God granted her the fruit of the womb (1 Samuel 1:9-19). Notice Hannah's words, "For this child I prayed; and the Lord granted me my petition which I asked of Him" (Verse 27). Notice that she prayed, but no one heard what she said. At this level, prayer happens within the prayer. It establishes contact with the divine essence without the physical world hearing what was said in the interaction between two spirits in prayer: the spirit of man and the Spirit of God. This is why I said that prayer helps strengthen our communion with God and consequently makes us stronger in spirit, mind, and body.

Subchapter II

2. Prayer increases our spiritual sensitivity.

In the physical sphere, natural men function based on five senses: sight (the eyes), hearing (the ears), touch, taste (the tongue), and smell (the nostrils and nose). So, we can say that combining these reflexes helps man become aware, conscious, and perceive the environment around him. He sees with his eyes, hears with his ears, feels by touch, tastes with his tongue, and smells with his nostrils. He needs these five senses, and it's from them that he derives knowledge about the world. This influences his communication and increases his vocabulary. For example, he knows how to say it's cold or hot because he feels it in his skin. He can tell the colors of objects because he sees them.

One must realize that the physical world was created from the spiritual world, so what is seen came from what is unseen (Hebrews 1:3). Faith helps to understand this. Therefore, if there are physical senses, there are also spiritual ones in parallel. The problem is that the natural man doesn't have these functional senses. All this came about because of the fall of man due to sin. He lost the faculties that gave him dominion over the earth. He became a natural man and not a superman that God had created. Sin humanized man, reducing him to function merely confined to the five physical senses.

However, the new birth and faith in Christ can make a man a new creature. So, the new birth divinizes him, reveres him, and enables him by the power of the Holy Spirit to function with five more spiritual senses. So he would have ten in total: five physical and five spiritual. Where you are limited naturally, you can trigger and activate the spiritual senses and win. How? Through prayer. Prayer helps increase our spiritual sensitivity to keep track and be aware of things happening in the spiritual world. Understand this: all things that exist in physical form have their correspondence in the spiritual world in the form of words. But to manifest themselves on earth and be visible and tangible, they must be given material bodies. Therefore, God made the physical body to accommodate the spiritual man He had created, to make him legal and functional on earth. Did you know that even the cars we drive used to exist in the form of thoughts and words in someone's mind? So when your spirit is sensitive to the things of the spirit, it can take possession of blessings and spiritual things that will become material things when confessed.

That's why when Hagar and her son cried for lack of water in the desert, the angel of the Lord just opened her eyes, and she saw a well next door. She drew from the water and drank with her boy (Genesis 21:19). The Scripture doesn't say that God made the well, but that He opened her eyes to see what was already there. The well was there in spiritual form and only materialized when her spiritual eyes were opened. Thus, Hagar had other spiritual senses that gave her access to the physical water that she and the baby physically drank. Please take note of this: the water was physical, drunk by the physical mouths of Hagar and her son Ishmael. However, in the first instance, that water was in spiritual form because although it was in the desert, she didn't see it. She could have died of thirst along with the baby, looking for something that was already there but not physically accessible. So God opened her spiritual eyes to see with spiritual eyes what she could not see with physical eyes but needed. Soon that which was spiritual (the water) became materially accessible. Have you ever stopped to imagine how much money, how many goods, and how many things exist in the spiritual world here on earth with us, but in spiritual form? If your spiritual eyes were opened, you would take possession of them. This is why Paul encouraged Timothy to take possession of eternal life (1 Timothy 6:12). You can only take possession of what already exists. Know this: God created the universe in six days and rested on the seventh. Therefore, he is no longer doing things as we imagine. Things materialize when we trigger spiritual principles, and things in the spiritual form will become physical-material. They will take on material form, and you will have them.

However, to get to this stage, one must pray with God. Prayer gives us access to the spiritual world.

In the New Testament, we find the example of the apostle Peter. God wanted to speak to him about some men coming to get him on behalf of Cornelius, a Roman centurion. This man was a Gentile, so God knew Peter would refuse to enter his house. He felt like going up on the terrace to pray while they prepared a meal for him. Suddenly, he went into a trance and saw a sheet with four ends and all kinds of animals and quadrupeds. The voice of God commanded him to kill and eat, which he declined because it looked unclean, and he had never eaten unclean things. But God told him that he shouldn't call unclean something He Himself had sanctified. When he was still thinking about the vision, the men sent by Cornelius were already arriving. The Scripture says, "While Peter thought about the vision, the Spirit said to him, "Behold, three men are seeking you. Arise therefore, go down and go with them, doubting nothing; for I have sent them" (Acts 10:19-20 NKJV). Notice that Peter saw what he saw and heard the Holy Spirit's voice directing him because he had been in prayer. Peter's prayer activated and increased his spiritual sensitivity to see and hear in the spirit to solve a physical problem. He went where he was supposed to go and did what he was supposed to do because he had God's direction. He prayed.

Dear reader, if you apply your heart to prayer, you can have the same results and much more, for Jesus Christ is the same yesterday, today, and forever.

Subchapter III

3. Prayer helps cancel out evil in the spiritual arena.

The spiritual world controls the physical world, and everything that happens in the physical world has its origins in the spiritual world: accidents where demons drink blood in large quantities, wars, fights in homes and marriages, young people addicted to drugs, the world of crime, and other alterations that plague humanity have their origins in the kingdom of darkness headed by the devil. All diabolical plans can be canceled through prayer.

We see this on several occasions in the Holy Scriptures. For example, Herod's plan to kill Peter was canceled when the Church prayed, and the angel of the Lord was sent to free him from prison (Acts 12:5-11). I will explain this in detail in the following chapters about the prayer of intercession.

The plans of King Sennacherib of Assyria to take Jerusalem, the nation of Judah, the captive, was foiled when Isaiah, the prophet, and King Hezekiah prayed. God sent an angel of the Lord, who destroyed all the mighty men of the Assyrian army, including the princes and the chiefs of the king's camp. He returned with a shameful face to his land, and his sons killed him (2 Chronicles 32:20-21).

Dear reader, if you pray too, evil plans can be canceled and aborted in the spiritual world before they happen in the physical. Use the name of Jesus. "I neutralize all the devil's plans against my life, family, and country in the name of the Lord Jesus Christ."

Subchapter IV

4. Prayer reinforces God's will on earth and in fulfilling the promises and prophecies.

Not everything God has promised in his word will pass just because he promised it. There is a part for us as humans to pray to strengthen its fulfillment. Daniel is one of the practical examples in this regard. He had read in the manuscripts the prophecy of Jeremiah, the prophet, that the desolation (slavery) of Israel would be only seventy years. At the end of this period, they would be free. However, he realized that although God had made the promise, Israel was still captive. In light of this, he held fast to God's promises and, relying on His many mercies, decided in his heart to pray and fast (Daniel 9:1-3). A word was revealed to Daniel about a protracted war, and he understood this word and understood the vision. For this cause, he was to fast and pray for three whole weeks, desiring no food (Daniel 10:1-4). Indeed, there was a prince of darkness responsible for influencing and controlling the physical prince of Persia to keep Israel imprisoned. Their prison would seem physical and dependent on the prince of Persia. Still, reality shows that there were spiritual forces behind it all. This is what the angel told him and that he had asked for help from the Archangel Michael, the prince of the armies guarding and fighting for Israel. Finally, Daniel won that battle through prayer and reinforced the fulfillment of Jeremiah's prophecy.

One must look at life from a spiritual point of view and trigger spiritual laws to change the situation on earth. And prayer is one of these laws. Even in Jesus' model of prayer, He said, "In this manner, therefore, pray: Our Father in heaven, Hallowed be Your name. Your kingdom come. Your will be done, On earth as it is in heaven" (Matthew 6:9-10 NKJV).

Did you notice that even God's will on earth must be reinforced through prayer? He gave the earth to the children of men. It is up to us as humans and citizens of God's kingdom to spend time with God's word, studying and meditating to decipher His will. Then, we must pray for what God said in His word about us to happen.

For example, it is God's will that you, as a woman, bear children because He said, "No one shall suffer miscarriage or be barren in your land; I will fulfill the number of your days" (Exodus 23:26 NKJV). Therefore, if the sister cannot conceive, she can claim the fulfillment of this promise in prayer. "Father, according to the word, I would not be barren, and I would not suffer a miscarriage. So in the name of the Lord Jesus, I receive grace to be a mother, I receive the fruit of the womb, and I rebuke the spirit of barrenness to leave me forever. Thank you for giving me the joy of being a mother."

If you are sick, you can claim your healing. "Father, you said in your word that you would take sickness away from me. Therefore, in the name of Jesus, I rebuke this illness and receive healing now."

Exercise

1. Look at the Holy Scriptures (Holy Bible) and look for God's promises concerning your life or situation;

Pray about them to the Lord, claiming their fulfillment in the name of Jesus.

Chapter IV
Spend time with God in prayer

"Now it came to pass in those days that He went out to the mountain to pray, and continued all night in prayer to God. And when it was day, He called His disciples to Himself; and from them He chose twelve whom He also named apostles" (Luke 6:12-13 NKJV).

We see that Jesus prayed all night. You cannot make important decisions without first praying. Learn to have solitary places to pray and dedicate days and weeks to praying. You can pray while fasting and not; be a champion in prayer.

When Jesus spent time with the Father in prayer, He absorbed the glory and virtues of heaven. When He came down from the mountain, everyone wanted to touch Him because what He had received was flowing from Him to the sick who were miraculously healed. Here, praying for people to be healed is no longer necessary, but anyone who thirsts will drink this glory. It was not Him praying for the sick; each sick person went to touch and received their portion of healing and blessing.

Looking at this scenario, you might think it's easy, but it's not. Before that moment of glory, those instantaneous miracles, healings, and forensic and extraordinary prophecies, there was a time to cast yourself before the Father, pray, pour yourself out, and surrender to the Holy Spirit.

It's no accident that our church headquarters is in a rural area. Still, people from various social classes, nations, languages, ethnicities, and races commute from cities and their countries and come to our ministry in droves. But, before I go up to the altar to minister, there is work to be done behind the scenes - time with God.

That's why Paul said, "Pray without ceasing" (1 Thessalonians 5:17). When you spend time with God, even unconsciously (not actively knowing), you receive a glory you don't see. Something happens every time we pray. You don't have to feel it, but your spirit absorbs the heavenly glories of the world to come. You begin to explode into creative and innovative ideas, visions, and revelations. An idea that couldn't have come in any way comes to your mind after you have prayed, and glorious projects are born in the process. So don't get poor or sickly, because as He is, so are we in this world (1 John 4:17b).

I often say, "Never joke, never threaten, never try to harm a man or woman who prays. These people are dangerous."

Take the case of King Sennacherib of Assyria, who had his soldiers invade Samaria and take everything they had. However, King Hezekiah and the prophet Isaiah prayed to God - the God of heaven who created the whole universe. As a result, the Holy Bible says that God sent an angel, who killed one hundred eighty-five thousand valiant men in answer to the prayer of two men who had faith and fellowship with God (Isaiah 37:36).

When you have a man or woman who prays and is intimate with God, don't touch him, it's dangerous for you. When I see a man who preaches the word of God, I recognize him. But when I find that man has intimacy with God and is a man of prayer, I respect him. Why? **Because he who kneels before God will always remain standing before the challenges and problems in this world.**

That demon that ripped your husband away doesn't know who he is dealing with. Your knees are running for him to return while you are in the room, on your knees, or standing in prayer. That colleague at work who tries to set you up for being close to the boss has no idea about the power of the prayers you say.

When I was younger, Jesus spoke to me and said, "Onório, be careful about one thing; you can't be angry. It's very dangerous to have someone on earth that makes you angry. No matter who they are, that person will be destroyed. So, if you want to spare some people, avoid getting angry with them." In fact, throughout my life, I have been cautious of two things: my tongue and **patience**. If I get angry with someone and they stay alive for a year, that's good luck. That's why some people who are around me think I get angry. What they don't know is that my anger has rounds. I can be sad about one thing, and it ends in my mind, but when that thing hits my spirit, I know that the person will not hold out for long or the situation I am sad about will not stand for long.

Most of the people who tried to persecute me are not among us.

One day in 2015, three armed thugs showed up at my house, and I wasn't there. They made a mistake and kidnapped the gardener. My wife was coming home from college and saw them leaving with an AKM47, taking the young gardener. When she told me, I became angry in spirit. That night, I had a vision in which God said the situation would be resolved in three days. After three days, they went into a gentleman's house in the area where we lived before, and as they were leaving, they ran into the police, and all three were shot dead.

On another occasion, armed people were in the church chasing a sister; I said only one word. But unfortunately, on their way home, they had an accident, and one of them lost his leg.

One should never play with the Lord's anointed. This is why God warned: "Do not touch My anointed ones, and do My prophets no harm" (Psalms 105:15 NKJV).

On one occasion, in 2003, if I'm not mistaken, a great healer from Boane, Maputo, Mozambique, threatened me. I told him to watch out for me. He went home and became seriously ill, and while he was dying, his wife asked me to forgive her husband. I said they shouldn't play with people they didn't know and told her, "Go; he is free." He was healed, and the family converted to Christ. People cannot abuse God and the church.

Of all the things you can do, never make the apostle angry.

There was a bishop of a particular church who started speaking ill of me. Days later, the church he leads was left with no one and to this day has no believers except him and his family.

Paul said, "If your enemy is hungry, feed him; if he is thirsty, give him a drink; for in so doing you will heap coals of fire on his head." Do not be overcome by evil, but overcome evil with good" (Romans 12:20-21 NKJV).

One must be careful with people who depend on God and nothing else. When someone depends solely on God and has put Him as his strong arm, he has no other recourse but God. Therefore, be very careful with such people, especially if the hand of God is with them as it was with the people of Israel when they left Egypt.

I am reminded of the prayer of Josaphat, king of Judah, when he said, "For we have no power against this great multitude that is coming against us; nor do we know what to do, but our eyes are upon You" (2 Chronicles 20:12 NKJV). So God bewildered the enemies who fought and killed each other, and God's people were left for three days to collect the loot in the form of gold, silver, clothing, and animals.

This is why I don't react when people speak ill of me. My missionaries know this; all the people who have tried to destroy the ministry have not prevailed! Do you know why? Because we carry greatness in us because we trust only in God.

Paul said, "If I must boast, I will boast of the things that show my weakness" (2 Corinthians 11:30 NIV). David said, "Glory in His holy name" (Psalms 105:3).

Spend time with God: praying to the Father in Jesus' name, worshiping Him, praising Him, saying He is good, He is holy. That time is beneficial. If you practice this starting today, there is a guarantee that even what you have not asked for, you will get it without having asked for it. The glory that you carry will bring things.

What to do?

Reading the text in Isaiah 36:37 carefully, we see that Hezekiah and Isaiah's prayer didn't take long. They did it once in faith; that very night, there was an answer, and God delivered his people.

Notice this: when you have a problem or a challenge in your family, at work, in your marriage, or your home, take that problem, write it down on paper, go to your place of prayer, get on your knees and present the problem to God. You have to be specific about what you want God to solve. If you have an issue today and can't write it down, put it on your tongue and present it to God. You will receive victory notes in your spirit. Prayer is the power that God has given us to move the heavens and the earth and alter the course of events.

Now, raise your hands and pray.

PART III
Principles for effective prayer in the New Testament

Introduction
How to pray and receive answers from God

Prayer is a spiritual law, a principle that works whenever we activate it. Furthermore, some sub-principles make prayer produce results. We will get results if we follow the same principles established in God's Word. The text of 1 John 5:14-15 NKJV attests: "Now this is the confidence that we have in Him, that if we ask anything according to His will, He hears us. And if we know that He hears us, whatever we ask, we know that we have the petitions that we have asked of Him." We will always have testimonies when we activate the principles that make prayer work. Moreover, we will be confident of two things:

1. That when we pray, God hears us,

2. That He answers and grants the petitions that we ask of Him.

However, we must pray according to His will, expressed in His Word. God has defined the lines of communication we should use to connect with Him in ways that He will answer us. This is why Jesus said, "If you abide in Me, and My words abide in you, you will ask what you desire, and it shall be done for you" (John 15:7 NKJV). What a wonderful promise from the Lord Jesus! He promises that the Father will hear and answer us. And in all this, our trust in Him grows, for He is a living, faithful God who hears and answers when His children pray. Now, let's see what the Word of God prescribes for us in the New Testament concerning prayer: how to pray correctly and receive answers. Otherwise, what the Scriptures we read indicate to us, is that God promises to answer and grant us what we ask of Him. This in itself should generate an expectation and a desire to talk to God.

Why do many ask but don't receive? James answers, "You ask and do not receive, because you ask amiss, that you may spend it on your pleasures" (James 4:3 NKJV). When you ask badly, you don't receive. Therefore, you must ask according to His will expressed in His Word.

Otherwise, someone might ask God to give you your sister's husband, your sister's husband's house, or your brother's wife. Anything you ask for that is not consistent with God's will expressed in his Word will not be granted to you. The Lord would violate the precepts of his Word and thus lose credibility. Glory be to God because he cannot lose credibility. After all, he is perfectly faithful, and you can trust him! As stated in Malachi 3:6 NKJV: "For I am the Lord, I do not change." "Heaven and earth will pass away, but My words will by no means pass away" (Matthew 24:35 NKJV).

Chapter I
Principle number 1

1. Recognize your need and dependence on God.

You need God and must depend on Him confidently in your heart.

According to the Holy Scriptures, everything starts from recognizing that you and I need God. There is no other motivation to pray and seek God if man considers himself self-sufficient and independent of God. You need Him. Whether rich or poor, healthy or sick, weak or strong, sinner or righteous, big or small - we all need God. This is the cradle of contact with divinity-hunger and thirst for God. Why is this principle important? The answer is simple: prayer must come from the heart - from deep within and not merely from the mind. In prayer, you must establish this contact of dependence on God and his provision, dependence on God and his direction, protection, help, and life. The prayer that moves God is the one that comes from a heart surrendered to Him, from a heart trusting and depending on Him. He told the people of Israel that after they had entered the promised land, lived in their new homes, and eaten grapes and honey, they were not to forget the Lord because He had brought them out of the house of bondage. Instead, they were to remember that He gives us the power to acquire "wealth" to confirm His covenant with their fathers Abraham, Isaac, and Israel (Deuteronomy 8:11-1).

Notice verses 12, 13, and 14 NKJV: "Lest—when you have eaten and are full, and have built beautiful houses and dwell in them; and when your herds and your flocks multiply, and your silver and your gold are multiplied, and all that you have is multiplied; when your heart is lifted up, and you forget the Lord your God who brought you out of the land of Egypt, from the house of bondage." Did you notice that God is interested in the state of our hearts, knowing that we always need and depend on Him? Therefore, He warned that our hearts should not rise above our needs and dependence because He gives us everything.

It's very easy for someone to pray when they have nothing to eat and nowhere to live. On the other hand, it's very common to see people without jobs, without homes or stable homes pray, fast, and seek God and not miss church services. They are always in the service, arriving early, no matter the distance. They wake up early to pray and study the Bible. They are faithful in the weekly or monthly programs of their congregation. Why? What is their motivation? One of the reasons may be their needs, hunger, sickness, misery, family curses, and bad luck in their professional, sentimental, or academic life. However, they forget about God when they are delivered, healed, and blessed. They think they already have everything and no longer need to pray or attend church services. They are already married, have houses, have good jobs, and their children are in elite schools. They drive the cars they want, and there is plenty of food in the house. Business is going well, and money is no longer a problem. Many of these brothers and sisters don't even pray anymore, either at home or in church. They think they don't need God. The blessings and riches have turned their hearts away from God. They don't know that they are heading for a great fall.

Just as God asked the farmer, who had gathered everything in his barns and didn't need God, the Lord asked him, "'Fool! This night your soul will be required of you; then whose will those things be which you have provided?" (Luke 12:20 NKJV). After that, the scales fell from his eyes, and he soon realized that man's life doesn't consist in the abundance of possessions he possesses but in the grace of God. That's why God told Paul, "My grace is sufficient for you, for My strength is made perfect in weakness" (2 Corinthians 12:9 NKJV). What weakness? The weakness of a heart surrendered to God's Word, a spirit thirsting for God, and a person dependent on God at all times and in all circumstances.

You must get to a level where even though you have everything you need or that others don't, you remain simple, humble, and of good character - dependent on God. Many people are not necessarily humble; poverty makes them look like they are. When someone has nothing, it's easy to show false humility and demonstrate false love. Give him the power, the money, the position, and the power, and you will see his true colors. As Abraham Lincoln once observed, "Power corrupts, and absolute power corrupts absolutely." On another occasion, he observed,

"Almost all men can endure/resist adversity, but if you want to test their character, give them power." This observation is almost timeless. Have you ever noticed that most people with some material power don't flock to churches almost every Saturday, Sunday, or other days of worship? Why? Because they are busy with the temporal things of this life. Power, money, and fame have given them a sense of false security - something sneaky, fleeting, and evaporating. It is all trivial, for nothing is firm and secure without God.

People tend to seek God when they are in despair, in a pinch, or at a dead end. A relative is terminally ill in the hospital or clinic, and the money and the doctors can no longer do anything to extend that person's life by at least one more day. The marriage is at risk, and they need restoration, a miracle. The employment contract is about to end; you are in a car at risk of an accident or a plane in a turbulence zone. Or because you are in a war zone and your life is in danger. When they are already well, they dismiss God as if He were disposable. God wants us to prosper and be healthy, but our spirit and heart must be steadfast in Him. As it says in 3 John 2 NKJV, "Beloved, I pray that you may prosper in all things and be in health, just as your soul prospers." It's God's will that you prosper and enjoy abundant health but that you never forget the Lord. So the Scripture testifies: "The blessing of the Lord makes one rich, and he adds no sorrow with it" (Proverbs 10:22 NKJV).

You don't need a blessing that brings pain or inconvenience. You need peace of the soul, and only God can give it to you. Therefore, you must surrender your heart to Him, trust Him, and be conscious of His presence.

This is how the principle of prayer is born - from a heart dependent on God. Even King David, who had all the best at his disposal, never discarded it from his life and heart. On the contrary, he said, "One thing I have desired of the Lord, That will I seek: That I may dwell in the house of the Lord All the days of my life, To behold the beauty of the Lord, And to inquire in His temple. For in the time of trouble He shall hide me in His pavilion; In the secret place of His tabernacle He shall hide me; He shall set me high upon a rock" (Psalms 27:4-5 NKJV). This is the habit of God's great men and women - to pray.

The Patriarchs Abraham, Isaac, and Jacob were men of altars. Therefore, men of prayer were in constant interaction and contact with heaven. Contact with God through prayer, dependent on Him.

A case study can be made by observing the attitudes of King Asa:

1. A heart dependent on God.

When Solomon died, the kingdom of Israel (all 12 unified tribes) split into two kingdoms: the kingdom of Judah, the southern kingdom with its capital in Jerusalem, and the kingdom of Israel, also described as the northern kingdom and with its capital in Samaria. In the period when Asa was king of Judah, the Ethiopians (kingdom of Ethiopia) came with a million soldiers and chariots and war horses vastly outnumbering the army of Judah. In this period, Asa's heart was turned to God, trusting in Him and depending on Him for his victory, protection, and provision. Facing this massive army, numerically superior to him, Asa had the most extraordinary God on his side, superior to the entire Ethiopian army. First, he took down the altars of the strange gods and the high ones, broke the statues, and cut down the groves. Second, he commanded Judah to seek the Lord, the God of their fathers (Abraham, Isaac, and Jacob), and to observe the law and commandment of God (2 Chronicles 14:3-4). This was righteous in God's eyes.

In short, he cleansed his heart and turned it away from idols to turn solely to the Lord. So, with a heart surrendered to the Lord and trusting in Him, he prayed, "Lord, it is nothing for You to help, whether with many or with those who have no power; help us, O Lord our God, for we rest on You, and in Your name we go against this multitude. O Lord, You are our God; do not let man prevail against You!" (verse 11). In response, the Lord smote the Ethiopians before Asa and Judah, and they fled. The people of Judah were left to gather the spoils of the victory God had granted them.

How could King Asa achieve such a victory in a disadvantageous situation for him and his people? The answer is simple: he trusted the Lord with all his heart and prayed to Him in total and complete dependence.

Dear reader, I want you to notice one thing: the prayer that Asa said took neither an hour nor thirty minutes, but it had a tremendous impact. "Why, Apostle Onório?" - you may ask. Well, because that prayer came out of the depths of his heart. There was nothing else he and his people could do in the face of such a frightening situation that presented itself as a dead end. So he fully settled his heart on God - Spirit, soul, and body. Therefore, he won the battle with God's help. This is what we call the "power of short prayers."

The power of short prayers

Understand this: prayer's power "or impact" is not in the long or short hours you pray, nor in the shout or low voice. It is not in the position of your body when you pray on your knees, your feet, your stomach, or your back, but in the state of your heart - which recognizes and depends entirely on God. This kind of prayer will come out of the heart with power and life and will indeed produce results. Why? Because your spirit is involved there. For this reason, the Scripture says, "For the eyes of the Lord run to and fro throughout the whole earth, to show Himself strong on behalf of those whose heart is loyal to Him..." (2 Chronicles 16:9 NKJV). Through the joy of victory, Asa and the people of Israel "entered into a covenant to seek the Lord God of their fathers with all their heart and with all their soul" (2 Chronicles 15:12 NKJV).

It had happened to me several times when I was in a very urgent health situation, someone between life and death. I was standing near the ambulance with the doctors, not knowing whether the person would make it to the hospital. And in that instant, I said a short prayer: "Father, show your glory and don't allow them to die. I rebuke the Spirit of death to let go of her soul now, in the name of Jesus Christ." And suddenly, the miracle happened. The person returned to life to the amazement of all the doctors and health care personnel. This kind of prayer goes out with all your soul because you have no choice or solution but to look to God. Josaphat said, "O our God, will You not judge them? For we have no power against this great multitude that is coming against us; nor do we know what to do, but our eyes are upon You" (2 Chronicles 20:12 NKJV).

Dear reader, has this ever happened to you? Have you ever been in a situation like this? I have, and several times. There was one that, given the urgency and emergency of the situation, I didn't even have time to open my mouth. I just prayed from the bottom of my heart, trusting and depending on God. I saw the power of God at work – even opening doors that were closed, touching tough people, and changing unfavorable situations into advantageous ones. So I wrote this book to help you too.

I remember when my wife gave birth to Esther, my youngest daughter. She was born prematurely and was so tiny that the doctors said she wouldn't live. We had to treat her like a kangaroo (put her inside my shirt on my chest or under her mother's blouse to warm her up). Three times she died, and we prayed. The Lord raised her from the dead. That day, the hospital had no ambulance or oxygen. It was one of the things that moved me later to buy an ambulance and offer it to the Matola provincial hospital to help others.

Many think that we, as men of God, don't go through trials and just sit around with a Holy Bible, waiting for people who have problems for us to pray for them. Many bring various cases and problems to us, and we must be teachers, counselors, firefighters, psychologists, psychiatrists, doctors, fathers, and mothers to these people. They don't realize that we are also human, superhuman, graced with a special grace to deliver and bless other people. Many people who come to us for help and are blessed never return to say thank you. This isn't a problem because we know who has called us. We are soldiers, and we are to spiritually defend those whom the devil has imprisoned or seeks to oppress.

We are often hated for things we have not done, just for doing good for others. Many have no concept of the life of a man of God. We can't go to certain places or do certain things that ordinary believers do. We are soldiers of Christ and are always on missions because the devil, the adversary of humanity, does not sleep. We always have to watch and pray, fast, and think about the people.

My daughter was in the hospital, and I had to go and visit her during the day; at night, I went and ministered to the large crowds waiting for me with their various problems. All or most were delivered, healed, and blessed without seeking to know what was going on with me and my wife. No one was coming to say, "Take this. Go buy fuel for your car or milk for the baby." Everybody was coming to be rescued. So, over the years, I have learned to trust God and depend solely on Him. Many think we live on church offerings; others look at the large crowds that flock to my crusades or our church services and see money. However, they don't know the reality on the ground, that people do come in droves, not with bags of money, but with burdens of sickness, problems, suffering, demons, and afflictions. God uses me to relieve them. My wife and I have our businesses that we do to support our family and support the vision God has given me for ministry. We love the Lord and people, and that love of Christ moves and motivates us - the unfailing presence of the Holy Spirit with us that gives us peace, joy, and victories. God said to Moses, "My presence will go with you, and I will give you rest" (Exodus 33:14 NKJV). And we have already entered into rest because we have learned to unload our burdens at the feet of Jesus and live with his peace. It's our calling - our heavenly calling and not a burden.

Dear reader, I have given you my example so that you will be encouraged that this God whom we serve and worship is faithful and answers prayers, even if they are short. My little girl is now big, slender, beautiful, and extremely intelligent. Yet, anyone who sees her today has no idea where she came from to be and be what she is today. So I am convinced of this God of ours and the power of the name of Jesus Christ. His name works, His power is real, and His love is real.

Have you ever imagined a situation where you see a child or an adult crossing a road and a bus or a truck approaching at high speed? You try to shout for that person to move away, but the voice is not enough, and danger is imminent. What will you do? Pray. But how long will you need to pray for the car to stop or save the person? In this situation, you will need to say a short prayer that comes out of the heart - an interventional prayer from someone who depends on God. "Father, in the name of Jesus, save that person. Nothing is impossible for you. Do something, O Father." And miraculously, the car stops, or an unknown force pushes the person, and soon they are saved. Circumstances like this and others will require your prayer to come out of a surrendered and dependent heart.

2. A heart estranged from God.

King Asa returned to his palace with spoils, joy, and celebration of the victory God had granted him - because he had prayed. However, sometime later, already very rich, prosperous, and full of gold and silver, his heart gradually stopped trusting God; he stopped depending on Him. He began to oppress the people God had entrusted to him (abuse of power). He changed his behavior and became boastful and proud. His heart was lifted. He already had plenty of money and didn't need God for anything. One day, he got sick - an infection got to his feet. Even so, he didn't seek the Lord. On the contrary, he requested the best doctors, given his financial means.

However, the doctors couldn't heal or help him until his feet rotted away and he died. That was the end of the story of a man who began with God and prayer and ended without God and rotten (2 Chronicles 16:12-14). The Scripture says, "His malady was severe; yet in his disease he did not seek the Lord, but the physician" (verse 12b NKJV). Nothing wrong with doctors, for they are a great blessing, and medical science has been a great help to humanity, and we need it. But the problem was that money had gone to his head to the point that he thought he could solve everything with money without needing God.

Did you know that there are diseases that even pills or injections cannot solve? Because demons cause them and no demon is detectable in an X-ray examination or an ultrasound scan - it takes the power of God to break the curses and destroy the works of the devil. In everything, trust God, regardless of your level of prosperity. Don't be so stubborn that the devil blinds you to see the way back to God - return to your heavenly Father while it's still early. So says the Scripture, "Seek the Lord while he may be found, call upon him while he is near" (Isaiah 55:6 NKJV).

In short, the first step or principle to an answered prayer is the predisposition of your heart to trust and depend on God. You may not be able to say everything you want, but God reads your heart and knows your spirit's intention. It all starts with the heart. The Scripture says, "Now He who searches the hearts knows what the mind of the Spirit is, because He makes intercession for the saints according to the will of God" (Romans 8:27 NKJV). With a heart surrendered to God, "...we know that all things work together for good to those who love God, to those who are called by his decree" (verse 28 NKJV). Remember God's words to the prophet Samuel: "Look not at his appearance, nor the height of his stature; for I have rejected him. For the Lord does not see as man sees. For man sees what is before his eyes, but the Lord looks at the heart" (1 Samuel 16:7 NKJV).

How is your heart now? Do you acknowledge that God exists and trust Him as your Redeemer, Protector, Provider, Savior, and Guide? If the answer is yes, then you can begin to pray. Remember that God has more than a thousand and one ways to help you out of any situation. The distance between you and your miracle is in your heart and your faith in God's Word. He is trustworthy. He is an eternal Rock: Abraham, Moses, Elijah, Paul, Peter, and Daniel trusted Him, and He delivered them. Take some time now and thank God for all He has done for you. Praise Him.

Chapter II
Principle number 2

1. Recognize your spiritual position or state before God: righteousness in Christ Jesus.

"The eyes of the Lord are on the righteous, and His ears are open to their cry" (Psalms 34:15 NKJV).

One of the essential things that the believer must have is the awareness of his righteousness before God. Righteousness, in this case, is the righteousness of man's spirit before God. In my book "Grace To Reign," I dwelt at length on this concept, and it will be worthwhile for the reader to purchase and read this companion work. In the text from Matthew 6:31-32, Jesus warned his disciples not to be concerned about what they would eat, drink or wear. Obviously, these three human needs are what drive the lives of many people on earth today. Everyone wants food, shelter, clothing, and something to drink. We wake up early, study, and work to meet these needs, which are human beings' primary concerns, coupled with need and security. Jesus, wanting to relieve us of this worry and give us a glorious life of inexhaustible provision of resources, left us a formula: "But seek first the kingdom of God and His righteousness, and all these things shall be added to you" (Matthew 6:33 NKJV).

The kingdom of God is God's rule in our hearts through his Word and Spirit, shaping our character and impacting us with his culture, will, and purposes so that we please him in all things as our King. By accepting Jesus as our Lord and Savior, we are born again in our spirit - our inner man - and become children of God and simultaneously citizens of the kingdom of heaven. Thus, God bestows upon us the gift of righteousness that serves as a certificate that we no longer have any guilt before Him, for all our sin has been unloaded upon Jesus Christ. Thus, God credits Christ's righteousness to our account, and we appear before Him as one who has never sinned. This is not the result of something deserving or some sacrifice we have made. Still, the result of his love toward us and our part is to receive what Christ's grace has made available to us. That is why the Scripture says, "For He made Him who knew no sin to be sin for us, that we might become the righteousness of God in Him" (2 Corinthians 5:21 NKJV). Therefore, the issue of sin was settled the day we accepted Christ's vicarious sacrifice; from the moment we accepted him as our Lord and Savior. Now we are in Christ, and the sin that separated us from God has been removed, and there is no longer any barrier between God and us.

Remember the text in Isaiah 59:1-2 NKJV: "Behold, the Lord's hand is not shortened, That it cannot save; Nor His ear heavy, That it cannot hear. But your iniquities have separated you from your God; And your sins have hidden His face from you, so that He will not hear." Before you accepted Christ and rested in his finished work, this was your condition. Now, this debt bill has already been removed because you have accepted the lordship of Jesus Christ. You have already been justified, that is, declared innocent by God because Christ paid the price necessary for our liberation and freedom. So now, we are new creatures in Christ and free from sin's consequences. As Paul says, "There is therefore now no condemnation to those who are in Christ Jesus, who do not walk according to the flesh, but according to the Spirit, for the law of the Spirit of life in Christ Jesus has set me free from the law of sin and death" (Romans 8:1-2 NKJV). For this cause, we have peace with God through Christ. Hallelujah.

Thus consciousness is born in us, a mentality: the consciousness of the righteousness of God in Christ Jesus. Say it like this with me: "I am the righteousness of God in Christ Jesus. I have been washed by the blood of Christ, justified and sanctified by the power of his love. I am free from sin. I am of Jesus." With this awareness, you can now pray and expect answers from God.

Notice our opening Scripture for this chapter "The eyes of the Lord are on the righteous, and His ears are open to their cry" (Psalms 34:15 NKJV).

The eyes of the Lord are upon whom? On the righteous. So think of it this way: "The eyes of God are upon me 24 hours a day and seven days a week." The eyes here refer to the Spirit of the Lord, to his attention and care. So the Spirit of the Lord is upon you now and every day. Moreover, his ears are attentive to our prayers.

The psalmist David said, "their cry" because, at the time, many of them needed to cry when they prayed, hence the constant use of this expression. God seemed distant from them; therefore, they must cry out, weep, or shout. This awareness stemmed from the fact that they had such reverence for God that they could not even call him by his name. He seemed a distant, fearful, and frightening God to them. They didn't deal with Jehovah directly, so the people of Israel asked Moses to go and speak to God on their behalf because they feared death.

However, it wasn't like that in the beginning. God always wanted to interact directly with us, with each of his children. But they asked for an intermediary, so it was only the priests and the prophets who ministered to the people on behalf of the Lord and took the people's problems to God. There was a rupture, a gap - the God who wanted to be near and alongside them was feared like a consuming fire. So no one else but this class of prophets, judges, priests, and kings could speak directly to God. Hence, this awareness of a distant God arose in them, even though He was with them daily. Day in a pillar of cloud, and night in a pillar of fire. He had to send the angel of His presence to go before the people in their place so that His wrath would not consume them. Therefore, the people's relationship in the Old Testament was not one of intimacy with God, but one of the laws, sacrifices, death for the sinner, a tooth for a tooth, and an eye for an eye. Even Moses, God's holy man, didn't get to enter the promised land because of the anger the people caused him. They were rebellious from time to time to the commandments of the Lord, turning their hearts away to worship a calf or other gods instead of Him.

Now, do you understand why in principle #1, we discussed the predisposition of your heart to recognize the Lord as the only God and trust Him dependently? Your heart must be turned toward God. When Jesus came, he was called Immanuel, which translates to "God with us." And when Christ ascended into heaven, he sent us the promise of the Father - the Holy Spirit to stay with us forever. The veil of the temple has been torn in half, and God's presence is now available to all who, with sincere hearts, seek him. Thus the Scripture testifies: "For God spoke to our fathers by the prophets many times and in many ways in olden times, but has in these last days spoken to us by his Son" (Hebrews 1:1 NKJV).

You have direct access to God's throne

In this day and age, God needs no intermediary to be able to speak to you. And you don't need one to be able to talk to Him. The way is clear for you, for Jesus is the way, the truth, and the life. No one comes to the Father except through Him (John 14:6).

With this awareness that you are in Christ, you don't need to cry or shout when you pray, for you are in Christ and God hears you as he would hear Christ.

In the following chapter, I will explain this in detail, but the main point here is that you must recognize the position and place you are in - in Christ, in the heavenly places.

I once heard a preacher say in a service, "Brethren, shout because God may not hear us because of the noise of the airplanes in space." Not necessarily. God is not confused. There is nothing in space hindering your prayers. Have you never read the text in Ephesians 1:3 NKJV where Paul says the following? "Blessed be the God and Father of our Lord Jesus Christ, who has blessed us with every spiritual blessing in the heavenly places in Christ." We are in Christ right now, seated with Him in the heavenly places. From this position, we pray, make prophetic decrees, and reign with Christ and in Christ with absolute authority over the devil and his entire demonic constellation.

Now note this: the ears of the Lord are attentive to our prayers. With this awareness, pray to believe and know that God hears you at any time: dawn, day, or night, for his ears are attentive to your prayer. He is close to you. In Him, we live, walk and move. Believe this fact and live in Jehovah Shammah's consciousness, which means, "God is here." He is present in us. Therefore, He is with us. Whenever we pray, He hears us and answers us.

You have an Advocate before the Father

We have come to a place in the spirit (in Christ) where we are righteous, and the Lord always hears our prayers and answers. So, don't let the devil attack your mind with false accusations that God can no longer hear you because of your past and mistakes. On the contrary, if you stumble into some sin or mistake, confess it to the Lord and receive His forgiveness. How to receive God's forgiveness? The text from 1 John 2:1-3 NKJV says, "My little children, these things I write to you so that you may not sin; and if anyone sins, we have an Advocate with the Father, Jesus Christ the Righteous. And He Himself is the propitiation for our sins, and not for ours only, but also for those of the whole world." Believe that. He is powerful to forgive us and to cleanse us from all evil. So, starting today, surrender your body to God, to the holy habitation of the Holy Spirit, and renew your mind through meditation on God's Word.

Know this: God is not up there in Heaven with a hammer or baton in His hands waiting for you and me to fail or slip into sin and then come running to punish us. On the contrary, He has hired two lawyers for us: one in heaven and the other on earth.

Jesus is standing with the Father in our defense and representation in heaven. Someone once said that the devil occasionally goes up to heaven and talks to God about us to tempt us as he did with Job. God occasionally allows the devil to punish us a little, so we stay in line. This thinking reveals ignorance about the Scriptures. Satan did this in the Old Testament, for it was before Christ died on the cross for us and bought us with his blood. The Scripture says of us, "But you are a chosen generation, a royal priesthood, a holy nation, His own special people, that you may proclaim the praises of him who called you out of darkness into his marvelous light; who once were not a people but are now the people of God, who had not obtained mercy but now have obtained mercy" (1 Peter 2:9-10 NKJV). Did you notice the repetitive employment of "now" expression as in "now the people... now you have obtained mercy?" Recognize that it was not by your own holiness but by grace. You and I have found favor in the eyes of the heavenly Father. Jesus is there in heaven for us. We are in Him, reigning together. And know this: the Judge, who is God, is our heavenly Father, and the Advocate, who is Jesus, is our big brother, Lord, and Savior. Glory, glory! We are immensely graced. The devil no longer has any way to go to heaven to accuse us. The text in Revelation 12:10-11 NKJV confirms: "Then I heard a loud voice saying in heaven, 'Now salvation, and strength, and the kingdom of our God, and the power of His Christ have come, for the accuser of our brethren is cast down, who accused them before our God day and night, has been cast down. And they overcame him by the blood of the Lamb and by the word of their testimony...'"

Satan has been overthrown and can no longer go to heaven to make any complaints. How was he defeated? By the blood of the lamb - by the blood of Jesus. The Scripture comforts us, "To him who loved us, and washed us from our sins in His own blood, and has made us kings and priests to His God and Father; to him be glory and dominion forever and ever. Amen!" (Revelation 1:5-6 NKJV). In heaven, Satan is a *persona non grata* - he is not welcome there and hasn't been around for two thousand years.

On the other hand, the Holy Spirit is with us and in us as our Advocate on earth. He helps us in our prayers and weaknesses. He gives us words, inspires us, and guides us into truth. He protects our minds through the Word of God on which we meditate. You must study and meditate on the Word, so the devil doesn't sow doubts or accusations in your mind. Pray using God's Word.

Prayer

"Heavenly Father, thank you so much for your eternal and unconditional love toward me. Thank you for your grace and mercy. I am the righteousness of God in Christ Jesus. Whenever I pray, you hear and answer me. Thank you because your ears are attentive to my prayers and grant my petitions. I am strong and stand firm in the grace that is in Christ. Thank you for protecting my mind and heart. I live with peace and joy, the joy of knowing that I am saved, protected, and loved by you in the name of Jesus."

Chapter III
Principle number 3

When you pray, forgive

"And whenever you stand praying, if you have anything against anyone, forgive him, that your Father in heaven may also forgive you your trespasses. But if you do not forgive, neither will your Father in heaven forgive your trespasses" (Marcos 11.25-26 NKJV).

Forgiveness is one of God's foundational principles for our prayers to be heard and answered. "But why does God want me to forgive those who offend me if I feel hurt by them?" - someone may question. God wants you to forgive because He is interested in your heart and therefore doesn't want it to be closed, bitter, or resentful. That would create a short circuit to the prayers you pray. Forgiveness benefits you, who forgive more than the person who offended you. God is interested in relationships and doesn't want anything interfering with the spirit of the man praying. Hatred, envy, resentment, and bitterness form such an enormous layer of weight in a man's heart that they can weigh against him at the moment of prayer. This is why God's Word says, "Be angry and do not sin; do not let the sun go down on your wrath" (Ephesians 4:26 NKJV). What happens when you stay angry for a whole day or extended days? The Scripture answers, "Nor give place to the devil" (verse 27). The devil gains power over the believer when he sees that his spirit (his heart) is weakened. Remember principle number two that we learned about having a heart turned toward God? Well, that's key because the part that matters most to God is your heart. That's why the Scripture urges, "Keep your heart with all diligence, For out of it spring the issues of life" (Proverbs 4:23 NKJV).

How to protect your heart?

One of the ways to protect and guard your heart is to practice the art of discounting offenses. This is to say that when an offense comes, you have to decide in your heart that you will not be dominated by it. Jesus made us realize that offenses must come; as long as you are in this world, you will always or occasionally be offended. The devil may move someone to say offensive words against you or do things that try to hurt your success or dim your shine. This is human nature, weak and fragile. We always want to be correct, and we always want to prove that we are right. Understand this: you don't need to justify yourself in front of the people who love you because they will understand you. Likewise, you don't need to try to justify yourself in front of your opponents because they will decide never to understand you. Therefore, no matter what you do or say, none of it will convince them to change their minds because they want you to fall or fail at all costs. So, guard your heart. You will have to make this important decision for the rest of your life. When you wake up every morning, decide that you will not lose your motivation or your cheer. This is why Jesus said, "In the world, you will have tribulation, but be of good cheer. I have overcome the world" (John 16:33 NKJV). He has overcome the world for us; we should rest in his victory. However, you need to look to Jesus as a model and see how He reacted in the face of His critics.

During the three and a half years of his earthly ministry, Jesus faced severe opposition from the religious constellation of Israel, who considered him to be a kind of deviation from the laws established by Moses in the Old Covenant. They loved the leadership positions and the praise of men who saw their interests and status being threatened by the popularity of Jesus and his ministry. They criticized him for everything and were always looking for a flaw, a loophole to accuse him and tear him down. Even healing the sick was a problem for them. But in everything, Jesus behaved wisely, was firm with a fortitude of character in the face of his detractors, and at the same time, with an attitude of love and compassion for the people suffering and oppressed by the devil. Moreover, he knew how to manage his emotions.

One of the problems with many people is that they don't know or haven't learned how to manage relationships or their emotions. They get angry over minor things and, out of the blue, give up on the important projects God has given them. Thus, they give occasion to the devil to keep them in the same place and at the same level in life. You cannot stay a whole day or life lamenting and feeding the sorrows because this can cause bitterness in your soul. A bitter heart cannot pray well because it is not involved in fellowship with God. Getting angry is not a sin, but what you do when angry can be. When you are offended, you become angry, and your mind becomes open and prone to the devil's manipulation. He can tell you to hit someone, break dishes, insult, and make decisions you may regret. So when you are angry, say nothing and speak nothing. Scripture gives us a prescription: "Is anyone among you suffering? Let him pray. Is anyone cheerful? Let him sing psalms" (James 5:13 NKJV). God always directs us in what we should do in every situation. This is why Paul exhorted that the word of Christ dwells abundantly in our hearts (Colossians 3:16).

Understand this: your heart is more important than anything else because that is where the Holy Spirit speaks and from where He guides us. As the Scripture says, "The spirit of a man is the lamp of the Lord, searching all the inner depths of his heart" (Proverbs 20:27 NKJV). Your heart is like a lamp; if you let bitterness, anger, resentment, envy, or hatred get in there, they can dim the power of this light or lamp so that it no longer shines. From then on, you no longer hear God's voice. As a result, you lose direction and motivation in life. The people who have offended you are living right in your corner, leaving you with their seeds that germinating may hold back your potential.

The Scripture encourages us, "Let us run with endurance the race that is set before us, looking unto Jesus, the author, and finisher of our faith, who for the joy that was set before Him endured the cross, despising the shame" (Hebrews 12:1-2 NKJV). What is the thing that motivates you to wake up each morning and say this? "This is the day that the Lord has made. Therefore, I will rejoice in it and make the most of God's opportunities today." When you constantly complain and think of yourself as poor, despicable, and a victim of everything around you, you will not see the opportunities God gives you. You will be like a tamarisk tree in the desert and won't feel it when the heat comes. God wants you to be like a tree planted by streams of water and always be fruitful and productive. If you understand this and put it into practice, your life will go from glory to glory, onward and upward only. There will be no ups and downs, only ups and forward.

Another thing you can do is not associate with the scoffers, gossipers, or mockers. Did you know that there are people who have nothing to do in life but go from house to house or sit somewhere to talk about other people's lives? Instead of taking action and making progress in their lives, they just react to the progress of others. They are cheap commentators on other people's lives. Therefore, God's Word advises you: "Blessed is the man Who walks not in the counsel of the ungodly, Nor stands in the path of sinners, Nor sits in the seat of the scornful; But his delight is in the law of the Lord, And in His law he meditates day and night. He shall be like a tree Planted by the rivers of water, That brings forth its fruit in its season, Whose leaf also shall not wither; And whatever he does shall prosper" (Psalms 1:1-3 NKJV). Therefore, you can prosper in everything you do.

Note this: forgiveness is vital because it determines the health of your soul, and this determines prosperity in life and the health of your body. This is why the Scripture in 3 John 2 NKJV creases, "Beloved, I pray that you may prosper in all things and be in health, just as your soul prospers." Why all this? Because God wants to see you always encouraged, motivated, and in good spirits since then you will hear his voice well, follow his direction and enjoy life.

Another thing you can do is to develop the habit of constantly meditating on the Scriptures, singing and praising God in your heart. This will create a heavenly atmosphere in and around you, which will cause you to experience the heavens on earth and carry God's presence everywhere you go. This is why Paul said, "Do not be drunk with wine, in which is dissipation; but be filled with the Spirit" (Ephesians 5:18 NKJV). Feeding bitterness in your heart is no way to be filled with the Holy Spirit. There remains only religiosity and not a living fellowship with God. Now, how to be filled with the Spirit? Paul prescribes: "Speaking to one another in psalms and hymns and spiritual songs, singing and making melody in your heart to the Lord, giving thanks always for all things to God the Father in the name of our Lord Jesus Christ" (verses 19-20).

Talk positively to yourself

Learn to speak to yourself in Psalms: "The Lord is my light and my salvation; whom shall I fear? I refuse to be afraid. The Lord is my shepherd. I shall lack nothing: joy, peace, health, and prosperity shall not fail me." And finally, learn to be grateful for all God does for you. Stop complaining and be grateful. Gratitude will open your spirit to opportunities that would never come into your life without it. Gratitude will make you appreciate God's glory and enjoy every stage of success in life. But this will spring from a clean heart that has forgiven and knows how to forgive. Forgiving doesn't mean that you haven't been offended, but that you no longer have the wound, only the scar, and it doesn't hurt anymore. Forgiveness doesn't mean that you must trust everyone. Love everyone with the love of Christ, but don't trust everyone. People are always likely to disappoint you, but always trust God, and you should never trust people using the trust with which you trust God. People change, but God doesn't. He will never disappoint you since you trust in Him. For people, create a margin of error, and expect they may change at some point. It may be because of the weakness of the flesh or the devil's influence, or even because they didn't watch out for potential evil in their lives. If you do this, you will be prepared not to be disappointed. You will not be surprised when your husband, wife, children, parents, siblings, friends, or colleagues suddenly demonstrate bipolar behavior and change.

One of the reasons why many are disappointed is because they trust people too much and not God and place their expectations on them when they should place them on God. Therefore, the Scripture exhorts, "Cursed is the man who trusts in man, and makes flesh his strength, whose heart departs from the Lord" (Jeremiah 17:5 NKJV). But it also encourages, "Blessed is the man who trusts in the Lord, and whose hope is the Lord. For he shall be like a tree planted by the waters, which spreads out its roots by the river, and will not fear when heat comes; but its leaf will be green, and will not be anxious in the year of drought, nor will cease from yielding fruit" (verses 7-8).

Forgive and don't be haunted by bitterness or sorrow if someone has offended you. Instead, say this prayer, "Heal me, O Lord, and I shall be healed; save me, and I shall be saved, for you are my praise" (Jeremiah 17:14 NKJV).

"I, the Lord, search the heart, I test the mind, even to give every man according to his ways, according to the fruit of his doings" (verse 10).

When you meditate on God's Word, your inner voice will become God's voice produced by His Word. Then you can bless yourself by thinking good, positive, glorious things about yourself and others. You won't have any voice accusing and gnawing at you from the inside. The spirit of sadness and bitterness will have no place in you. Instead, you will be a cheerful, lively, and animated person. And even as you pray in your heart, God will hear and answer you because you constantly interact with Him through His Word and His Spirit. Train your heart and tongue to speak consistently with God's love. The Scripture says that God has poured his love into our hearts through the Holy Spirit he gave us (Romans 5:5). Love like your heavenly Father. God's love is the greatest way to guard your heart. As the apostle Jude (not Iscariot) said, "Keep yourselves in the love of God, looking for the mercy of our Lord Jesus Christ unto eternal life" (Jude 21 NKJV).

Chapter IV
Principle number 4

Pray to the Father in the name of Jesus

"And in that day you will ask Me nothing. Most assuredly, I say to you, whatever you ask the Father in My name He will give you" (John 16:23 NKJV).

The Scripture above reveals to us one of the fundamental principles of praying in the New Testament. We must understand that before the Word became flesh and was called Jesus, no one in the Old Testament had the privilege of calling God "Father." Think of the patriarchs like Abraham, Isaac, and Jacob, who had a covenant with God. Think of these great men of God like Moses, Elijah, and Daniel, who walked with God and constantly listened to his voice. Yet, none of them ever referred to God as Father. Furthermore, one of the reasons why the religious Jews hated and handed Christ over to be crucified was because He claimed to be the Son of God, and to them, this was regarded as blasphemy. Jesus brought about a dispensation, an era, a new time when the God who seemed far away would be near us, establishing intimate fellowship with us.

In his prayers, he always referred to God as Father. He let his first disciples know they have a heavenly Father to whom they should pray. That is why in the model of prayer in Matthew 6:9, he said, "In this manner, therefore, pray: our Father in heaven..." Here we are presented by the Master how we should address the God with whom we walk, serve and worship, "Father." Of course, this Father is omnipresent, omnipotent, omniscient, holy, God of armies, peace, Lord our flag, and self-sufficient God, among many other attributes. However, despite all these facets of himself, he is still our Father.

Suppose you look at most of the prayers of the men of the Old Covenant. In that case, you will notice that they usually use the term

"Lord," "Lord God," but in the New Covenant, Jesus brought us the presence of the Father. We are in the Father's presence now, and we live there. So whenever you pray, pray to the Father. You can worship him, praise him, "Father, you are holy, powerful, merciful, and compassionate. There is no God like you." Calling Him Father reveals a level of intimacy we have with Him. When did He become our heavenly Father? Well, not everyone is a child of God. There are creatures of God and children of God. So the Scripture testifies, "But as many as received him, to them he gave the right to become children of God, to those who believe in his name" (John 1:12 NKJV). We are made children of God when we believe in Jesus and accept him as Lord and Savior. We are children with the word of faith we have heard. "Having been born again, not of corruptible seed but incorruptible, through the word of God which lives and abides forever" (1 Peter 1:23 NKJV).

Dear reader, notice this: something happens in our spirit when we become children of God. There is an adoption of sonship. So the Scripture says, "And because you are sons, he has sent forth the Spirit of His Son into your hearts, crying out, Abba, Father!" (Galatians 4:6 NKJV). "Aba" is an Aramaic expression meaning "Father." Aramaic was the language Jesus spoke in the region where he grew up. Note that before Jesus, no one was called a son of God. The expression "son of God" doesn't mean that God had a woman and she became pregnant and had a human or divine child, but rather, "God in human form." Note that Jesus wasn't Jesus before He became incarnate. He was always the Word, the eternal Word proceeding from the Father. Now, this Jesus, through the Holy Spirit, became a seed sown into our hearts by faith, which also made us children of God. Our adoption as children of God occurs in Christ by faith in Him, and thus we come to receive the Holy Spirit. Through this Holy Spirit - who came in place of Jesus to glorify Him and convince the world of judgment, righteousness, and sin - man can be regenerated and call God Father. Anyone who doesn't have God's Spirit is only a creature of God, not a son.

For example, whenever I call God by Father in prayer, I feel his love, warmth, and power that manifests his presence. My spirit is activated, and I am filled with anointing. My spirit recognizes him as the self-sufficient God and surrenders completely to him. I do not need to cry out, for the Father hears me and answers. Therefore, as children of God, we should call Him Father in prayer.

Pray in the name of Jesus

In the text from John 14:6 NKJV, Jesus said, "I am the way, the truth, and the life. No one comes to the Father except through Me." This statement clearly shows that Jesus Christ is the only way to God the Father. Furthermore, the Father Himself approved Jesus as the mediator between God and men by raising Him from the dead and placing Him at the right hand of His majesty, above every government, kingdom, and name. It is through Him that we come to the Father; there is no shortcut. The Father is so holy that we could not come near Him by ourselves. We were sinners and deserved His punishment. But our punishment was upon Jesus, and by His stripes, we were healed (Isaiah 53:4-5).

Jesus has given us power of attorney to use his name in prayer before the Father.

Notice the opening Scripture, "And in that day you will ask Me nothing. Most assuredly, I say to you, whatever you ask the Father in My name He will give you" (John 16:23 NKJV). What day was Jesus referring to here? Well, it should be noted that before He died on the cross of Calvary and rose from the dead, there was no New Testament, and the church didn't even exist on earth. Jesus lived and ministered under the Old Covenant. The New Covenant was ratified by his blood when he died on the cross, and the church was born in his resurrection and the descent of the Holy Spirit. So when he said, "In that day," he didn't mean heaven; he meant the day of salvation, the New Testament day. And we are on that day today, in this dispensation of saving grace in Christ. So when Jesus uses the expression "most assuredly," he wants to emphasize the value of what he wants to communicate to his disciples; he wants to establish a principle that needs to be noticed, believed, and accepted.

"Whatever you ask my Father in my name, he will give it to you." To whom do we ask? To the Father. What do we ask for? Whatever we want, following his will. How do we ask? "In Jesus' name." The underlying principle here is that when we pray to the Father, we should do so in the name of Jesus. By saying "in the name of Jesus," you are literally saying the same as "by Jesus' authority, in Jesus' place." This is because Jesus has given us power of attorney to use his name. The Father hears us as if it were Jesus praying. We are members of his body; we are his voice, ears, and eyes. He has given all his authority to the church. Therefore, you should not pray to Jesus in Jesus' name. The correct way is to pray to the Father, in the name of Jesus, because you are in Jesus' place now.

Jesus' disciples had already cast out demons and healed the sick in the name of Jesus, but none had even used Jesus' name in prayer. They were still under the Old Testament because Christ had not yet suffered. That is why He said to them, "Until now you have asked nothing in My name. Ask, and you will receive, that your joy may be full" (verse 24). Did you notice here that God is interested in answering prayers and granting our petitions? With these words, Jesus banks on the disciples' faith in the infallibility of his name. As if to say, "If you ask the Father for anything in my name, he will give it to you. Speak directly to the Father, but use my name." The name of Jesus gives us access to the throne of the heavenly Father. The name serves as a channel in prayer, and in ministering to the sick or casting out demons, the name is an instrument. You can trust in the name of Jesus.

Starting today, you can pray to the Father in the name of Jesus and see positive results. Just use the name in faith and fellowship with Jesus. God desires to see us joyful. This is why Jesus told us to ask for our joy to be fulfilled. Joy comes whenever we pray, and God answers us positively. Pray in the name of Jesus; do not use the names of saints or dead people. Use the name of the One who rose from the dead, overcame, and lives forever. Use the name of Jesus. Take some time now, raise your hands and start praying—practice using this great name. Ask God for whatever you want and, by faith, receive it now.

Chapter V
Principle number 5

When you pray, believe you have already received what you requested

"Therefore I say to you, whatever things you ask when you pray, believe that you receive them, and you will have them" (Mark 11:24 NKJV).

Jesus' first disciples were amazed to see a fig tree, which the day before, Jesus had cursed, had dried up completely. Jesus showed them that they could have the same results in the sense that whatever they said would come to pass, and whatever they asked for would be given if only they would believe. The issue of faith is so fundamental that the Scriptures say, "Without faith, it is impossible to please him, for he who comes to God must believe that he is, and that he is the rewarder of those who diligently seek him" (Hebrews 11:6 NKJV).

Faith is thus one of the essential principles governing prayer.

Two reasons why you should have faith in God when you pray

First: because the believer must believe that God exists.

How would you pray and trust a non-existent God? He is not a Judeo-Christian mythology - he is a reality. For example, a sister told me she felt weak in prayer because her husband wouldn't pray with her. Furthermore, her husband thought she was paranoid, talking to someone he couldn't see. This is common if you are saved and your family members or colleagues are not. They may think you are crazy because you are there talking to someone they don't see, but God is more real than the clothes you wear.

The Holy Bible says that in Him we live and move and exist (Acts 17:28). His presence is not far from us. This is why Jesus begged the Father to send us the Holy Spirit. In turn, the Holy Spirit carries God's presence and His love for us to where we are praying, and we come to feel the power of that presence, His love, and His glory. He is real.

When I pray alone, even at home, a wind suddenly seems to blow, and my clothes flutter. I know I didn't turn on any fan or air conditioner at that moment. What could this phenomenon be? It is the presence of God brought and reproduced by the Holy Spirit. The extent of God's presence accompanies us and manifests itself whenever we pray to the Lord. This presence of God produces a feeling of safety, security, and protection. No wonder David said, "Though I walk through the valley of the shadow of death, I will fear no evil, for You are with me. Your rod and your staff, they comfort me" (Psalms 23:4 NKJV). It was the assurance that God was with him. Otherwise, he would not have had the audacity to face Goliath, the giant, without trusting in the Lord - his God. This is why Paul encouraged us, "Finally, my brethren, be strong in the Lord and in the power of his might" (Ephesians 6:10 NKJV).

Dear reader, you can strengthen yourself in the Lord and the strength of his power. Always acknowledge God's presence with you; you will see his manifestation.

Understand this: the men and women who revolutionized the world of their time brought revival, worked great miracles, left great legacies of faith and way of life, and impacted past generations. They had no honorific or academic titles, but they were people who had experiences with God. Men who knew how to hear God's voice and walked with Him. Because of this awareness of God's presence, they weren't afraid of anything or anyone. This is why Abednego, Meshach, and Shadrach were rescued from the fiery furnace because they dared to have faith in their God. So likewise, Daniel escaped from the lion's mouth because he trusted God.

When done in faith and with the recognition of God's power and greatness, prayer produces extraordinary experiences.

Prayer produces experiences with God

I remember that in 2010, I was in my room in prayer one morning when the roof of the house suddenly disappeared. I was taken in a spiritual vision - a trance or ecstasy. I was between heaven and earth, and from space, I looked and saw my body lying in bed, and at the same time me in bed, I could see myself in space. It was a great experience. And I started having visions of what would happen next and information about people, events, and situations. And everything was happening in the same way.

I remember that on one of those beautiful mornings, around 7:00 a.m., I saw a young man named Páida, broken-hearted, sad, and almost thinking about committing suicide because the devil completely barred his life and his family's life. His father had died, and he was living with his mother and sister. He was in tears. I saw his face very clearly in that vision. Then I went out to evangelize around my neighborhood and found the young man the same way I had seen him in the vision: with the same clothes, countenance, and condition. So I prayed for him, and his life and that of his sister were never the same again.

I am giving these details to help you realize that moments of prayer are moments of spiritual elevation and that God is real, His Word is faithful, and you can trust Him.

Now, from this His nature of being faithful, all-powerful, merciful, omniscient, and omnipresent, and at the same time, taking an interest in humanity, you can have faith in Him in prayer, which never fails. That is why Jesus told His disciples, "Have faith in God" (Mark 11:22 NKJV). Faith in God produces results.

Second: pray with faith because God is the rewarder of those who seek him.

This means that whenever we seek the Lord, He rewards us, or something of value is always credited and added to us whenever we pray to God.

Many people pray but don't receive answers because they don't believe. However, Jesus said, "Whatever you ask for by praying, believe that you will receive it, and you will have it." This isn't a promise, but an assurance, a statement of spiritual reality. Sometimes I ask some people, "does the brother or sister believe that he or she has already received what he or she asked for?" and the response of some is, "I don't know whether I have received it or not, nor do I know yet whether I will receive it." So why do you pray if you don't believe God will answer? As I said, it's God's will to answer our prayers, but He wants you to believe.

Why is faith necessary?

As we read in Hebrews 11:6, it's impossible to please God without faith. Therefore, prayer must be made with faith, expectation, and trust. Furthermore, in the spiritual world, believing is synonymous with receiving. You receive what you ask God for when you believe you have received it. The ability to believe that God has granted you what you have asked for in prayer is the proof you have received. Therefore, you should no longer be worried. By the way, the text in Hebrews 4:3 says that we who believe have entered into rest. Which is equivalent to saying that we are no longer worried; we are not apprehensive or afraid.

For example, if you pray for employment, you can say, "Father, I ask for this job, and I get it now, in the name of Jesus." You can now see yourself working even before you are called to sign the contract.

Faith is an attitude, that is, you must not only believe but also act as one who has already received. You must manifest the attitude of one who already has what you asked for. You must confess what you have already received.

In another chapter, we will go more in-depth on this matter when we learn about the typology of prayers. For the moment, I want you to understand and retain that when you pray and ask for something, believe first that you have received it before you see the manifestation of the thing you have asked for. One thing is certain: when we pray, God examines our hearts to see whether we believe He can do what we ask. As Jesus asked the two, who were asking for healing from their blindness, "Do you believe that I am able to do this? They said to him, 'Yes, Lord.'

Then He touched their eyes, saying, 'According to your faith, let it be to you. And their eyes were opened." (Matthew 9:28-30 NKJV). Did you notice how simple the healing of these blind men was? They responded positively to Jesus, saying that they believed He was able, and it was soon done to them as they believed.

May God grant your request according to your faith! All things are possible to those who believe. Therefore, when you pray, pray with faith.

Chapter VI
Principle number 6

When you pray, give thanks as one who has received

In principle number 5, we learn the value and necessity of faith when we pray. Faith gives us access to what Christ's grace has made available. For example, salvation, health, prosperity, and a life of glory are available to us. These aren't things we must sacrifice, for they are already available to all humanity of those who come to God in Christ with a surrendered heart and faith.

Knowing that whatever we ask for in prayer, we must believe we have already received implies that there must be an attitude on our part right after we have prayed.

This question remains: what do you do after you have prayed? If you believe you have already received what you asked for in prayer, giving thanks is the best way to manifest a receiving attitude. Actions of grace should punctuate the believer's prayer because only with this attitude will you have the peace and joy of knowing that God has already answered all your worries.

Notice the text to Philippians 4:6 NKJV: "Be anxious for nothing, but in everything by prayer and supplication, with thanksgiving, let your requests be made known to God." So what the Spirit of God is saying here, through Paul, is that you should give thanks when you have delivered your petition to God in prayer.

From God's point of view, as His son or daughter, you should not be worrying. You shouldn't have something that worries you or causes you to worry. Worry is one of the reasons why many people are sick, weak, and lack the appetite to eat. Because of worry, people lose their peace, quiet, and joy in life. Some are worried about what they will eat, wear, or drink, and others are worried about their businesses, jobs, family, and many other things. The prescription God's Word gives us is, "Be anxious for nothing." What a desire God has for his children! That is why Jesus said to let the children come to Him because theirs was the kingdom of heaven. One of the characteristics of children is that they trust and forgive easily and are grateful for little things.

Furthermore, children aren't worried about how they will pay their school fees, what they will eat tomorrow, or where they will sleep the next day. Something inside them quiets them down, knowing that mom and/or dad will take care of the rest. So most of their time is reserved for studying, eating, and playing while their parents are losing weight from worrying so much.

This is the happiest phase of life. They enjoy life, play and can express their emotions. The adult is not like this; he is always reflective and often defensive. He likes to worry about things that shouldn't even occupy his mind. They stay up all night thinking about how to pay the electricity, water, and rent bills. During the day, you have no quiet, and at night, you have no peace. They are looking for an alley to hide from life's challenges and problems because they haven't learned to cast their burdens on the Lord. They haven't learned to trust or to depend on God. They want to do what only God can do. Many are still worried after praying, sometimes even more than before the prayer. At the moment of prayer, instead of giving their burdens to the Lord or making their petitions known, they remember their suffering and complain all the time. So even though they pray, they receive nothing, and even if God gives them instructions, they aren't attentive to listen and follow. The reason? They are worried. You must learn to rest in the Lord.

Rest in the Lord

The peace of Christ - the inner sign

The Scripture, in Psalms 55:22 NKJV, says, "Cast your burden on the Lord, and He shall sustain you; He shall never permit the righteous to be moved." How do you cast your burdens on the Lord? By surrendering your petitions to God in prayer and with thanksgiving. Thanksgiving is a sign that, by faith, you have already received what you have asked the Lord for. What does someone who has already received what he asked for do? Obviously, he gives thanks. Now, in the things of God, that is, in the kingdom of God, the principle is that you should give thanks for what you have asked for as one who has already received. You aren't trying to receive or assume that you have received it. The fact is that when you believe you have received, in the spiritual arena, you are granted the petition in the spirit before it is manifested in the physical.

Look at the example of Hannah, Samuel's mother; the Scripture says that she was barren and her rival, Penina, had children. Because of this, she humiliated her. Once, when they went to Silo to worship the Lord, she stood in the temple and prayed without saying any audible words. Only sighs and groans came out of her because she prayed from her heart. The man of God, Eli, noticed that she was babbling words, but nothing could be heard from her. Therefore, he considered her to be drunk. However, she explained why she was petitioning God, saying she wanted to have children. In fact, she didn't even exactly tell the man of God that it was a child that she wanted, but that she was pouring out her soul before the Lord. Note the words of Eli, the priest of the Lord, "Go in peace, and the God of Israel grant your petition which you have asked of Him" (1 Samuel 1:17 NKJV). That was all she wanted to hear - a word from God for her case. She knew that God's Word never fails. Notice her reaction: "So the woman went her way and ate, and her face was no longer sad" (verse 18).

Did you notice that sadness disappeared and joy came into her heart and manifested on her face? Why? Because she knew how to receive. In fact, she conceived and had a boy whom she named Samuel, and he was a judge, priest, and prophet. He anointed the first king of Israel, Saul, and later anointed David, from whose lineage came the Savior - Jesus Christ. In addition, she had other sons besides Samuel, but she dedicated Samuel to the Lord.

Dear reader, don't be worried. Just pray in faith and then give thanks as if you already had what you asked for. What is your request to the Lord today? Use these principles and present your requests to the Lord by prayer and thanksgiving.

There is one thing that happens when you give thanks: God gives you peace - a peace that reassures you and lets you know that the matter is settled.

Do you understand why we talk about the importance of keeping your heart clean and forgiving? So that it can pick up the signals emitted by the Holy Spirit.

For example, when I pray and ask the Lord for something, He gives me a sense of inner peace. Notice that we already have the peace of Christ in us. Still, there is a kind of peace that comes after we have unloaded whatever burden to the Lord in prayer and with thanksgiving. This peace serves as a sign that everything is already settled. And when you continue to worry even after you have prayed, you lose that peace and consequently lose the ability to receive what you have asked God for in prayer. This is why Scripture assures, "And the peace of God, which surpasses all understanding, will guard your hearts and your minds through Christ Jesus" (Philippians 4:7 NKJV).

When will you experience this peace? When you pray with thanksgiving. This peace is a note of victory that comes from God to His children - a way of communicating the answer in man's heart before what you have asked for is physically manifested. Now, if you are still worried after prayer, it is a sign that you prayed in vain and fasted in vain because you did not follow this divine principle. See the magnitude of this peace: it will guard your heart and mind. Where does the devil usually put worries? In the mind of man. Where does Satan put fear in man? In his heart. Now, this peace solves all that at once so that you live every day without worry or fear in your mind and heart. Receive peace now.

I have noticed that many brethren are worried and afraid even after praying because they consider the problem they face or their situation to be bigger than God and more serious and severe than their faith. When this occurs, prayer comes out of a heart frozen with fear and plagued by circumstances. God said, "Behold, I am the Lord, the God of all flesh (humanity). Is there anything too hard for Me?" (Jeremiah 32:27 NKJV). Of course there is not! Everything is possible for the believer before God, to whom nothing is impossible.

Understand that we are dealing here with spiritual laws that cause prayer to be answered by God. God doesn't answer simply because someone cried but because he believed and gave thanks.

Look at Jesus' reaction. Before the tomb of Lazarus, the prayer was, "Father, I thank You that You have heard me. And I know that you always hear me, but because of the people who are standing by I said this, that they may believe that You sent Me" (John 11:41-42 NKJV). Notice that Jesus thanks the Father for Lazarus' resurrection long before he is resurrected. Why? Because this is a spiritual principle, and it works very well. Many believers have already received from God what they have asked for but have not taken and manifested it yet because they don't believe and have not given thanksgiving. They say, "I will give thanks when I see the thing come true." But it shouldn't be like that.

For example, if you are sick, you can say, "Father, your Word says that Christ took all my infirmities and pains. Therefore, I refuse to be sick and reject this pain, sickness, and virus in the name of Jesus. Thank you for removing all pain and sickness from me. By the stripes of Christ, I have been healed. Thank you for healing." From there, demonstrate the fruits of your faith. Start acting like one who is healed, and do what you didn't do before by faith. Is it employment, marriage, finances, or the restoration of your home? Transformation of your husband, your wife, or the salvation of your family members? Start thanking them for their salvation now. Even before they start coming to church, they recognize that it is already done.

Don't forget: whenever you pray, believe that you have received and give thanks. Receive the peace of Christ now. Don't be worried. When you rest, God works for you, but when you are worried, you work, and He ceases to deal with your busyness. As Peter once said, "Casting all your anxiety on him, for he cares for you" (1 Peter 5:7 NKJV). Cast your care on the Lord, give thanks and receive peace.

After learning all these six spiritual principles, it's time to put them into practice now and see results in your life and your walk with God.

PART IV
Types of Prayer

Introduction
Types of prayer

"Praying always with all prayer and supplication in the Spirit, being watchful to this end with all perseverance and supplication for all the saints" (Ephesians 6:18 NKJV).

The Word of God commands us to pray at all times and never faint. Therefore, we can find ourselves in various situations where we should pray. Situations of challenge and temptation because we face an obstacle that threatens to jeopardize our life, stability, family, or nation. Or because we want to reverse the course of an event or event or situation that seems unfavorable to us. Or even because we are happy about an achievement or a victory and are in celebration. At various moments in life, we will always have to pray. For each situation, a type of prayer is recommended or applicable. Therefore, knowing the different types of prayers is very important to know how to pray in each situation. Although many take it as a silver bullet, we need to know when to use it and know how to match the type of prayer with the situation we are in, what we feel or when we want divine intervention, which puts the believer at a great advantage over those who don't know.

For example, nine of Jesus' disciples stayed behind when He took Peter, James, and John to the mountain to pray. When they were alone, a boy was brought to them who was lunatic, deaf, and dumb, and his father asked for their intervention. But, unfortunately, they couldn't cast out the unclean spirit, much less heal the boy. It's only when Jesus comes down from the mountain, after having been in prayer, that he ministers deliverance to this young man with words of authority, short but potent in their impact: "Deaf and dumb spirit, I command you, come out of him and enter him no more;" immediately, he came out. The nine disciples were amazed because they probably must have tried to use the same method as Jesus "of issuing commands to the spirits to come out, and so it happened." In their turn, however, out came powerless words and unresolved shouting, and it took them a long time to try to cast out a demon that, for Jesus, took only a few seconds. Faced with this frustrated and astonished attempt, the disciples asked Him apart why they hadn't cast out the demon. The Master's answer was revealing: "However, this kind does not go out except by prayer and fasting." They thought that just because they had authority, they could talk, and things would happen without regard to the importance of prayer and fasting.

Understand this: some situations will require only prayer, and others prayer and fasting to resolve. So don't take the issue of prayer lightly.

In the opening scripture in Ephesians 6:18, Paul urges us to pray with every kind of prayer and supplication. This scripture suggests that there are various kinds of prayer, and we should use them at certain times in life. If there is one area in which every Christian should develop, it should be prayer.

Now, before this verse and recommendation, Paul clarifies the context in which these various types of prayer are to be employed. In verse 12, he makes us understand that we are at war - spiritual warfare - and this means that there is an opposing force whose intention and mission is to do everything to make the lives of humans unbearable by fighting against their happiness, success, health, and prosperity. This is the kingdom of darkness headed by the devil with his spiritual hosts of evil in the heavenly places. On this matter, I advise the reader to acquire and read my ninth book: "The Spiritual World: Understanding the forces that dictate the life of humans on earth" (CUTANE, Onório, 2021).

The critical point here is that Paul speaks of an "evil day," and the Spirit of God wants you and me to be able to resist the onslaughts and snares of the devil and stand. Have you ever had an evil day in your life? A day when it feels like the world has come crashing down on you, and it feels like you are at the end of the tunnel? Have you tried everything and called everyone you know, but it seemed like everything was closed, and your opponents stepped up against you? It seemed like everyone was against you, and it was the end of the world for you. Well, I have, but knowing the various types of prayer and fellowship with Jesus gave me victory. Jesus said to His disciples, "Indeed the hour is coming, yes, has now come, that you will be scattered, each to his own, and will leave Me alone. And yet I am not alone, because the Father is with Me" (John 16:32 NKJV). Jesus enjoyed a deep fellowship with the Father, and even though his disciples abandoned him, he was not shaken. Paul once said, "I know whom I have believed" (2 Timothy 1:12 NKJV). There are those days when the devil decides to make an onslaught after several failed attempts to bring you down. He launches his best missiles against your life, family, people you love and cherish, or your job or nation. The problem is that if you don't know that there are different kinds of prayer, you may walk around worried, even shaken, because you prayed but saw no change.

However, you need to realize that God has already given us the solution to everything in the provision of his word. This is why Paul urges us to pray with every kind of prayer. Prayer is listed in this context as one of the believer's spiritual armor against the cunning snares of the adversary - Satan. As a properly prepared and vigilant soldier of Christ, you must have the discernment to know what kind of weapon to employ in the face of a negative situation. Will you use a small caliber pistol, or will you use a long-range weapon? Which one will you use? A bazooka or a spiritual missile? Knowledge of the various types of prayer is essential. Several men and women of God from ancient times prayed and prevailed when confronted with various life challenges. The book of Psalms is a typical example of men who, even poetically and lyrically, prayed in moments of the war, surrounded by their enemies when they were hated, or even in moments of euphoria, of joy - in everything they called upon the Creator of the universe and He answered them.

In this chapter, we will learn some of the most common types of prayer. Aware that I couldn't exhaust this subject of prayer and its typology and that I may have to write a second or third edition of this book with more spiritual aids and inputs, I will stick to only eight. Namely: the prayer of petition, the prayer of thanksgiving, of faith, of praise and worship, in tongues, of consultation, of intercession, of agreement, and the prophetic statements. I repeat, this typological set of prayers doesn't exhaust everything there is on this subject. Still, I believe it will be helpful to the reader. They work and never fail because the God who recommends them in the Scriptures never fails. Suppose others in Biblical times walked with God and overcame everything. In that case, you too couldn't be an exception, for Jesus Christ is the same yesterday, today, and forever (Hebrews 13:8). The Scripture encourages us to imitate those who, by faith and patience, have inherited the promises of God (Hebrews 6:12).

Chapter I
The prayer of petition

"Until now you have asked nothing in My name. Ask, and you will receive, that your joy may be full" (John 16:24 NKJV).

In this scripture, Jesus encourages his disciples to ask and, at the same time, assures them that these petitions will be fulfilled, that is, they will be granted.

The prayer of petition is one in which the candidate sets out to ask God for something. The purpose of this type of prayer is to ask. We will learn along these lines the procedures that accompany this type of prayer so that what we ask for will be given to us.

I once heard a preacher say, "Don't bother God with multiple requests because He must be exhausted from having people worldwide asking for something." Well, this doesn't correspond with the truth as far as God is concerned, for He is omniscient and omnipotent. He is not confused because people ask Him for things in various parts of the world. Asking is not bad because He is the one who invited us to ask. The text in Matthew 7:7 says, "Ask, and it will be given to you." God wouldn't invite us to ask if He didn't have the will to give. It's the way we ask that needs to be revised. In the opening text of John 16:24, Jesus noted that the disciples had not yet taken advantage of this openness of God, this opportunity to, without any intermediary, use Jesus' name to put their petitions to God.

Why does God want to answer our petitions?

Let's look again at part b of verse 24: "Ask, and you will receive, that your joy may be full." Here, it is clear that God wants to grant us our petitions: *your joy may be full.* These words of Jesus reveal the Father's heart toward us: He wants to see us joyful, not sad. Did you notice the use of the possessive pronoun "yours?" Our what? Joy. O glory! God wants to see us rejoice in the fact that we asked for something in Jesus' name, and He granted it to us.

For many years, I grew up hearing that God wasn't very interested in our joy but in His joy. This verse knocks down that argument. The joy He wants to see is ours, for God is the owner of the gold and silver. Everything belongs to Him and lacks nothing. Therefore, there is no darkness, sadness, or bitterness in Him. It is we here on earth who need Him and His provision. He was the one who fed Elijah with bread brought by crows and water from the brook of Kerith. When the stream dried up, He multiplied the flour and oil of the widow of Zarephath, thus delivering her from death and the famine that lasted for three and a half years.

He multiplied five loaves and two fish to feed a hungry crowd, and the second time He multiplied seven loaves. He is the God of provision, which is why King David exclaimed, "The Lord is my shepherd; I shall not want" (Psalms 23:1 NKJV).

Look at the words of David in his old age   the words of a man who has walked with God and seen his faithfulness: "I have been young and now am old; Yet I have not seen the righteous forsaken, nor his descendants begging bread" (Psalms 37:25 NKJV). And Jesus seizes here in John 16:24 to say that the disciples had asked for nothing in his name. The fact is that there is a joy that springs from the heart of a person who has asked God for something, and He has given it to him. He has many gifts and wants to give them to His children. Don't be sad when you ask Him for something because His will to give is greater than your ability to ask. He encourages us, "Ask, and it will be given to you." The reason you should ask is that the Lord wants to give you. So there is an interconnection between the asking (the petition) and the giving (the act of giving). Both are interconnected, and you must know how to ask and, simultaneously, how to receive. Many brothers don't know how to receive. That is why they keep asking for the same thing every day when God has already given it to them. God has many infinite treasures. The Scripture states, "Every good gift and every perfect gift is from above, and comes down from the Father of lights, with whom there is no variation or shadow of turning" (James 1:17 NKJV). When you ask God for something, He will not give what is no good as humans do, but rather, every good gift. This is why Paul said, "And my God shall supply all your need according to His riches in glory by Christ Jesus" (Philippians 4:19 NKJV).

Notice the way God will supply all our needs in glory? Through Christ. Now I want you to notice two expressions in this verse:

Accessing the Lord's provision

a) "In glory."

This expression suggests that the riches with which God will supply our needs don't depend on the world bank or some physical source on earth. Instead, they depend on his glory, for they are housed in his glory. It is easy to understand this by looking at the first man, Adam. The Bible says, "What is man that You are mindful of him, or the son of man that You take care of him? [...] You have crowned him with glory and honor, and set him over the works of Your hands" (Hebrews 2:6-7 NKJV). Before Adam sinned and fell from dominion, he didn't know what want, hunger, misery, or need was. Why? Because he had been crowned with glory. And what did he lose when he sinned? Romans 3:23-24 NKJV answers, "For all have sinned and fall short of the glory of God, being justified freely by His grace through the redemption that is in Christ Jesus." When man sinned, he lost his glory, and that loss stripped him of the place of provision, blessings, and all that was glorious. Did you notice that the first thing Adam discovered when he sinned and his eyes were opened was that he was naked? "Being naked" means "lacking clothes, something to cover himself with." Therefore, we can say that the first manifestation of sin from man's point of view was: " need, want," in other words, "poverty."

Poverty is the lack of means of subsistence. It's said that everyone living below a dollar a day is on the poverty line. But when did Adam discover that he had nothing? When he sinned and became disconnected from God. That's why Jesus' first message when he quoted from the book of Isaiah 61 NKJV was, "The Spirit of the Lord God is upon Me because the Lord has anointed Me to preach good tidings to the poor; He has sent Me to heal the brokenhearted, to proclaim liberty to the captives, and the opening of the prison to those who are bound; to proclaim the acceptable year of the Lord." Did you notice that the first problem that the anointing on Jesus (on the Messiah) would solve would be "poverty?" If the Gospel is the Good News, what is it for the poor? Surely God wants to see him prosperous. Moses told the people of Israel, "And you shall remember the Lord your God, for it is He who gives you power to get wealth, that He may establish His covenant which He swore to your fathers, as it is this day" (Deuteronomy 8:18 NKJV). What would God give? "Strength" "power," that is, a special grace to prosper in whatever man does. In verses 12 and 13, God speaks of his people being able to eat and be satisfied, build good houses and dwell in them, and have their farm (cattle and sheep), gold, and silver (symbols of money) increase.

O glory! This reveals that God wants to see you rich and prosperous so that you can finance the preaching of the Gospel. Did you know that Jesus was a Jew, as were the first 12 apostles? Do you know something? Even today, the Jews believe in these promises of prosperity. That is why they are rich, in the class of the greatest inventors of technology, owners of banks, and have a lot of intellectualities. They know and believe that they are children of Abraham. Christians have been taught a gospel that disconnects them from daily life here on earth. That is why some brethren are lazy and do not believe in prosperity. Preachers of poverty criticize God's ministers who have received the grace to prosper and prosper God's people. Many Christians say that they are children of Abraham. Still, they would rather imitate the poor and sick Lazarus than their father Abraham, who was rich in cattle, gold, and silver, and at the same time, was a friend of God. To their amazement, even Lazarus went to Abraham's bosom when he died because there was comfort there. The gospel of poverty is not biblical. Jesus became poor so that in his poverty we might become rich (2 Corinthians 8:9). Still, he didn't become poor spiritually, but materially, for he was born in a manger, sharing accommodation with animals.

It is time to believe in the real gospel. The problem is that if your belief is wrong, your life will also be wrong. If your theology is wrong, your way of life and destiny will also be wrong. All because you didn't study God's word for yourself, you preferred to be tied to dogmas of men ignorant of the Scriptures. Jesus rebuked the then-religious constellation, saying, "You are mistaken, not knowing the Scriptures nor the power of God" (Matthew 22:29 NKJV). When God's word brings light to your mind and heart, God's power will materialize what you believe in the Scriptures. If you believe in poverty, it will manifest that poverty in your life. And you will become a good Christian, but poor and miserable, and in the end, you will go to heaven. If you believe in prosperity, God's power will manifest prosperity. You will be prosperous and happy on earth, and then you will also go to heaven. Have you noticed that the question of heaven has long since been settled? "When?" -you may ask. When you gave your life to Jesus and accepted him as your Lord and Savior, he took away your sins and made you a prince and priest to God (Revelation 1:5-6). Refuse to be enslaved when you are a child of the King. Refuse to be poor when your heavenly Father owns the gold and silver. Believe the truth.

Did you notice that God wants to see you prosperous and not miserable? It's a fact; believe it. Adam was prosperous because he had the glory of God upon him. But because of sin, he lost such glory, and all humanity at birth inherited the fallen and despicable nature. But thank God for Jesus Christ, who came to solve this poverty. What did man lose? Glory. And what did Jesus do through his death and resurrection? The Scripture answers, "Bringing many sons to glory" (Hebrews 2:10 NKJV). So our provision is in his glory. Don't look at people because they may disappoint you. Look to Jesus. Receive the grace to prosper now, in your spirit. From today on, you will see the light and glory wherever you go.

b) "By Christ Jesus."

This expression is profound, for it reveals how God will give us his provision. The answer is that it will be through Christ. The text in Hebrews 2:10 says that Christ, through his suffering on the cross, brought many sons to glory. How? Through his suffering. Now understand this: the life of glory follows after Christ's sufferings (1 Peter 1:11). Christ accomplished this by his death on the cross is made available to the believer through his grace. We take possession of it by faith.

Understand this, too: you don't need to suffer to have what Christ has already conquered for you on the Cross. It's yours; just take possession of it (1 Timothy 6:12). The health, prosperity, and life of glory are yours. Notice this scripture: "...And by his stripes, we are healed" (Isaiah 53:5 NKJV).

Looking at this scripture and seeing its fulfillment in Christ on Calvary's cross, Peter took hold of his healing portion. That's why, when quoting the same scripture to the brethren of the Church, he said, "Who Himself bore our sins in His own body on the tree, that we, having died to sins, might live for righteousness—by whose stripes you were healed" (1 Peter 2:24 NKJV). He didn't say, "we were healed," but rather, "you were," because he wanted them to understand what he himself had understood. He wanted them to take possession of the health he himself had taken possession of. So when he ministered healing to Aeneas, who had been bedridden with paralysis for eight years, he just said, "Aeneas, Jesus the Christ heals you. Arise and make your bed.' Then he arose immediately" (Acts 9:34 NKJV). You can also say, "In the name of Jesus, I take possession of my healing now and declare that I am healed." Then, get up and walk - you are free. You can say, "I take possession of my job, my victory, and my marriage in the name of Jesus." You are now.

The main point I want you to pick up here is that you must understand what Christ has already conquered for you and take hold of it all. You must know that Christ has won for you and take hold of that victory. So, next, we are going to study two principles that govern the prayer of the petition:

1. Be filled with the Word of God. Be a friend of God's word.

"If you abide in Me, and My words abide in you, you will ask what you desire, and it shall be done for you" (John 15:7 NKJV).

Given that the nature of the prayer of petition is really to ask the Lord for something, knowledge of God's word becomes fundamental in this process. The reason is that this type of prayer is more comprehensive in terms of meeting the needs of the candidate or proposer. This means that you can ask for anything. In the text from John 16:23 that we read in the introductory part, Jesus promises that whatever we ask the Father in His name, He will grant it to us. Now, because of this, "you will ask what you desire," the believer must know God's will concerning what to ask. For example, we already know how to pray, but the problem for many is what to ask for as it is fitting. In the text of Romans 8:26 NKJV, Paul says, "Likewise the Spirit also helps in our weaknesses. For we do not know what we should pray for as we ought, but the Spirit Himself makes intercession for us with groanings which cannot be uttered." The apostle Paul, who, even though he is an experienced minister of God and distinguished by having gone to the third heaven and heard ineffable words that no man is allowed to speak, hints that our asking God shouldn't be done just anyhow.

There is a great responsibility with the prayer of petition, for one can pray and ask for what he shouldn't, that is, what is not fitting. For example, if a brother in the church prays that God will give him his brother's wife in faith or a sister in the church asks God that her sister in the church gets divorced so that she can be with her sister's husband; this kind of prayer request will not be granted by God. Imagine you pray to the Lord that your neighbor has an accident so that you will take his place at work or his house; you would be praying in contravention of God's word. "But didn't Jesus say that anything I ask the Father for, He would grant it to me?" Yes, Jesus made this promise, but the entitlement to the perks behind it requires that you know God's will about that matter. John adds light to the same subject when he says, "Now this is the confidence that we have in Him, that if we ask anything according to His will, He hears us. And if we know that He hears us, whatever we ask, we know that we have the petitions that we have asked of Him" (1 John 5:14-15 NKJV).

John advocates that God hears us and grants us petitions if we ask for something according to his will. However, the question remains: "How will I know if I am asking according to his will?" The answer is in the introductory verse of this chapter: "If you abide in Me, and My words abide in you, you will ask what you desire, and it shall be done for you" (John 15:7 NKJV).

The condition for asking anything you want according to God's will is to know his word. God's word reveals his expressed will for humanity in general and his children in particular. Therefore, it must take root in our hearts and become the standard that guides our choices, requests, desires, and will until God's will is ours. In this way, we will be praying within his will. This is why Paul said, "Let the word of Christ dwell in you richly in all wisdom, teaching and admonishing one another in psalms and hymns and spiritual songs, singing with grace in your hearts to the Lord" (Colossians 3:16 NKJV).

What to do with God's word?

1. Study it.

Make time daily to study the Scriptures. It is vital.

2. Meditate on it.

Meditation on the Word is like the digestion we do of food. Meditation is repeatedly thinking about God's words that you have read until they become part of your subconscious and dominate your mind and heart. In this sense, God's word will remove thoughts contrary to God's will until your mind and heart are flooded with divine light. With this, meditation will help you renew your mind - your way of thinking - and consequently your behavior until you reach the level Paul preached when he said, "Whatever you do in word or deed, do all in the name of the Lord Jesus" (Colossians 3:17 NKJV). The negative thoughts, the ideas whispered by the devil, and all the impurity of this world that enters a man's mind and heart through his ears and eyes are filtered out and prevented from entering his psychic system so that they no longer contaminate his spirit. This has great benefits because his mind is no longer manipulated by the devil but is guided by the Holy Spirit. The Scripture says, "And do not be conformed to this world, but be transformed by the renewing of your mind, that you may prove what is that good and acceptable and perfect will of God" (Romans 12:2 NKJV).

In this condition shaped by God's word, you can already ask for anything you want, and it will be given to you. Why? Because you will ask within the boundaries of the word - according to his will. The greatest advantage is that it stimulates your faith because faith is born and strengthened when we know God's will. With this knowledge, we can refuse what is not from God and claim what is from Him for us.

For example, as we learned in the introductory part, if you know that God's will is to heal you, bless you, prosper you, protect you, and grant you victory, then it will be easy to be motivated to ask for these things in prayer, claim them, or take possession of them. This may even help you to speed up God's response. Remember Elijah's words when he prayed to God to send down fire on the altar of stones he had made? "Lord God of Abraham, Isaac, and Israel, let it be known this day that You are God in Israel, and I am Your servant and that I have done all these things at Your word. Hear me, O Lord, hear me, that this people may know that You are the Lord God, and that You have turned their hearts back to You again" (1 Kings 18:36-37 NKJV).

In this prayer, in front of the four hundred and fifty prophets of Baal and the people of Israel, Elijah wasn't embarrassed because he was firm in God's word, his will, and what he was asking for was going to give glory to God. It was a simple, short prayer full of faith, surrender, and heart. As a result, without delay, the Scripture records, "Then the fire of the Lord fell and consumed the burnt sacrifice, and the wood and the stones and the dust, and it licked up the water that was in the trench" (verse 38). How long did it take God to answer this prayer of Elijah? Minutes. How long did it take Elijah to pray this prayer? Minutes. This is equivalent to saying that the prayer (the petition) and the answer did not take long to correspond because he prayed from his heart according to God's word. This story inspires faith in us.

I remember the year 2008. I was with a group of young people doing a crusade of salvation and miracles in the Zona Verde neighborhood, on the outskirts of Maputo city, in Mozambique. There were many people, big and small, and it was afternoon, around 6:00 PM. Suddenly, it started raining, and the rain was spoiling the event because some people didn't want to get wet and would leave the crusade site. We didn't have a stage; we used the back of a truck as a stage because that's where I would stop and preach. So I got a group of brothers together, and we started interceding. At the same time, some religious adults laughed at us, as if the rain wasn't going to stop and that I was defying the laws of nature. One of them even told me to cancel the event and reschedule it for another day. But I was convinced that it was God's will for us to do it to win souls.

The Holy Spirit had given me this indication and confirmed it several times. Knowing the will of God and remembering what Elijah had done and that I also worship and serve the same God that Elijah served, I told everyone who had umbrellas to put them down because the rain was going to stop. Then I started to pray, "Father, we are here because of you and your kingdom. I like the rain because my parents are farmers and we need it to produce in our fields, but today I have a job for you to do. Let this rain stop, in the name of Jesus." Then I turned, looked up at the sky, and said, "Rain, stop now, in the name of Jesus!" Immediately, the rain stopped, to everyone's amazement. I heard some saying, "This young man is a sorcerer; how did he manage to stop the rain?" Because I prayed, that is, I asked according to his will. With this knowledge, you can stop the devil's plans and claim to do only God's will. Whatever you ask for will be given to you because you will not ask for selfish motives. As James said, "You ask and do not receive, because you ask amiss, that you may spend it on your pleasures" (James 4:3 NKJV).

Put your request objectively and precisely before God

2. Be specific and objective in what you are asking.

"Do not be anxious about anything, but in every situation, by prayer and petition, with thanksgiving, **present your requests to God**" (Philippians 4:6 NIV).

The word "petition," employed by Paul in Philippians 4:6, comes from the Greek term "aitēma," which means "thing asked for," "object desired," and generally means that which is requested. It's a term synonymous with "supplication," derived from the Greek "deesis," meaning to make known a specific need.

The use of the terms "Petition" and "Supplication" in the same context of asking God for something to supply our needs, as we see in the verse mentioned above, indicates that the request must be objective and specific. Therefore, the fundamental principle for the believer to be able to pray the prayer of petition or supplication is that he must be clear in his mind and heart about the thing he wants to ask God for, specifically.

For example, it's common to hear someone say, "Father, in the name of Jesus, I ask for a house or a job. No, Father, actually, I want a car; oh no, I want marriage." Up to this point, you aren't being specific or objective. The prayer of petition requires you to be objective in what you want to ask God for. Many ask for so many things at once that they no longer know what they really need. So they don't receive it because it wasn't clear what they wanted. They are wandering in the thickets. This is one of the reasons why their prayers become repetitive. Someone may say, "But God knows what we need; he reads our hearts. So He will grant me my request because He has already read what is happening inside me." Logically, it's a fact that God, being omniscient, knows everything we think even before the thought enters our mind. In the spiritual arena, thoughts and words are synonymous = both are visible objects in the spirit and not necessarily abstract things, as in the physical world.

However, the very definition of prayer implies communication. Although you can communicate with God in your heart, at the highest level of that intimacy, the rule is that you give voice to that communication, needs, or things you want to ask the Lord for. This is to avoid getting worried in your mind or your heart. Therefore, the biblical guidance is, "Do not be anxious about anything, but in every situation, by prayer and petition, with thanksgiving, **present your requests to God**" (Philippians 4:6 NIV). The principle here is that your petition must be known before God. How? By prayer and supplication with thanksgiving. You must deliver this petition personally to God through prayer and supplication. And we define supplication as a specific request that comes from a man's heart. If God had to constantly read what we desire in our hearts without praying, He wouldn't recommend us to pray. But the fact is that prayer is giving God legal permission to intervene in the affairs of the earth. He knows what we need, but He wants us to pray.

How do you know God has answered your petition and when to stop asking?

The answer to this question is in verse 7 of our opening scripture, "And the peace of God, which transcends all understanding, will guard your hearts and your minds in Christ Jesus." When we pray in faith and ask God for something, He gives us inner peace, a sense of peace like no other. The word "peace" here comes from the Greek "eirene," which is the deposit of God's tranquility and rest in our hearts. This peace is a sign that the matter has already been received and processed, and its manifestation is about to occur. The reason why Paul uses the expression **"peace of God which transcends all understanding"** is founded on the fact that even though you don't see the answers physically and don't yet have those things you asked for in the physical form, you are as peaceful and rested as one who already has them in visible form. This creates an attitude, a way of being, and a life called "the life of faith." You come to live by faith, and because you have faith in your heart, worry and fear are cast out, and God's peace begins to reign in your heart. You can already begin to thank God for the things you have asked for, knowing they have already been granted to you. You already have that job, the business is going well, and your family is healthy and stable. Now, you need that peace. How do you receive it? By faith because Christ has already earned it on the cross of Calvary. He has given us access to the throne of grace through His blood. Have you noticed that carnal people can only have peace when they already have the things they have physically asked for? However, as a spiritual person, the peace that God gives you is the assurance that the thing you asked for has already been granted and awaits its manifestation. And when you give thanks, you speed up the manifestation because you have shown an attitude of faith. If you are still worried and restless, it's a sign that you didn't believe when you prayed and didn't receive what you asked for. Not because God didn't hear or didn't want to give, but because you blocked the channels with a lack of faith and trust in God's ability. It's a matter of the mind and the heart because He said this peace would serve as a preservative and guard our hearts and minds.

Count your blessings

God's desire is for each one of His children to ask Him for something, and He will positively grant it. Thus, the believer accumulates blessings and moments of victory and glory in a dark world. He becomes the light of this world. With this comes the responsibility to remember the things God has done for us so that we can have times to do other kinds of prayer, such as praise and worship prayer, and not just keep asking. God wants you to develop confidence in this communication channel called "prayer" to ensure that He hears and answers whenever you pray.

So it's vital to have two things:

1. Prayer points.

Prayer points are the sequence of those things we will ask God for, the matter on which we want his intervention. What is or what are those things that you want to ask Him?

Exercise 1

List below three specific things about which you wanted God's intervention or that you wanted Him to grant you.

I.

II.

III.

2. Praise and thanksgiving points.

The points of praise and thanksgiving are the sequel to the things God has already granted us, and we already have them in the physical arena. They are those prayer requests that God has already answered and upon which we have already seen results or God's positive intervention. In this sense, you shouldn't keep asking for the same thing. Instead, you should note what He has done and start with each point. This is called "counting blessings." The psalmist said, "Bless the Lord, O my soul, and forget not all his benefits" (Psalms 103:2 NKJV). In the following verse, he enumerates, that is, counts the sequence of these blessings:

1. Forgiveness of sins;

2. Health: cure all illnesses;

3. Protection;

4. Favor and mercy;

5. Material goods and provision of spiritual, emotional, and material needs;

6. Rejuvenation.

Exercise 2

In your case, too, dear reader, I want you to take note of all the specific things God has done for you. Then turn the points of prayer or request into points of thanks and praise.

Now, list below the three specific things you have asked God for and received. Then thank Him for them.

I.

II.

III.

Chapter II
The Prayer of Thanksgiving

"Bless the Lord, O my soul; and all that is within me, bless His holy name! Bless the Lord, O my soul, and forget not all His benefits" (Psalms 103:1-2 NKJV).

The Scripture mentioned above is one of the typical examples of thanksgiving prayer. In this type of prayer, the principle is the recognition of God's deeds in our lives, and out of that recognition comes thanksgiving. In practice, this type of prayer's goal is to render thanks to God in recognition of his goodness, mercy, and love toward us. The prayer of thanksgiving reveals man's high sensitivity to God's deeds in his life.

The main point is that of all that God does in your life, from salvation and protection to provision, you should acknowledge him at all times and exalt his deeds.

In Luke 17:11-19, we read the story of ten lepers who Jesus had healed. It was customary for Jews that people suffering from leprosy should be socially isolated, as was the case with covid-19 since leprosy was seen as an impurity and a contagious disease. Therefore, these men were socially rejected and couldn't be with others. Can you imagine the pain of being separated from your wife and children? Of being separated from your co-workers, neighbors, and the rest of your family members because you posed a threat of infection and were spiritually regarded as unclean? No one was allowed to touch the clothes they wore or their linens, much less their cutlery. It was a difficult life. But thank God, they had contact with the word of the Master, for Jesus had compassion on them and commanded them: "Go and show yourselves to the priests. And it came to pass that going they became clean." Did you notice that they believed Jesus' word and acted on it? They didn't wait to see if the leprosy was gone or not. They just went on believing God was faithful and that the word out of Jesus' mouth did not fail. Because of this act of faith and their action on the Master's word, leprosy went away from them, and they were all cleansed and purified of leprosy.

Although all ten were healed, only one, a Samaritan, returned and prostrated himself at Jesus' feet to worship him as a gesture of thanksgiving for the miracle he had received. The others didn't bother to come back and give thanks because they were more focused on the gift of healing than on the Giver of the gift; they were more focused on the miracle than on the Worker of the miracle. Scripture describes the attitude of the thankful man: "And one of them, when he saw that he was healed, returned, and with a loud voice glorified God, and fell down on his face at His feet, giving Him thanks. And he was a Samaritan" (Luke 17:15-16 NKJV). The Lord Jesus knew that God the Father likes to receive thanksgiving because He wants men to know He is among us and also cares for us. So, amid that crowd, He said, "Were there not ten cleansed? But where are the nine? Were there not any found who returned to give glory to God except this foreigner?"

If you look closely at this passage of Scripture and the Master's words, you will realize that Jesus expected the ten to return to give glory to God. God wants the glory, and every time He works a miracle in us, delivers us, or blesses us, we should give Him thanks.

Dear reader, how many times a day do you take the time to thank God for all he has given you? From the gift of eternal life to salvation and other gifts. The problem with human nature is that we just want to continually ask and receive without first stopping to see what God has done for us thus far. David well stated, "The Lord, who delivered me from the paw of the lion and from the paw of the bear, He will deliver me from the hand of this Philistine" (1 Samuel 17:37 NKJV).

Thanksgiving, A Weapon of Spiritual Warfare
What to do when faced with a challenge

Faced with the new challenge of Goliath, who for forty days had been harassing the armies of Israel - day and night - David drew strength from God simply by remembering the past victories the Lord had given him: "Our servant used to keep his father's sheep, and when a lion or a bear came and took a lamb out of the flock, I went out after it and struck it, and delivered the lamb from its mouth; and when it arose against me, I caught it by its beard, and struck and killed it. Your servant has killed both lion and bear; and this uncircumcised Philistine will be like one of them, seeing he has defied the armies of the living God" (verses 34-36). In verse 32, David encouraged King Saul not to faint or be discouraged because of this significant problem that threatened the entire nation of Israel.

Notably, David's courage in the face of this tormentor who psychologically threatened the army of Israel and thwarted every possible conventional war (battle) strategy that Saul and his military commanders had was the fruit of God's recognition. David remembered all the battles the Lord had delivered him and thanked him. With this formula, he won not only Goliath but also all the battles he had in his life. He said, "The young lions lack and suffer hunger; but those who seek the Lord shall not lack any good thing" (Psalms 34:10 NKJV).

Dear brother or sister, take this example of David; recognize every victory and deliverance God gives you and use them as points of thanksgiving. When faced with a new challenge, don't be afraid or worried. Don't be intimidated by the severity of the problem, the scary medical report (which causes despair); think of the bigger challenges in the past that the Lord has delivered you from; think of His greatness and how He has helped you so far, and begin to thank Him. Thanksgiving activates the power of God because it places the Lord above the circumstances of life. Know this throughout your journey here on earth. You will always have challenges, some seemingly greater than others, depending on the level of glory you have achieved or want to achieve.

In everything, acknowledge God, continue to count your blessings, and sing victories because Jesus Christ is the same yesterday, today, and forever. He doesn't change. He has already defeated the devil for us. Unfortunately, human instinct often makes you forget the wonders of God and His mighty hand. When confronted with new challenges or the devil in another guise, we tend to get scared as if there is no solution to any problem and forget what God did yesterday.

Acknowledge God at all stages of your life. This will help you develop trust in God and strengthen your fellowship with Him. That is why David wasn't afraid to face Goliath because he knew his God and wanted that God to be glorified. David's solution to solving the "Goliath" dossier was not conventional (sword, spear, and shield) but a sling and a pebble (flat stone). Because he had intimate fellowship with God and was grateful to Him, the Lord gave him out-of-thought strategies and standard methods to slay Goliath. God hasn't changed. Even today, He can give you innovative ideas for the businesses you do, open doors to work, and provide for your needs outside the regular doors you expected. But you must recognize Him first and note what He does in your life.

The prayer of thanksgiving serves as a record of past victories and, simultaneously, as a force of attraction for the desired glorious future to keep God's intervention in our lives constant, yesterday, today, and forever.

A typical example was when Jesus was confronted with the death of Lazarus, who had been buried for four days and was already stinking of decomposition. In a situation that seemed to have no way out, He prayed the prayer of thanksgiving: "Father, I thank You that You have heard Me" (John 11:41 NKJV). Then He commanded Lazarus to come out of the tomb, and to everyone's amazement, the miracle happened - Lazarus was resurrected. Did you notice that Jesus thanked the Father for Lazarus' resurrection long before he issued the command, "Lazarus, come forth" (verse 43)? The prayer of thanksgiving empowered the words of command he gave, and everything he said materialized. There is power in the prayer of thanksgiving.

On another occasion, when there was a crowd of about five thousand hungry men (not counting children and women), he said a prayer of thanksgiving, and the bread and fish of the boy who had brought them were multiplied to feed everyone present until there were twelve baskets of bread left over. We can conclude that in the face of the greatest challenges, Jesus prayed the prayer of thanksgiving for the working of the greatest miracles.

Why is the Thanksgiving Prayer Powerful?

The prayer of thanksgiving brings the revelation of the Lord's provision - the revelation that God has already solved the problem, healed the disease, and brought relief and victory to his children - even if this has not yet physically happened. This moves God's heart and causes God's eternal purposes to materialize in our lives. This is why Jesus said to the Samaritan who had been healed of leprosy, "Arise, go your way. Your faith has made you well" (Luke 17:19 NKJV). The word "healed" denotes a state in which the person is completely restored. Although the ungrateful ones were healed of leprosy in the sense that the disease or infection was removed from their skin, this man received the resurrection of his limbs (fingers) that he had lost because of leprosy.

The thing is that when you give thanks, God gives more than what He gave before you thanked Him. So don't be ashamed to stop in front of the brothers and sisters of the Church and testify about what God has done for you. Don't be afraid to tell that to people at your workplace, in your family circle, or even schoolmates. In everything, glorify God, and have a thankful heart. If you have prayed about an issue and apparently it hasn't been resolved, raise your hands to the heavens, get down on your knees if you can, and start thanking God for what He has already done and will still do.

Finally, when saying the prayer of thanksgiving, be specific; tell God what He has really done for you. Count your blessings and sing your victories.

Exercise

Take a few minutes of your time and think about all that God has done for you. Think of at least three glorious things the Lord has done or three critical moments in your life where you saw God's hand at work. Thank Him objectively.

Chapter III
The Prayer of Faith

"And the prayer of faith will save the sick, and the Lord will raise him up. And if he has committed sins, he will be forgiven" (James 5:15 NKJV).

In our opening Scripture, we see mention of the prayer of faith and its impact on the salvation of the sufferer. Obviously, this salvation can encompass other areas of life, for even forgiveness, can be granted when this type of prayer is made.

Now, one must realize that all the types of prayer we have studied involve faith, for without faith, it's impossible to please God. However, when it comes to the prayer of faith, we are faced with a type of prayer that resolves even cases thought impossible to the human eye. The very nature of this kind of prayer requires that the believer or candidate has a bold and unshakable faith in the power of God and His word. On many occasions, believers pray, but there are times when the situation may defy the possibilities of any human solution.

For example, imagine a situation in which a family is told by doctors that their sick family member - who is terminally ill - is no longer curable and there is nothing that can be done; that they only have a few days to live. How would a Christian member who walks with God react? Well, it's normal for them to be shaken and perplexed, especially when they see that there seems to be no improvement in the patient's medical condition. At that moment, the impending situation may challenge everything they have learned in church services, seminars, conventions, and even what they have read or studied in the Holy Bible. Notice that many brethren in this situation may resort to prayer, but praying without faith, thinking that it's possible to reverse the medical condition of this sick family member. For this and other types of challenging situations, you should pray the prayer of faith. Scripture states that everyone who believes (trusts) in Him will not be put to shame, that is, will not be disappointed (Romans 10:11).

One must remember that prayer will not be answered because we pray but because we pray in faith. In this sense, it is not only what we say that counts, nor the fact that we pray, but the state of the heart of the one who prays. The believer's ability to fully trust God's power above any contrary report counts. To do this, we must follow the diet of faith.

Principles of the Prayer of Faith

A principle is a law, a norm that makes something work. Whenever this law is triggered, there is the predictability of its results. For example, one of the famous laws of physics is the law of gravity, which states that each body with mass and volume, that is, with weight, is attracted to the ground by the law of gravity. With the naked eye, you won't see this law, but if you climb to the roof of a ten-story building and launch yourself into the air, you will suddenly find yourself pulled to the ground. You neither see the law nor feel it, yet it's there and works all the time, regardless of a person's color, race, age, or ethnicity. The law is universal and across the board. The principles you will learn here have been tested by the men and women we read about in Holy Scripture, and they have all had positive results.

Furthermore, the Scripture attests, "Jesus Christ is the same yesterday, today, and forever" (Hebrews 13:8 NKJV), and in Malachi 3:6a NKJV, God states, "For I am the LORD, I do not change..." Below are three fundamental principles that make the prayer of faith work. If you trigger them, you will get positive results.

1. When you pray, don't doubt in your heart.

In Mark 11:14 NKJV, Jesus curses a fig tree so it will no longer bear fruit: "Let no one eat fruit from you ever again." And His disciples heard it." As God, Jesus could not feel hunger or thirst. However, He had not come as God but as a man. In this state, He was hungry, and seeing a fig tree in the distance, hungry, He approached it to see if He could find some figs to eat. Notice one important thing: "it was not the season for figs" (verse 13b). So Jesus curses the fig tree and then leaves.

The next day, as they were passing by the same place, His disciples were amazed that the words the Master had spoken had materialized. His answer was, "Have faith in God. For assuredly, I say to you, whoever says to this mountain, 'Be removed and be cast into the sea,' and does not doubt in his heart, but believes that those things he says will be done, he will have whatever he says" (verses 22-23).

Here is the principle of the prayer of faith: when you pray, believe that what you say will be done. So we see that the prayer and the decrees of faith depend on the condition of man's heart when he prays or speaks. Do you understand now why I said in the introduction that in the prayer of faith, the state of the heart of the one who prays counts more and not only the words they speak? Anyone can pray or speak, but we have been given a high standard, a higher level of functioning as God, enacting things, and they happen, asking for something in prayer and it being done. So the prayer of faith serves much better for complicated cases because it puts God into action. The rule is that when praying, do not doubt in your heart but believe that what you say will be done. Jesus guarantees that whatever we say will be done if this condition is met. The prayer of faith suspends times and epochs. It produces new times and epochs, causing the believer to live in an atmosphere of glory and light even amid turmoil and crisis. This is why Jesus said, "All things are possible to him who believes" (Mark 9:23 NKJV).

Let's see: from a natural point of view, it was not fig season, so the fig tree was not expected to have figs. But Jesus cursed the fig tree for not producing figs for Him to eat. Why? The reason is simple: when faith is present, it suspends the laws of nature to accommodate the miracle. With faith, miracles can happen anytime and at any time, regardless of the circumstances. For Jesus, the fig tree should have produced figs, and because it was unproductive, it was cursed and withered.

There is a narrative that can make it easier to understand this principle. There was a man named Jairus who was the head of the synagogue. His daughter was sick and on the verge of death, so he went to the Master to visit her house and heal her. However, on the way, Jesus lingered because of the hemorrhagic woman who had touched his clothes and been healed. What moved Jesus to go with Jairus? His faith that he would heal his daughter. What stopped Jesus in his tracks for a while? The faith of the sick woman. So He said to the woman, "Daughter, your faith has saved you." Did you notice that what moved Jesus was the faith of those who needed God's intervention and His compassion for them? Because Jesus lingered a while along the way, Jairus' daughter died.

Some of those in the synagogue came to tell Jairus not to disturb the Master anymore because the girl was dead. As if they wanted to say, "give up, it is too late." These words almost sowed fear in Jairus' heart; thus, he would lose faith in Jesus because of despair. So Jesus quickly said, "fear not, only believe." Jesus wanted Jairus to keep his faith in Him; otherwise, the miracle wouldn't happen. Some of His disciples were also desperate. For this reason, He took only Peter, James, and John as they showed faith at the time and were part of His inner circle. Jesus resurrected the little girl.

How to do the Prayer of Faith?

The prayer of faith can turn situations of despair into testimonies of victory. The requirement is simple: believe in God's power and don't doubt in your heart.

Now, what do you do so that doubt and fear do not enter your heart? Go forward with faith.

1. Locate yourself in God's word.

Find a scripture from God's word that has to do with the thing you are praying for.

2. Believe firmly in it.

To believe means to agree with what God says. But believing is not yet faith.

Many brothers believe, but because they stop at believing, their miracle is not completed. Then they complain and say: we prayed and believed, but God didn't act. But, of course, this isn't true; the problem is that these people confuse faith with believing. Believing is a part of faith, but it isn't complete without the other parts that I will show you here.

3. Meditate on this scripture.

Think about it until it shapes your mind and dominates the emotions of your spirit. Then, meditate on it until you begin seeing it with your heart's eyes. When you reach this level, you will see that the situation before you no longer moves you, for all that matters is what God has said in His Word.

4. Confess the scripture.

Give voice to that scripture. Speak in conformity with what God says. God's word says that you will be saved if you confess with your mouth to the Lord Jesus and believe that God raised him from the dead. When will you be saved? When you believe and confess. Do you see that believing alone does not solve the situation? It must be accompanied by action. When God's word is confessed, it shapes the spiritual world and changes the course of events. Something happens whenever we confess or declare God's word. This is why Jesus said heaven and earth will pass away, but his word will not pass away (Matthew 24:35).

5. Act on God's Word.

Faith is an action. It has nothing to do with emotions or reason. This means it's neither emotional nor rational but based on what God says in his word. You pray from a basis, which is God's word. This is your firm foundation. "Now faith is the substance of things hoped for and the evidence of things not seen. By it, the ancients have obtained witness." You can have testimonies if you pray based on the word. So pray, trusting solely in God's word.

We have an example in the Bible of King Hezekiah. Isaiah, the prophet, came with a message from God that he should put his house in order because he would die. But instead, he decided to knuckle down and pray to God in faith. The expression knuckle down means that he applied himself earnestly to this prayer and looked to God as his only solution.

Now, in this kind of prayer, you must be specific as he was, and he also argued why he wanted to be healed. So he reminded the Lord of all the good things he had done. And before long, God told Isaiah to return with a new word: he would live another fifteen years.

The main thing is that despair and declared death was reversed. How? Through the prayer of faith. The prayer looks to God as the only alternative. Generally, this kind of prayer does not take long to be answered. Furthermore, after having prayed this prayer, the believer is no longer moved by circumstances by medical reports but by the Word of God, which is the source of faith. As the Scripture says: "So then faith comes by hearing, and hearing by the word of God" (Romans 10:17 NKJV).

So make a habit of always listening, studying, meditating on the word, and attending worship services. This will condition your heart to always believe in God confidently, and when you pray, there will be a positive answer. The prayer of faith is the fruit of a heart convinced in the faithfulness and infallibility of God's word.

2. When you pray, believe that you have already received what you asked for before you have it physically.

In Mark 11:24 NKJV, Jesus left the secret of the prayer of faith when he said, "Therefore I tell you, whatever you ask for in prayer, believe that you have received it, and it will be yours."

The principle of the prayer of faith is that the believer must believe that he has already received what he has asked for. In the spiritual arena, to believe means to agree with God that what He has said in His word is real and existing. Following the same tune, it should be noted that in prayer, believing also means receiving. We will receive nothing from God if we do not believe. Therefore, believing is a form of receiving. The fundamental point to understand here is that when praying the prayer of faith, don't expect the answer to be given in the future but believe that it has already been given even before it is manifested. Do you understand now?

For example, when Jesus thanked the Father for hearing Him about the resurrection of Lazarus, this was before the stone was removed from where Lazarus had been buried. But why did Jesus thank the Father for hearing Him on the subject of Lazarus? Because He prayed the prayer of faith. This implies that you must believe you have already received what you asked for before physically seeing it. Therefore, believing also means seeing.

The Scripture states, "For we live by faith, not by sight" (2 Corinthians 5:7 NKJV). That is, we walk by faith and not by what we see. So, to believe means seeing the reality of the thing we ask for and acting as one who already has it. For example, if you pray and ask for a job, believe that you already have it. Then start thanking God and acting accordingly. Likewise, if you pray for healing from an illness, believe that you are already healed and start doing what other healthy people do. So, faith is an attitude; it's an action.

The Bible says that faith without works is dead (James 2:17). Faith requires an action corresponding to what you believe. You speak and act as one who already has the thing compelled by faith. It never fails and always has guaranteed results because it is the active and positive response of man's spirit. For example, if you are praying for the fruit of the womb, that is, to conceive (get pregnant), believe that you are already a mother, and buy the baby's trousseau and clothes immediately. People will say that you are paranoid, but it doesn't matter because this is an attitude of faith. True faith believes, receives, acknowledges, acts, confesses, and thanks. It puts God into action. Pray with faith, with expectation. With conviction in your heart, through the revelation of the provision of what you have asked for in God's word.

3. When you pray, don't be repetitive.

In Matthew 6:7-8 NKJV, Jesus gave a fundamental principle in the prayer of faith. He said, "And when you pray, do not keep on babbling like pagans, for they think they will be heard because of their many words. Do not be like them, for your Father knows what you need before you ask him."

The underlying principle here is that you should not repeat the same request you have already made to God after you have prayed. You shouldn't use repetitions because you believe God heard your prayer when you first prayed it. Remember: faith doesn't fail. It always works, regardless of the circumstances. Therefore, the reason why the believer repeats the same prayer over and over again is that he doesn't believe that God heard and answered it from the first moment. So, even this time you are praying, you may not receive it if you keep repeating the same thing repeatedly.

To pray the prayer of faith, you need it to spring from the heart, be on time, and get to the point. Once done, you will feel in your spirit (heart) that that burden you had is gone. Then you will know that it's done. It's done. The Bible says: "If clouds are full of water, they pour rain on the earth. Whether a tree falls to the south or to the north, in the place where it falls, there it will lie" (Ecclesiastes 11:3 NKJV). You know and are sure that the clouds are already formed in your heart. It's only a matter of time before the rain begins to fall. Repeating the same thing in prayer signifies a lack of faith and trust in God. Don't forget that God doesn't fail, and true prayer doesn't. If there is any failure, it will always be human and not divine.

The Bible tells us about Elijah, a man just like us who felt thirsty, hungry, and tired, just like us. But he prayed a prayer of faith, and it didn't rain for three and a half years. Then he prayed, heaven gave the rain, and the earth produced its fruit (James 5:17-18). This shows what a human being who walks with God and has faith in Him can do. Thus, we are given an example of faith so that by imitating or being inspired by him, we can likewise perform feats in our time in this dispensation we are in. You, too, can pray with faith and change circumstances; just believe. There is no limit to what faith can accomplish or can solve and do. Have faith in God.

Chapter IV
The Prayer of Praise and Worship

"Give praise to the Lord, proclaim his name; make known among the nations what he has done. Sing to him, sing praise to him; tell of all his wonderful acts" (Psalms 105:1-2 NIV).

The prayer of praise and worship is one of the highest ways to have fellowship with God. The communion with God that is given through praise and worship constitutes the highest and highest level of walking with Him.

First: praise prepares the atmosphere for God's moving, and worship attracts his manifested presence. Both produce extraordinary miracles and manifest God's glory. In all places and at all times when God's presence is manifested, praise and worship are activated automatically as a reaction to God's attributes.

Second: in this kind of fellowship in praise and worship, no requests are made, but God's nature is extolled. This is the kind of prayer that angels pray in heaven before their throne, revealing how God and man were to relate to each other long before the fall of Adam. The prayer of petition wouldn't be necessary if all believers reached this level of communion with God.

Third: at this level of communion, the believer is transformed into an instrument of God - a worshiper, not a simple beggar or victim of circumstances. This is because in this type of prayer, the awareness of God's greatness, faithfulness, love, and other attributes is activated, and the awareness of needs and problems is ignored. In essence, the devil is ignored in this kind of prayer since nothing he does interests us or moves us because we only see God at all times.

Fourth: the prayer of praise and worship can help the believer to receive in great measure what he hasn't come to ask God for since he has come to the throne of grace. His needs are supplied without any request.

It's like someone who is immersed in the water at the beach doesn't need a shower or bucket to bathe because water is available everywhere. Just jump in and take the plunge.

In worship, the worshiper immerses himself in the glories of God, receives and walks in the victories of the eternal, and lives in the inexhaustible supply of God's blessings. Therefore, God wants us to be worshipers. But many believers haven't yet reached this level because they are always aware of the devil and his needs and not of God. They can't see God in everything. They have a victim mentality and not an overcomer mentality; they are aware of poverty and not the Lord's provision, and they see the devil instead of seeing God. They haven't understood the power of praise and the power of worship: worship is the spirit of man in intercession with God without any bother or need. Praise is the awareness of the revelation of God's attributes. When God reveals Himself to man, man becomes worshipful and adores Him.

In the text from John 4:23 NKJV, Jesus said to the Samaritan woman, "But the hour is coming, and now is, when the true worshipers will worship the Father in spirit and truth; for the Father is seeking such to worship Him." In this passage, Jesus reveals the heart of God the Father: he is looking for worshippers; for men and women with hearts surrendered to him and aware of his greatness and mercies. Men and women who will recognize him at all times and at all times exalt him. This becomes a service to God. That is why there were Levites in the Old Testament whose job was only to minister in the temple, leading the worship of God.

The fact is that worship and praise reveal the activities in heaven by God's angels and affirm that God is present, has worked, and is on the throne.

What is worship, and what is praise

Usually, these two concepts are seen as one, but in practice, they aren't the same. However, one can lead to the other, as praise can lead to worship and be practiced simultaneously.

Praise is the recognition and appreciation of God's attributes, usually expressed through the lips - the mouth. Praise doesn't always come out of the heart, but worship compels the involvement of the heart. Praise falls into the category of prayer because it can be done directly to God.

For example, when the psalmist said, " Bless the Lord, O my soul; and all that is within me, bless His holy name" (Psalms 103:1 NKJV). In this context, it's the soul of man that, through his lips, blesses or praises the Lord. Thus, direct communication from man to God expresses appreciation and recognition of what God is or what He has done. Through the lips, man praises God. Therefore, praise can be defined as speaking well of God, exalting God. That is why the psalmist used the term "bless," which means "to speak well of God." In the prayer of praise, you speak well of God, telling Him that you are thankful for what He has done in your life and what He is. This type of prayer must be specific because you must tell God literally what He is to you. For example, looking at your life, where God took you from, and where you are now, you can see God's operations, His love, and His mercies. What do you do? You praise him. Have you noticed that praise is an active and positive reaction of man's heart to God's attributes and deeds?

You can say, "Father, thank you so much for your eternal and unconditional love toward me. You are holy, just, and merciful. Thank you for being so kind to me. Thank you for being so gracious in my life. You are faithful, unfailing, and invincible. Therefore, I will always trust in you. Thank you because your mercy has no end; new is every morning."

In this context, we are faced with the prayer of praise, not just praise per se. You can praise God without communicating that directly to Him but by exalting or superimposing deeds before men. You are communicating with people, informing them what God is and what He has done or can do. For example, in Psalms 107:01 NIV, the psalmist says, "Give thanks to the Lord, for he is good; his love endures forever." He is communicating with people by extolling the attribute that the Lord's love is forever. This separates God from human beings because people's lovingkindness is circumstantial and sporadic. That is, it changes because it depends on circumstances. However, God is always gracious, always kind. That's why verse 8 says, "Oh, that men would give thanks to the Lord for His goodness, and for His wonderful works to the children of men."

Understand this: when you pray the prayer of praise, you need to be objective and specific in saying why you praise Him and what He has done for which you praise Him. It is not enough to say, "I praise you, Father; I praise you, Lord." The question is, "why do you praise Him?" What has He done, or what is He to you? What wonders has He done in your life? That must be said word for word, ipsis verbis. So the verse says, "Then they cried out to the Lord in their trouble, and He delivered them out of their distresses. And He led them forth by the right way, that they might go to a city for a dwelling place. Oh, that men would give thanks to the Lord for His goodness, and for His wonderful works to the children of men! For He satisfies the longing soul, and fills the hungry soul with goodness" (Psalms 107:6-9 NKJV). Here he explains why they should praise the Lord.

Therefore, for the prayer of praise to be effectively one of praise, it's necessary to connect the praises to God's attributes or his deeds in your life. For example, "I praise you, Father, Creator of heaven and earth because you have healed me from sickness and delivered me from the snare of death. I praise you, Father, because you are my provider and supply all my needs." The prayer of praise can be done in conjunction with the prayer of thanksgiving because there is a need to mention God's deeds in both. But in the prayer of praise, the deeds are mentioned in connection with His attributes - "He did this for me because He is this or that."

As a child of the kingdom, you should always praise God. One of the reasons many believers don't pray is because they say they have nothing to say and their prayers are seconds. And why don't they have anything to say? Because they only know how to pray the prayer of petition and pray when they have needs. What should you do if God has already supplied your needs? Pray. Which prayer? The prayer of praise or adoration. This is why the psalmist David said, "I will bless the Lord at all times. His praise shall continually be in my mouth" (Psalms 34:1 NKJV). Avoid complaining all the time that life is complicated. God doesn't like to see His children complaining but praising.

How to express the praises

We can express the praises of God using words. In the text we just read, David said that the praises of God would continually be on his lips, that is, in his mouth. No wonder he had a glorious life - he had the praises on his lips. He was always ready to praise, and the anointing was upon him. Even as he touched the harp, the anointing drove out the demon -the evil spirit- that tormented Saul. With this praise ministry, you will never live tormented by the devil. You will always live in the peace of God.

In the text of Hosea 14:1 NKJV, we read, "O Israel, return to the Lord your God, for you have stumbled because of your iniquity." Here, Israel is called to turn and turn to God. How? Verse 2 says, "Take words with you, and return to the Lord. Say to Him, "Take away all iniquity; receive us graciously, for we will offer the sacrifices of our lips."

It was customary in the Old Covenant, commonly known as "The Old Testament," to offer to God animal sacrifices: sheep, lambs, etc. This was a service that the priests performed in shifts, and there were morning and afternoon sacrifices. Great importance was attached to this service rendered to God so that animals were killed daily, and incense was burned to offer sacrifices and offerings to the Lord. Because of this, their sins were forgiven and delivered from their enemies around them. In addition, God sent rain so that their fields would produce, removed their diseases, and gave them victories in battles.

Now, you and I can have this kind of glorious life when we apply ourselves to the ministry of praise. Note that praise can be done through singing, music, hymns, and other instruments in recognition of God.

King David, one of the great poets of the Old Testament, had this habit of sacrificing to the Lord. In Psalms 141:2 NKJV, he said, "Let my prayer be set before You as incense, the lifting up of my hands as the evening sacrifice."

Hosea and David were prophets, each in their own office because of the Spirit of Christ in them. David also had the prerogative of being king of Israel. They looked prophetically and saw a time in human history, our time - when it would no longer be necessary to offer animal sacrifices and calves or burn incense to God. However, in place of these sacrifices, we would offer God sacrifices of praise expressed through our mouths.

We see this statement in the New Testament, in Hebrews 13:15 NKJV: "Therefore by Him (Jesus) let us continually offer the sacrifice of praise to God, that is, the fruit of our lips, giving thanks to His name."

Through words, we should always praise God. Suppose there were teams and shifts of priests doing this daily morning and evening in the Old Covenant. In that case, we should also do it consistently.

Benefits of the Prayer of Praise

The primary benefits are the opening of the heart and spiritual dimensions to hear the voice of God.

Praise and worship prayer can lift man's spirit and enable him to hear God's voice and guidance for his life. We read this in Acts 13:1-4, when Saul (Paul), Barnabas, and other prophets and teachers in the Church in Antioch ministered to the Lord in prayer and fasting. The Holy Spirit spoke to them to set apart Saul and Barnabas for the work that God had commanded them to do. And they were sent forth by the Spirit and did exploits.

Subchapter - The Power of Praise
Praise as a weapon of war

How to Win Without Struggling and Prosper Without Sweating

In the Old Testament, we find a vivid example of the people of Judah and their king Josaphat. Threatened by an attack by three united kings against this few in several people, Josaphat decided to put singers in front of the army to sing and exalt the Lord. The Scripture says, "Then the Levites of the children of the Kohathites and of the children of the Korahites stood up to praise the Lord God of Israel with voices loud and high" (2 Chronicles 20:19 NKJV). Can you imagine what the armed soldiers thought that, in the place of an ambush, they were being exposed to the noise caused by the praise songs of the Levites? Well, this was God's strategy to give them the desired victory. They praised the Lord. Thus the Scripture attests, "And when he had consulted with the people, he appointed those who should sing to the Lord, and who should praise the beauty of holiness, as they went out before the army and were saying: "Praise the Lord, for His mercy endures forever" (verse 21).

A few aspects to note:

1. He commanded a group of singers to stand before God. To do what? To sing and praise the majesty. This was their work, their ministry before the Lord.

2. These singers were to go before the armed ones. The weapon of the armed ones wasn't the spears, arrows, and shields they carried but the praise of the singers who stood before them.

3. So God fought for them by confusing the minds of the enemies who started fighting against each other until they killed one another, and no one was left alive.

4. The people of Judah collected much spoil in the form of garments, camels, gold, and silver left behind by their enemies.

Conclusion:

1. They worked for the Lord by ministering praise to Him;

2. They won without fighting, only praising the majesty of the Lord;

3. They became rich without fighting, without sweating, just praising the Lord.

In all this, we see the power of praise manifested. If you create this habit of always having a place or anywhere to praise and worship the Lord, you will have the same results.

Released from prison without using human force

In the text from Acts 16:25-31, we read about the incident in which Paul and Silas are arrested and put in jail, having their feet tied to a tree trunk. What crime had they committed? None, Paul had merely cast out a demon - a divining spirit of a girl who read people's hands and predicted their future. She was a slave, and they took the money from that profit. Seeing the girl free, they accused Paul and Silas of making a riot before the magistrates, who ordered them to be beaten with unclothed rods and thrown into prison. Even in this deplorable situation, Paul and Silas didn't complain before God, nor did they despair. The Bible says, "But at midnight Paul and Silas were praying and singing hymns to God, and the prisoners were listening to them. Suddenly there was a great earthquake, so that the foundations of the prison were shaken; and immediately all the doors were opened and everyone's chains were loosed" (Acts 16:25-26 NKJV).

Did you notice that not only Paul and Silas but everyone was set free? Their attitude brought deliverance to all the prisoners. It led to the salvation of the jailer responsible for keeping them imprisoned. As a result, he and his family were saved. You may be the only Christian in your home and ridiculed by other family members or even at school. However, suppose you are firm and persevere in praying the prayer of praise. In that case, you will see the light, victory, and everyone can benefit.

Consider this: you can free yourself from any kind of spiritual prison by praising the Lord because praise is a weapon of spiritual warfare.

If you have prayed and fasted for an issue that doesn't seem to be resolved, pray the prayer of praise. Then, raise your hands and praise the Lord; exalt Him. When praise goes up, glory comes down. In that glory are your victory, peace, provision, and success.

Understanding Worship

Worship is at a higher level than praise.

First, because it necessarily involves the creation of man. For example, if to praise is to speak well of God, someone can speak well of God and live a life contrary to what he says. For instance, someone can say, "You are beautiful," while he says the opposite in his heart. This doesn't happen in worship. Worship implies that everything expressed to God comes from a sincere heart and is surrendered to Him. This is why Jesus said that the Father seeks true worshipers who worship Him in spirit and in truth (John 4:23-24).

To worship means to pay homage, to prostrate oneself, to revere. Worship is a sign of surrender to God and deep respect for Him. In worship, the worshiper is shaped to conform to God's words and His will. Therefore, worship goes far beyond words; it comes from the heart. For example, you can worship God without necessarily saying a word. Worship is an attitude of reverence before God. It's a way of life of one impacted by God's greatness, his culture, and his purposes. Hence there are many believers worldwide but few true worshipers. Everyone can profess to love God, but in worship, what counts is what you do because you love him, not just what you say with your mouth. Jesus said, "If you love me, keep my commandments" (John 14:15 NKJV). In verse 23, He adds, "If anyone loves me, he will keep my word; and my Father will love him, and we will come to him and make our home with him."

God wants to dwell in humans through his word and his Spirit. The weight of God's word in our lives and our reverence for him makes us worshippers, people ready to execute his will.

Benefits of Worship Prayer

Among the many benefits of worshiping God, here are the following:

1. Worship brings God's presence into the life of the believer (John 14:15);

2. Worship draws the manifestation of the *shekina* "of God's manifested glory" to where we are;

3. Worship connects heaven to earth and transports the earthly environment into a heavenly one;

4. Worship causes the light of the believer to shine continuously, regardless of the forces of darkness;

5. Worship attracts God's attention.

In Matthew 15:21-28, we read about a Canaanite woman who had come to Jesus asking for healing and deliverance of her daughter. She cried out to the Master, "Have mercy on me, O Lord, Son of David! My daughter is severely demon-possessed." (verse 22). Jesus answered nothing, even though he saw her crying out. She thought that her cry or scream would get the Lord's attention. This is what many brothers and sisters in Christ think. They think that if they scream enough or cry copiously, God will be touched emotionally and rescue them. Well, He does it for spiritual babies, but you must learn to trigger the divine principles when you grow up and become a mature man or woman. Jesus' disciples, seeing this, told him to send her away because she had been screaming after them. This shows that the woman was desperate for her daughter's situation, and the cries for help were loud. When the woman noticed that there was no response from Jesus, she triggered the principle of worship.

We read in verse 25: "Then she came and worshiped Him, saying, 'Lord, help me." In verse 26, Matthew records, "But he answered..." When did He answer? When she worshiped Him. She prostrated herself at His feet in reverence, recognizing that He was the Messiah and capable of working a miracle. Jesus told the woman that it wasn't good to take her children's food and give it to the puppies, and she replied that even the puppies eat the crumbs that fall from their master's table. She received the healing and deliverance of her daughter through faith and worship.

The problem is that when many brothers and sisters in Christ pray to God, they start by begging and whining when they should be getting His attention -adoring Him.

How to do the prayer of adoration?

First: meditate on God's attributes. Attributes are characteristics of God - they are qualities that describe Him. For example, He is holy, all-powerful, kind, merciful, compassionate, etc. Think about these qualities of God. As you meditate on these in tune with the revelation of the Scripture, you will see God greater than the devil, more extraordinary than everything and everyone, and you will see that nothing is impossible for Him.

Second: surrender to Him completely; let yourself be carried away by Him. Surrender to His love, His power, and His mercies.

Third: speak to Him from your heart. You can use words expressed through your lips just as you speak into your heart without even opening your mouth. It is common and normal for tears to begin to fall from your face as the Holy Spirit begins to reveal to you who God is. You become increasingly involved in Him, and your whole spirit, soul, and body are flooded with God's presence.

One of the things you may experience is:

1. You will be filled with the Holy Spirit, the glory, and the presence of God;

2. You will gain faith, courage, and boldness, and all fear and worries will vanish;

3. You will see God's love for you and recognize that without Him, you are nothing and can do nothing;

4. You will be more willing to pray, to spend time with God in His presence;

5. You will be more thirsty to study and hear his word;

6. Will always be conscious of your presence;

7. Will be positioned to hear God's voice at all times;

8. Your spiritual eyes may open, and you will begin to see in the spirit;

9. You will be more and more transformed;

10. Whatever you determine or declare with your mouth will come to pass;

11. You will live in the conscious presence of God;

12. You will see yourself as God sees you: protected, strong, blessed, and more than a conqueror. And the world will become small for you;

13. You will be filled with joy and praise.

Exercise

1. Sing a song in praise of God, or put on a gospel song that exalts God's attributes;

2. Study some Scriptures from God's words or listen to some teaching or preaching message;

3. Think about God's attributes, who He is as you have heard in preaching or studied in the Word - the Holy Bible;

4. Worship Him in your heart. Then, if necessary, open your mouth and exalt Him. Think of all the glorious things He has done for you.

5. Have a notebook with you and write down everything He reveals to you.

Chapter V
Prayer in Tongues
A Brief History

In the text from Acts 2:1-4 NKJV, we read, "When the Day of Pentecost had fully come, they were all with one accord in one place. And suddenly there came a sound from heaven, as of a rushing mighty wind, and it filled the whole house where they were sitting. Then there appeared to them divided tongues, as of fire, and one sat upon each of them. And they were all filled with the Holy Spirit and began to speak with other tongues, as the Spirit gave them utterance."

This text reveals a supernatural phenomenon that has become part of the Church of believers who have become new creatures in Christ by receiving the gift of the Holy Spirit. This supernatural phenomenon is called "speaking in tongues" and "praying in tongues." But what were these tongues? Strange languages; foreign languages because they were initially not spoken by believers.

Generally, those who speak in tongues have been called Pentecostals because the Holy Spirit descended on the day of Pentecost. This has been assumed for many centuries to the point where denominations have been created that are called Pentecostals because they speak in strange tongues. However, this understanding is inconsistent with the Holy Scriptures, so it's wrong. According to the Scriptures, Pentecostals are not those who spoke in tongues, for on the day of Pentecost, Jews had come from various parts of the world: from Asia, Africa, Europe, and the East, as attested in verses 8, 9, and 10 of Chapter 2 of Acts. These were religious men who had come to Jerusalem to celebrate Pentecost; none were among those who received the gift and the baptism in the Spirit, nor among those who spoke in tongues. Only 120 disciples were in the upper room in prayer for fear of the Jews, for their Master Jesus had been crucified, resurrected, and ascended into heaven. They were waiting for the promise of the Father - the Holy Spirit.

Furthermore, Pentecost was a Jewish festive and ceremonial date celebrating the 50-year harvest. It was called the feast of the harvest. It was a custom for Jews from all over the world to go to Jerusalem to celebrate this date. These were the real Pentecostals because they were there celebrating the day of Pentecost. Jesus' disciples were not celebrating Pentecost; they were in prayer in the upper room, waiting to receive the empowerment of the Holy Spirit for the work Jesus had commissioned them to do, which was to go and preach the Gospel to every creature and make disciples of all nations. For instance, I speak and pray in tongues. Still, I am not a Pentecostal because Jesus' apostles were not Pentecostals in the sense that many describe them: that group of Christians who believe in speaking in tongues and the gifts of the Holy Spirit, in contrast to the orthodox who don't believe in these phenomena.

Why did the Holy Spirit descend on the Day of Pentecost?

Well, everything God does follows a wise plan as the Creator of the universe for the salvation of humanity and the fulfillment of His purposes. Since the day of Pentecost symbolized the harvest feast in the Jewish fields, the Lord of the harvest - the Holy Spirit - would be sent at this time. This was to let the disciples know that while the rest of the Jews from all nations were celebrating the feast of physical harvests, of the physical fields, the apostles of Jesus and the early Church began a new form of continuous harvest that would reach all nations - the harvest of souls for the kingdom of God, through the preaching of the Gospel, baptism of believers and discipleship. He had already said, "The harvest truly is plentiful, but the laborers are few" (Matthew 9:37 NKJV). Then he gave a direction, "Therefore pray the Lord of the harvest to send out laborers into His harvest" (verse 38). That is what they were doing, praying and interceding. That's why, before He ascended into heaven, He told His disciples, "But you shall receive power when the Holy Spirit has come upon you; and you shall be witnesses to Me in Jerusalem, and in all Judea and Samaria, and to the end of the earth" (Acts 1:8 NKJV). "But stay in the city of Jerusalem until you have been clothed with power from on high" (Luke 24:49 NIV). When the Holy Spirit came, they would be changed into new creatures, be born again, and be empowered to go and preach the Gospel all over the world with the same power that Jesus had - the power of the Holy Spirit.

God is omniscient, proactive, and highly planned and organized - all events unfold according to his designs and purposes - he is the Lord.

Now, on the day of Pentecost, while they were all gathered together in one place in prayer and ministering to the Lord, a mighty rushing wind filled the whole house. It reminds me of the phenomenon that happened to me in June 2008 when I was in the temple leading worship. First, there was a master of ceremonies who had been appointed to lead the worship service and a whole liturgy scheduled for that day; then came the preacher who was going to preach. So I was standing at the altar in front of everyone, directing the moment of praise. Then, as we were worshiping and praising the Lord, a rushing wind suddenly filled the whole church building. All this wind came and filled me completely so that I couldn't even walk; I was like a ball full of air. Everything in me was flooded with power, anointing, and the Holy Spirit: my hands, legs, mouth, everything.

I remember my first words, "God is in this place." Suddenly, demons started manifesting and coming out of people. Furthermore, when I looked at a bunch of chairs where the church brothers were sitting, the power went there. When I stretched my hand in one direction, the anointing went there, and people fell like dominoes. That day, extraordinary miracles of healing and deliverance occurred. Since that very day, my ministry life has never been the same. In every salvation crusade and miracle, every service, seminar, conference, and vigil where I would minister, there was one common characteristic: the supernatural always happened. Since then, I have been given more tongues than I spoke before. I was promoted in the spirit and was highly recharged and enlightened by the Spirit. The Lord told me I would pass into the "heavenly atmosphere." He said that he had anointed me with the anointing that he had given to his apostles in the early church to preach his second coming, to reach the nations of the world for Christ, and to expand his kingdom, demonstrating his power and his love to humanity. And he has always been faithful to this day.

Therefore, when I read the text from the Acts of the Apostles (chapter two) about the experiences that apostles had at the descent of the Holy Spirit, I always vividly remember the experiences I had on the day I was baptized in the Holy Spirit. I had been preaching and teaching the word. I prayed for the sick by faith, as Jesus said. Still, from that day on, I began to minister through the anointing, a special anointing for my ministry. However, before this experience, I had continuously sought and prayed to the Lord. I had a great hunger and thirst for the person of the Holy Spirit, a burning desire to know the Lord Jesus and to walk in His presence and will. To me, nothing in this world matters more than the Holy Spirit; nothing matters but Jesus. He is all that matters to me.

Prayer is essential, and God will move whenever He sees hunger and thirst in our hearts. He said, "And you will seek Me and find Me, when you search for Me with all your heart. I will be found by you, says the Lord..." (Jeremiah 29:13-14 NKJV).

I have written this short excerpt of my story and experiences with the Holy Spirit so that you can understand that I have mastery of the subject we are dealing with. Not from the theological point of view of one who has read about it in books or heard stories but as one who has had experiences with the Holy Spirit. One who has found favor before heaven to walk with God in the heavenly arenas.

The Holy Spirit descended upon them on the day of Pentecost like a mighty rushing wind. Each one in the upper room received an impartation: a sharing of fire tongues. Their natural tongues were clothed with tongues of fire to enable them to speak the new languages and preach the word of God (the Gospel of the kingdom of God) with power. When they received the Holy Spirit that day, they were utterly flooded by Him, in Him, and He clothed Himself in them. They began to speak in other languages as He granted them to speak. The Jews who had come to worship and celebrate Pentecost heard this sound because it was a noticeable, audible phenomenon that caught the attention of everyone who curiously approached Jesus' disciples to see what this was all about to see what that was. Their greatest astonishment was that they heard them speaking in their languages, knowing beforehand that these disciples hadn't learned them. Luke records, "Then they were all amazed and marveled, saying to one another, "Look, are not all these who speak Galileans? And how is it that we hear, each in our own language in which we were born?" (Acts 2:7-8 NKJV). This means that the languages the apostles spoke existed in the lexicon of some countries on earth. Still, they had no concept or mastery of these languages. However, they spoke because the Holy Spirit granted them the words, for He knows all.

Now, I want you to notice one thing too: although on the one hand, these languages existed as vocabulary in a human lexicon, native to a country, on the other hand, there was a miraculous ministry of the Holy Spirit that caused a word spoken in a particular language by the apostles to be heard by others in their own language. In short, they would hear it in their native language. When it reached many ears of the people who spoke that native language, the sound was the translation of the original language the apostles used. So this means that the Holy Spirit was doing double work:

1. He gave the disciples words that were not part of their native vocabulary.

Verse 4 explains this when it says, "...and began to speak with other tongues, as the Spirit gave them utterance." Who gave them utterance? The Holy Spirit. Who was speaking? The disciples. Therefore, He gave them the ability to speak in these other languages, but in an unintelligent way, because they didn't even understand what they were saying in these languages.

2. The same Holy Spirit interpreted to the ears of the recipients in their native languages what the apostles said under their inspiration.

He served as an interpreter for them, interpreting the words he allowed the disciples to speak.

It has happened to me. I remember one of the occasions when I was preaching in the main church in Maputo, in Portuguese, when an elderly lady, who had never been to school and couldn't speak Portuguese, understood the whole message without knowing the Portuguese vocabulary. I was a little worried about her because I thought she wouldn't understand what I was saying in Portuguese. Still, suddenly

I prayed for the Spirit to do something about it. And miraculously, when I heard her comments in Tsonga, my native language, she replied that the service had been glorious and that she had learned a lot. God is not limited, and according to his will, he does extraordinary things that go beyond our understanding and rational human logic: speaking and/or praying in tongues. It's a supernatural phenomenon carried out by the empowerment of the Holy Spirit.

Strange languages, the new language of the new creation

Other strange or unknown languages are the same phenomenon - languages given by the empowerment of the Holy Spirit to the spirit of man. They are so called because they do not come from man's mind, but rather, from his inner man, by being a new creature.

The text from 2 Corinthians 5:17 NKJV says, "If anyone is in Christ, he is a new creation; old things have passed away; behold, all things have become new."

As a disciple of Jesus and a citizen of the kingdom of heaven, you need to understand that when you surrendered to the lordship of Jesus and accepted him as your personal Lord and Savior, a miracle happened to you - you were born again. Your spirit was recreated, enlightened, and regenerated by being born again. As a result, you took on another active and functional nature - the divine nature. So, in addition to functioning humanly on earth like other normal human beings who eat, sleep, and exhibit normal emotions, you, to function spiritually, became a partaker of the divine nature (2 Peter 1:3-4). From that moment on, you began to see, hear and speak in the spirit from your spirit. He was given new tongues, spoken not by his natural mind but by his spirit, the new divine nature. Therefore, strange tongues are a language of man's spirit recreated, inspired, or given by the Holy Spirit to man's spirit and not to his mind. You can know Portuguese, English, Spanish, French, Mandarin, or even your native language that you learned at home, in school, or developed in the environment or community you grew up in.

The Holy Spirit teaches spiritual languages, and when they are spoken, the mind is unfruitful because it doesn't understand them. They are not part of your vocabulary but of the vocabulary of the angels.

They understand and act when we pray in tongues. Because the human mind doesn't understand them, many think we who speak in tongues are crazy and out of our minds. According to the Scriptures, the natural man doesn't understand the things of the Spirit because they seem crazy to him. They are understood and discerned spiritually by spiritual men. We can say that the strange languages given by the Holy Spirit are languages of enlightened, recreated, updated spirits, that is, born again - new creatures.

Looking closely at the texts of Acts, we can notice these kinds of occurrences frequently whenever the Holy Spirit descended on believers, when the apostles laid hands on them, or when they spoke or prayed. The presence of the Holy Spirit in the believer would mark a new stage in his life - that he would no longer be what he was before, but a new creature, a new person on the inside who has received salvation and the divine nature. Your spirit - the inner man - or the man hidden in the heart as the apostle Peter describes him in 1 Peter 3:4, is programmed to begin to function in the spiritual world by being able to hear God's voice, to have heavenly visions, to have divine revelations, and to be led by the Holy Spirit. So you come to understand the things of the Spirit, and everything that God does or speaks makes sense. Miracles begin to make sense to you, even without any logical-rational explanation. You no longer use only your mind but tune into the antenna of the spiritual world, of the throne of God - by the empowerment of the Spirit. Stephen could see the heavens open, the glory of God and Jesus standing at the right hand of the Majesty, while others could only see a blue or cloudy sky. How could he see? By the Holy Spirit, he was filled with the Holy Spirit (Acts 7:55). Without the Holy Spirit, everything will seem crazy to unbelievers, to natural men guided only by what they see, hear and feel naturally. We also operate supernaturally in two worlds: the physical world and the spiritual world.

Speaking in tongues became common whenever the Holy Spirit descended on believers.

For example, in Acts 2, we read that the apostles and the rest of the disciples spoke in other languages as the Holy Spirit gave them utterance. The second occurrence, we find in chapter 10:44-46 NKJV "While Peter was still speaking these words, the Holy Spirit fell upon all those who heard the word. And those of the circumcision who believed were astonished, as many as came with Peter, because the gift of the Holy Spirit had been poured out on the Gentiles also. For they heard them speak with tongues and magnify God." Notice that when the Holy Spirit descended on these Gentiles (non-Jews) who had believed in Jesus through Peter's preaching, they also began to have this experience of speaking in tongues. In Acts 8, they probably had the same experience. Still, Luke doesn't emphasize this because a confident Simon, the magician, wanted to pay money to have this power to lay hands on people and for them to receive the gift of the Holy Spirit. This is because demons can also give strange tongues to their faithful, as witches do when they treat people.

But we are talking about the heavenly languages, the languages of the angels, the languages of the spirits of the saints. So the third occurrence, we find it in Acts 19:6 NKJV when Paul evangelized twelve men who had been disciples of John: "And when Paul had laid hands on them, the Holy Spirit came upon them, and they spoke with tongues and prophesied."

So we see these occurrences and manifestations in the ministry of Jesus' first apostles, emphasizing Peter and Paul's ministry. Whenever the Holy Spirit descended on believers, they spoke in other languages. Suppose this phenomenon was so frequent and regular in the early church. In that case, it must have the same importance in the church of Christ of the twenty-first century, which has not yet realized this and has not drawn from it. Paul prayed a lot in tongues, saying, "I thank my God I speak with tongues more than you all" (1 Corinthians 14:18 NKJV).

The importance of praying in tongues

"He who speaks in a tongue edifies himself, but he who prophesies edifies the church" (1 Corinthians 14:4 NKJV).

This wonderful God-inspired text to the apostle Paul reveals the importance of tongues to the believer. If many believers understood the power generated when praying in tongues, they would invest much in this in their spirit and find themselves walking in dominion in the spiritual arena.

From an impact standpoint, Paul argues that "speaking in tongues" is equivalent to "prophesying" - speaking under God's inspiration - when tongues are interpreted. A believer can speak in tongues without understanding what he is saying. Then he may need someone with the gift of interpreting tongues to help him understand, especially if he speaks to other believers in public. And when tongues are interpreted, they become equivalent to a prophecy. Some brethren can be given gifts of speaking strange tongues and interpreting them simultaneously. In this sense, they are encouraged to do it in public in front of the congregation, but when there is no one to interpret, it is better to speak to oneself. In this sense, Paul advises: "Therefore let him who speaks in a tongue pray that he may interpret" (verse 13).

Praying in tongues is more important than praying in our mental or intellectual language. "What happens when we pray in tongues?" - someone may ask. The Scripture has already stated, "He who speaks in a tongue edifies himself." The word "edifies" employed here is synonymous with the word "recharges himself" or "builds a building with very high floors." With this, we can see how powerful and enlightening it is to pray or speak in tongues. When you pray in tongues, you activate the power generator in you. Remember what Jesus said in Acts 1:8 NKJV, "But you shall receive power when the Holy Spirit has come upon you; and you shall be witnesses to Me in Jerusalem, and in all Judea and Samaria, and to the end of the earth." The word "virtue" used here comes from the Greek "*Dunamis*," which means "miraculous power, inherent power or dynamic ability, effective power." With this power, you can effect change as a believer in any area of your life. Dunamis is associated with Dynamo, which converts mechanical energy into electrical energy.

In areas or countries with electrical problems, many businesses and households use generators so that when there is a cut in the general electrical supply, the generator is started automatically and produces an electrical current. This way, homes remain lighted, and industries continue to operate thoroughly. Why? Because they have generators. Therefore, the generator serves as a backup or reserve of electrical production, so there are no electrical problems. Now, God knowing that we would need to shine as the light of the world and be effective as the salt of the earth, gave us the Holy Spirit, a reservoir of energy and power within the believer. This power is dynamic and miraculous. With it, the believer can effect any change he wants: job, business, ministry, health, or family. Furthermore, you can activate this power anytime and become recharged and full of energy whenever you speak in tongues.

When we speak in tongues, this power is activated, and the Holy Spirit gives revelations.

Therefore, if you want to have an active and productive spiritual life, you need to speak in tongues.

In the spirit, we can speak, sing or pray in tongues. For example, when we speak in tongues, many glorious things can happen:

1. Your spirit is recharged, strengthened, and filled with power.

With this power and spirit activated, whatever you say comes to pass. Your spirit gets in tune with the Holy Spirit, and you connect to the source of inexhaustible power.

Have you ever noticed that after the Holy Spirit descended on Jesus when He came out of the waters of the Jordan River, He never said a prayer asking God for more power or more anointing? Why? Because He already had the power generator within Him: the Holy Spirit. In every born-again believer, there is a reservoir of energy that can make him a spiritual giant. Now, whenever you pray in tongues, this power fills your spirit and your mind and permeates your flesh, removing all evil.

2. You are built up and strengthened like a strong city when you pray in tongues.

3. When you speak in tongues, instructions are given to the angels to act on your behalf because you are speaking in a spiritual language.

The Scripture says, "For he who speaks in a tongue does not speak to men but to God, for no one understands him; however, in the spirit he speaks mysteries" (1 Corinthians 14:2 NKJV). Did you notice that when you speak in a strange tongue, you speak mysteries, that is, secrecy? They are mysteries to men but not mysteries to God. God hears and knows what is being said, and events and situations are moved in the spirit world. Angels take a position and come down on earth to heal, protect, deliver and fight on behalf of God's people when we speak in tongues.

In prayer, we can use words from our intelligence and our minds. That is, we think about what we want to say, ask or speak to God. And by praying this way with faith, God hears, answers, and manifests His glory. However, you may feel that you have not said everything you wanted to say as you wanted to say it. In other words, we know how to pray but often don't know what to ask for as it is fitting. In Romans 8:26 NKJV, Paul says, "Likewise the Spirit also helps in our weaknesses. For we do not know what we should pray for as we ought, but the Spirit Himself makes intercession for us with groanings which cannot be uttered." Have you ever stopped to imagine that a great man of God of Paul's size who had gone to the third heaven said that we don't know what we shall ask for as we ought? It's possible because our minds limit our humanity. God said that what the eye has not seen, what the ear has not heard, and what has never ascended to the heart of man is what God has prepared for us (1 Corinthians 2:9). This reveals that there are particular unattained glories that our minds have not yet even imagined; things that have not even ascended to our hearts. It means that all that you have today and are today and where you are today is still very little compared to where God wants to take you.

We are often tempted to pray and ask for things that are not connected to God's purposes for us, and therefore we ask wrongly. However, when we pray in tongues, we ask for what we should ask for as it is fitting. This is why Paul said, "For if I pray in a tongue, my spirit prays, but my understanding is unfruitful" (1 Corinthians 14:14 NKJV). See what he says, "My spirit prays." So if you want to pray, pray in tongues. When we pray in tongues, our minds become unfruitful. However, don't be sad or worried if you don't understand what you are saying when you pray in tongues. What is important is what is happening in your spirit now; it's what happens in the spirit world when you pray in tongues that matters.

Furthermore, when you pray in tongues, you become more spiritually productive than when you pray in your intelligible language. Paul prayed a lot in tongues and saw countless benefits from this. That's why he said, "What is the conclusion then? I will pray with the spirit, and I will also pray with the understanding. I will sing with the spirit, and I will also sing with the understanding" (1 Corinthians 14:15 NKJV).

Paul concludes that between praying in tongues and praying with understanding, the priority is to pray in tongues which also means to pray with the spirit. So when you pray, you will use more of the spirit and less of the mind. Have you ever prayed in your tongue, and in the end, you thought there were things you should have asked for that you didn't, and it seemed like something was still missing? This happens because our mind can limit the spirit. After all, we can forget. But when we pray in tongues, we ask for everything we should ask for and how we should ask for it. So:

1. Praying in tongues helps you pray in conformity with God's will for your life;

2. Praying in tongues aligns man's spirit and his life with God's purposes;

3. Praying in tongues activates your prayer life.

For example, if you feel weak or don't know what to say in prayer, or even feel that you have lost that fire you had before when you prayed, pray in tongues. As you do so, you will notice in your spirit that the weak energy soon grows stronger; you will move from the low voltage to the high voltage of the spiritual electric current. Soon your will to pray is revived, and the Holy Spirit begins to give you words to speak in prayer. Suddenly it's customary to start receiving visions and words from God, and when you receive them from Him, prophesy them, declare them, and you will see victories.

4. Speaking in tongues is a way to praise and magnify God.

We read in the past texts that when the first disciples received the Holy Spirit, they spoke in tongues magnifying God. However, the words from our lips may not express everything our spirit wants to express to God. This is because we are men with unclean lips, and our human vocabulary wouldn't do justice to the greatness of God. This is why Isaiah said, "Woe is me, for I am undone! Because I am a man of unclean lips, and I dwell in the midst of a people of unclean lips; for my eyes have seen the King, the Lord of hosts" (Isaiah 6:5 NKJV). Can you imagine we praise God with our tongues, and when we are sad with someone, we speak words that we shouldn't speak? Therefore, praying in tongues helps to magnify God in a pure language, for it is the language of the spirit of the recreated man. The language of the new creation.

5. Praying in tongues builds up your spiritual life and strengthens your faith in God. So the apostle Jude, not Iscariot, exhorted: "But you, beloved, building yourselves up on your most holy faith, praying in the Holy Spirit, keep yourselves in the love of God, looking for the mercy of our Lord Jesus Christ unto eternal life" (Jude 20-21 NKJV).

The most holy faith is the leverage God gave you when you accepted Jesus as your Lord and Savior. This faith can grow as you study the word and spend time with God in prayer. Praying in the spirit helps build up your spiritual life and strengthen your fellowship with God. In this way, you grow as a building from glory to glory and faith to faith.

6. Praying in tongues prepares a man's spirit and recharges him for spiritual battles.

Spiritual tongues are also used in spiritual combat against the forces of evil. This is because of the armor of warfare in spiritual battles given to us in Ephesians 6:13-8. We find prayer in the spirit as part of it. Verse 18 says, "Praying always with all prayer and supplication in the Spirit, being watchful to this end with all perseverance and supplication for all the saints." When you pray in the spirit or in tongues, your spirit is activated and in a state of spiritual alertness. You start receiving notifications from the Holy Spirit to your spirit, telling you what you should do and how to do it. As a result, you escape the enemy's snares and cancel the evil one's plans in the heavenly regions. For example, if an accident or a witchcraft attack was planned against someone close to you, it's normal for the Holy Spirit to give you a sudden urge to pray. And if you don't know what to say at that moment, but your spirit tells you that something evil is being planned against you, start praying in tongues. Sometimes you may have inexpressible groaning, and the words may not come out of your mouth. Still, the Holy Spirit will be praying through you using your spirit at that moment.

"How can I pray in tongues?" - you may question. Well, if you have already received the Holy Spirit, one of the things you can do is to start singing some praises and or worship hymns. Then, focus your attention on God, meditating on him and his word and pushing away all negative thoughts that are not in line with his will and his word. By faith, open your mouth and start praying in tongues. Sometimes, the Holy Spirit may prompt you to pray in tongues, and suddenly you find yourself praying. In others, you will have to start the process when your spirit is already in tune with Him; as you open your mouth, words will be given to you, and then you will start using them in prayer. They may initially be few, but the more you pray and are persistent, He will give you more words, and your vocabulary will grow. As with a language you learn, you will only speak the words in your mind. In the spirit, you will only speak those already recorded in it. But you can have more and grow in it. Speak by faith. Scripture says, "And they were all filled with the Holy Spirit and began to speak with other tongues, as the Spirit gave them utterance" (Acts 2:4 NKJV). Who was speaking? The disciples. Therefore, it is you who must speak.

Many brethren have had difficulty speaking or praying in tongues because they expect the Holy Spirit to pray for them. But we see here that they were the ones who found themselves speaking by faith, moved by the fire they had received when those tongues of fire landed on each of their heads. They all began to speak in tongues as the Holy Spirit granted them. What did the Holy Spirit do? He gave them the ability to speak. He gave them the power to speak, and they spoke.

Understand this: speaking in tongues or praying in tongues is an act of faith. You believe and already see yourself praying in the spirit. It doesn't pass through your mind; it isn't something thought. Remember what Paul said, "For if I pray in a tongue, my spirit prays, but my understanding is unfruitful" (1 Corinthians 14:14 NKJV). The mind doesn't enter into this process. It's as if you decide to close and open your eyes. It is instantaneous because you are already connected to the Holy Spirit.

Believe and start talking. "But what if I don't understand what I'm saying?" Well, no problem because God understands. That's why it is said, "pray in the spirit, with the spirit, from your spirit." Your mind doesn't ruin it unless God decides to reveal to you the meaning of what you are saying. For example, many times when I pray in tongues, I receive interpretation in my spirit as to what I'm saying. If I want to speak in tongues at any time, I can start with the empowerment of the Holy Spirit, and I'm already speaking. Why? Because the spirit is ready, and I'm connected to the Holy Spirit. I don't dwell on the words I'm going to say; I start speaking by faith, and words are given to me at that moment.

Chapter VI
The Prayer of Consultation

Like other types of prayer previously studied, the prayer of consultation is one in which the petitioner wants to seek or know God's direction in which he will have to make a decision or choices. In this, we seek God's will and guidance on what direction to take so that we will be successful in what we want to undertake. But, on the other hand, this is the kind of prayer that the believer can make when facing situations in which the devil seems to have the legality of action against him, even after he has prayed, sowed, and done everything he should, the adverse situation prevails and seems to defy the prayer that was made. Or, better explained, this happens when you have a recurring situation that seems to abandon you stubbornly. To this end, you pray the prayer of consultation to see what you have done wrong or what doors have been opened to the devil to cause these evils even after Jesus defeated him on Calvary's Cross. Next, we will study these two foundations on which the prayer of consultation is based.

1. Consulting god's will to obtain victory.

The prayer of consultation is essential and powerful, for it can help the believer access God's wisdom and strategies to overcome barriers, circumvent obstacles, and solve problems that seemingly have no solution through God's wisdom. God's wisdom is essential for a life of glory and success. The Scripture says, "If any of you lacks wisdom, let him ask of God, who gives to all liberally and without reproach, and it will be given to him. But let him ask in faith, with no doubting, for he who doubts is like a wave of the sea driven and tossed by the wind. For let not that man suppose that he will receive anything from the Lord" (James 1:5-7 NKJV). This Scripture makes it very explicit that God wants to give wisdom to his children without distinction and that the requirement is to ask in faith, without doubting. So pray, believing that God hears and answers. This practical wisdom is necessary to solve problems and overcome everyday challenges. Knowing what to do in every situation is the most valuable virtue of a citizen of the kingdom of God, who seeks from the supernatural, divinely inspired strategies to solve a problem that has no solution in the material world or whose solution has not flashed in the minds of natural men.

Generally, people are panicked when facing battles in their marriage, business, jobs, or even health, and they don't know what to do. Not knowing what to do is in itself frustrating, and even more so, if you have to do something wrong, the frustration and remorse are greater. They can reach proportions that lead a man to commit suicide, lose his appetite for food, and consequently lose his health. Therefore, you must know what to do in each situation. The prayer of consultation serves precisely this purpose: to help you take possession of the inexhaustible wisdom of God, under whose direction you make your decisions. From now on, you will succeed in life by being in the right place, with the right people, and making the right choices and decisions. As a result, you will begin to tell more testimonies and avoid the damaging scars of life. What to do?

First: Surrender completely to god.

The text from Proverbs 3:5-6 NKJV says, " Trust in the Lord with all your heart, and lean not on your own understanding; In all your ways acknowledge Him, and He shall direct your paths."

You must surrender your life to the Lordship of Jesus, trust Him with all your heart and acknowledge Him in all your ways, projects, plans, and purposes. This is the first step in making the prayer of consultation. Recognize that He knows everything and knows the end from the beginning. This is why Peter said, "Therefore humble yourselves under the mighty hand of God, that He may exalt you in due time" (1 Peter 5:6 NKJV). One of the mistakes many believers make is ignoring the warnings that the Holy Spirit gives to our hearts when we stray from the ways prescribed in God's word. Jesus promised that He would go to the Father and ask to send us another comforter - the Holy Spirit, to stay with us forever. John records the Master's words, "If you love Me, keep My commandments. And I will pray the Father, and He will give you another Helper, that He may abide with you forever" (John 14:15-16 NKJV).

The word "Helper" employed in this context comes from the Greek "*Paraclete*" and means "Someone sent to accompany us." It's like a tour guide who knows the way ahead and is accredited to guide us through life in God's plans and purposes. Understand this: the Holy Spirit was sent by God to be a part of our daily lives. Unfortunately, many have limited Him only to church services when His ministry goes beyond that. As a result, many make wrong decisions and choices that they later regret because they haven't consulted their tour guide, their travel companion who knows the way out in every situation - the Holy Spirit. The Scripture says, "Blessed be the Lord, who daily loads us with benefits, the God of our salvation! Selah Our God is the God of salvation; and to God the Lord belong escapes from death" (Psalms 68:19-20 NKJV). This is the glorious life that God has prepared for his children. He can deliver you from any kind of crossroads or alley and bring you out of any labyrinth. However, you must first acknowledge Him, and you do that by surrendering to Him.

Surrendering means giving yourself entirely to Him as David said, "I was cast upon You from birth. from My mother's womb you have been My God" (Psalms 22:10 NKJV). Another part says, "For this is God, our God forever and ever; He will be our guide even to death" (Psalms 48:14 NKJV). No wonder David was a successful man, a champion. He recognized the ministry of the Holy Spirit in his life. So he prayed, "Do not cast me away from Your presence, and do not take Your Holy Spirit from me" (Psalms 51:11 NKJV).

Dear reader, surrender yourself completely to the Lord and trust in the guidance of the Holy Spirit. God, because He loves us, has already provided us with a guide and a counselor who knows all the ways to escape death and misery and live a life of glory, health, prosperity, and victory. In addition, some of the synonyms for the word "Helper" derived from "Paraclete" are counselor, helper, and advocate.

Second: Present your issue clearly, in prayer to the Lord.

Once you recognize him, it's time to trust him with your projects. The Scripture in Psalms 37:5 NKJV exhorts, "Commit your way to the Lord, trust also in Him, and He shall bring it to pass." Proverbs 16:3 NKJV says, "Commit your works to the Lord, and your thoughts will be established." With these Scriptures, it's remarkable how guaranteed success is when God is involved in every aspect of your life. For in Him, we live and walk and move. If you want to decide or choose a partner for your marriage, invest in some kind of business, choose an academic course or technical-vocational training, or even face the opportunities that open up along the way, consult the Holy Spirit. Talk to Him. Trust Him with your works and give glory to God for success. Don't get confused or frustrated; follow the voice of the Spirit of God speaking in your heart. The Scripture assures, "Your ears shall hear a word behind you, saying, 'This is the way, walk in it,' Whenever you turn to the right hand or whenever you turn to the left" (Isaiah 30:21 NKJV). What is that voice? It's the voice of the Holy Spirit. In other circumstances, He can speak through circumstances. So you must be sensitive to Him and pay attention to His hunches in your heart.

For example, a man comes along and says he wants to marry you, but you don't know if he is serious, or two come along at the same time saying the same thing. So what do you do? You pray, "Father, in the name of Jesus, show me which of these is the right person." If it's not the right person, chances are your eyes will be opened, and you will begin to see or discover things about him that he was hiding all this time. From there, you make your decision right before you become disappointed. The same may be true of a man concerning a woman. Generally, the Spirit will put peace in your heart when God's approval or response has been given to you. As the Scripture says, "And the peace of God, which surpasses all understanding, will guard your hearts and minds through Christ Jesus" (Philippians 4:7 NKJV).

One of the vivid examples of a man who consulted God and was successful was King David. We will look at two situations in which he consulted the Lord and received different answers and strategies for each moment and situation. For you to have the same results, you need to be an attentive and sensitive listener to the Holy Spirit

First: Green Light. God gives David the go-ahead to attack the Philistines.

When David was finally anointed king over all of Israel, the Philistines charged against him and came to attack him. They pursued David and spread out across the valley of Rephaim. But the Scripture says, "So David inquired of the Lord, saying, "Shall I go up against the Philistines? Will You deliver them into my hand?" And the Lord said to David, "Go up, for I will doubtless deliver the Philistines into your hand" (2 Samuel 5:19 NKJV). David and his men defeated the Philistines, who, leaving their idols behind, fled in a stampede.

In this situation, God's answer was that he could go on the offensive and succeed. And, so it happened.

Second: Red Light. God forbids David to use the same strategy as in the past.

The defeated Philistines went to regroup and some time later came back to attack Israel and David. However, there was something they had left behind, their idols. In other words, they were physically defeated. Still, they had left elements of spiritual connection with Israel, which attracted them to attack again, hoping to achieve victory this time. But our God is a Master-strategist. And for every situation, He gives us a direction, a solution, a way out. So there are always inspirations for success when you walk with God.

So the Scripture testifies: "The Philistines also went and deployed themselves in the Valley of Rephaim. So David inquired of the Lord, saying, "Shall I go up against the Philistines? Will You deliver them into my hand?" And the Lord said to David, "Go up, for I will doubtless deliver the Philistines into your hand."

What an ingenious strategy from God to David! Indeed, we serve an incomparable God whose strategies for solving any situation are never-ending. David wanted to use the strategy he had used before when he won the first time. But God had another way of granting him victory. He is a God who speaks and inspires. He delivers and protects. King David didn't want to make the mistake that Moses had made of continuing to use the rod to smite the rock and give the people water to drink when the instruction was to speak to the rock the second time. This simple disobedience to God's voice for today, and for now, cost him entry to the land of Canaan. This is why I said that you must always be listening for God's voice and direction. That is why you must be a man or woman of prayer - who has intimacy with God. Sometimes we get attached to the preceding word when God is giving us today the proceeding word. In Deuteronomy 8:3, Luke 4:4, and Matthew 4:4, we are taught that: "Man shall not live by bread alone, but by every word that proceeds from the mouth of God." Did you notice the use of the verb tense "proceeds"? This suggests that there are two kinds of God's word:

1. The Proceeding Word.

The one that God speaks or says now, in the now of every situation you find yourself in. This is called **Rhema** in Greek, and it's that inspired word for the moment. **Logos** is the written word, the one recorded in the Holy Scriptures. Still, when you meditate on **Logos,** you receive **Rhema,** and by acting on **Rhema,** the solution comes to a head, and light shines on your paths.

2. The Preceding Word.

The word spoken yesterday, or the instruction given yesterday, becomes the preceding word because it precedes the one God will speak today. Jesus said that you couldn't pour new wine into old wineskins; otherwise, it would ruin the wineskins. Therefore, the preceding word is a dormant potential. Nevertheless, it has power because when we meditate on it, it will produce the *rhema*. However, when the new strategy comes, that is, the proceeding word, we must act on it; otherwise, we risk becoming attached to the preceding word. It becomes a religion, a lifeless tradition. Thus, it becomes a ritual. Like someone who says: "I had always used the rod to open the red sea when I stretched out my hand over it, and to make the rock spring up water as I did the first time. I will always use the stick." Thus, the rod became more important than the word coming from God. Therefore, Moses lost the opportunity to glorify God before the people who unnerved him and consequently lost his passport to enter the promised land.

Back to David. He has most likely read about all these epics of Moses and learned a lesson. So he is now watching and consulting God again for this new battle.

One of the mistakes many Christians make is that when God gives them a victory strategy in a situation and they win, they forget the Lord and start using their mental logic and strategies of men. Consequently, they are defeated because they have forgotten the importance of consulting the Lord. This is why the Scripture we read exhorts us not to lean on our understanding. When they are already married, or their businesses prosper, some brethren no longer find it necessary to pray or consult. This is dangerous because our adversary, the devil, doesn't sleep. He is always scheming something against someone. Therefore, you must always be connected with God at all times.

Speaking of David, the Scripture says, "And David consulted the Lord." As a result, God gave him a different strategy to overcome the same kind of problem he had previously faced. Thus the Scripture attests, "And David did so, as the Lord commanded him; and he drove back the Philistines from Geba as far as **Gezer**" (2 Samuel 5:25 NKJV).

Dear reader, follow these principles, and you will always win. Consult God in prayer and follow the strategies and inspirations He gives you. He knows the way out of any situation.

In summary, the prayer of consultation is employed when we need God's direction to move forward with a plan of action or to get out of some situation.

The word consult, used in this context, comes from the Hebrew "Sa'al" and means to inquire or to ask for advice. It also means to get permission or to request. In this case, it's to God that we make the petition or consultation, not to urns, tombs, or a mystical wooden object. Then it forbids us to consult the dead. Some people often go to the graves in cemeteries to consult their ancestors about their life or to ask for luck in their sentimental, professional, or any area of their life. This is sinful and saddens God. You shouldn't go to consult the witches or orishas. Instead, consult God in prayer, and He will answer you. Cling to His word, which is our compass on this journey of life. Put God as your strategist, and you will never stumble in the face of life's obstacles.

2. Identifying the root of the problem and pulling it out by prayerful consultation.

The prayer of consultation can also be done to make an inquiry into the spirit, that is, a probing to see what doors have been opened that have given the devil the legality to continue to attack the person's life or afflict his family, even after Jesus has defeated him. The Scriptures are abundantly clear about Christ's victory over the devil and his principalities at Calvary's Cross. So attests the text in Colossians 2:15 NKJV "Having disarmed principalities and powers, He made a public spectacle of them, triumphing over them in it." This Scripture portrays Christ's triumphant victory over the kingdom of darkness. The expression Paul uses when he says he exposed them publicly is derived from the Greek *"Deigmatizo"* and means "to disgrace someone publicly" or "to make them ashamed." Paul is writing in a context historically dominated by the culture of the Roman empire. In their battles of conquest and annexation of new territories, the Romans had a habit of public exposure in the arena (large public stage) of the kingdoms or leaders of defeated territories. This served in part as proof that the victory was resounding and exposed the glory of Rome to the Romans watching in the great arenas. Therefore, Paul uses another term, "disarm," derived from the Greek *"Apekduomai,"* meaning to strip off.

In this context, it means to strip off clothes, armor, and authority. The use of these two expressions in the same sentence hints at what Jesus actually did when He died on the cross and rose from the dead - He routed the devil. Jesus disarmed the principalities and powers and stripped the devil of his authority over the believer. Satan had usurped authority over the earth from Adam when he sinned, disobeying God's word. So he became the prince of this world and the god of this age, ruling over the children of disobedience, blindfolded from seeing or accepting the Gospel of the glory of God in Christ Jesus.

Furthermore, after His resurrection from the dead, the Lord Jesus said, "And Jesus came and spoke to them, saying, "All authority has been given to Me in heaven and on earth. Go therefore and make disciples of all the nations, baptizing them in the name of the Father and of the Son and of the Holy Spirit" (Matthew 28:18-19 NKJV). Glory to God! Jesus has all authority, and the devil was left with zero authority. And, Jesus bestowed this authority under his faithful custodian: the Church. That is why He said: "...and on this rock I will build My church, and the gates of Hades shall not prevail against it " (Matthew 16:18b NKJV).

As a believer and a citizen of God's kingdom, you are seated with Christ in the place of authority, reigning with Him. By faith, you can use the name of Jesus to cast out demons and destroy the devil's works. Victorious and glorious life has been given to you in Christ. You must set your heart on this victory, for the Scripture says, "For whatever is born of God overcomes the world. And this is the victory that has overcome the world—our faith" (1 John 5:4 NKJV). Faith is the response of man's heart to God's word. It's the assurance of things hoped for and the evidence of things not seen. Through it, you can attain God's approval and walk in victory. However, faith is directly proportional to your knowledge of God's Word because this is its basis.

Many believers haven't experienced the glories and victories God's Word speaks of. And others, even though they have been born again, continue to suffer oppression from the kingdom of darkness and don't know the root of this suffering. They quote the Scriptures, fast, and give their offerings, but the old problem persists. That covenant of the devil in the family destroying homes and marriages, jobs and businesses, those supposed curses and the carelessness of the tongue, seem to continue to exercise dominion over this brother or sister. They may even think that the devil is more powerful than God and wonder, "Why don't these sorcerers and witches die instead of continuing to kill innocent people in the family?" Perhaps you have experienced the same situation and wanted a permanent solution to the problem. Well, you need to distinguish between the problem and the root of the problem.

The problem is like a branch of a tree that produces sour fruit, and the root is the support of the trunk from which the branches sprout. What many people do is graft a different branch onto the same trunk of the tree—for example, grafting an orange tree branch onto a lemon tree trunk. This works, naturally. However, in the spiritual arena, you must pull out the root of the problem. The root is fundamental. For example, to save humanity, God planted the Jewish nation - the people of Israel - by calling Abraham, Isaac, and Israel (Jacob). Through them, he brought us Jesus, who became the salvation for all humanity. This is why Jesus said to the Samaritan woman, "You worship what you do not know; we know what we worship, for salvation is of the Jews" (John 4:22 NKJV). Because salvation comes from the Jews, and Jesus was a Jew, when they rejected him, God grafted us onto them, like olive trees (Romans 11:24).

In an ongoing, stubborn problem that, even after you have prayed and fasted, doesn't seem to want to let go of your life, you can turn to consultation prayer. Especially if you are facing an ongoing problem or a persistent attack from the devil in which you always seem to be a victim. It could be the case that whenever you are about to get married officially, sign a big job or business contract, or even take exams to pass a class or subject in college, that persistent dream appears, or the same problem happens. Things get messed up, and everything goes wrong. Or whenever she gets pregnant, she loses the fetus almost in the same months as the gestation phase. In other words, when a problem is so recurrent that even when you pray and go to deliverance, it doesn't seem to want to leave you, you need to seek the root of that problem. This is done with the prayer of consultation.

Some merchants were on a business trip, carrying their merchandise, as they probably always did. However, this time, a man named Jonah is on the ship, running away from God's command to go to Nineveh to warn those people about their sins and proclaim God's judgment.

Instead, he took the ship that was going to Tarshish. Suddenly there was a terrific gale, and the sailors and merchants had to throw their merchandise into the waters to appease the sea's fury. They thought that some water god was furious with them and that perhaps he would be calmed by the gifts from the merchandise on the ship. Even with this, there was no tranquility. As an alternative, they each began to pray and invoke their god, who obviously couldn't answer. For a moment, they lost all their merchandise, their business went bankrupt, and their time, money, and merchandise investments evaporated in the blink of an eye. They are left loaded with goods and merchandise, and now, they are trying to save their lives, for the ship is sinking. What is the problem? The fury of the wind and the sea hurled itself against the ship while the sea swallowed the merchants' business products. Every attempt they make as a way to solve the problem seems to be unsuccessful. Why? Because they have not yet located the root of the problem. Who was the root of the problem? An unknown passenger - Jonah. Notice that according to the Scripture, all the passengers and merchants on the ship were worried, each praying to their god and throwing their goods overboard to see if they would relieve the fury of the raging waves. Jonah, however, was sleeping, not praying, and not speaking. All this punishment is coming to innocent men because of him. That's when they approach him and ask him questions: "Please tell us! For whose cause is this trouble upon us? What is your occupation? And where do you come from? What is your country? And of what people are you?" (Jonah 1:8 NKJV).

Many marry without identifying the family background of the person they are marrying. Others invest in businesses without investigating the type of partners and the origin of the funds involved, whether it's blood money or covenant money. Many people seem blind and inattentive and only wake up when a hurricane rolls over them. Jonah answers, "I am a Hebrew; and I fear the Lord, the God of heaven, who made the sea and the dry land" (verse 9). The following verses narrate: "Then the men were exceedingly afraid, and said to him, "Why have you done this?" For the men knew that he fled from the presence of the Lord, because he had told them. Then they said to him, "What shall we do to you that the sea may be calm for us?"—for the sea was growing more tempestuous. And he said to them, "Pick me up and throw me into the sea; then the sea will become calm for you. For I know that this great tempest is because of me." For a moment, they hesitated to do with Jonah what he had told them because they felt so sorry for him. So they tried to use their strength, experience, and intellect to solve a problem with spiritual connections.

The Scripture says: "Nevertheless the men rowed hard to return to land, but they could not, for the sea continued to grow more tempestuous against them" (Verse 13). Did you notice that they wanted to ignore the root of the problem to accommodate their feelings? They saw the goal they wanted to achieve. They had clear, objective goals and knew where to go, but their efforts were not resulting in anything positive. Victory and prosperity were before them, but they couldn't achieve them. They knew they had the potential to be something. Still, they were neutralized by problems beyond their capacity whenever they tried. How many people today find themselves in this kind of situation? Probably many. Unfortunately, they have been formatted not to see. The Spirit of God has inspired me to add this particular type of prayer to help you come out of the pit unscathed and to program you for a successful life so that you make your journey here on earth gloriously and say like Paul: "I have fought the good fight, I have finished the race, I have kept the faith" (2 Timothy 4:7 NKJV).

Dear reader, be serious about your life and always take God seriously. Don't waste your time counting the years, but make the years count by God's grace. Receive the grace and courage to face any challenge and defeat it. To do so, you need to pray, identify the root of the problem, face it, and pluck it out in the name of Jesus.

That's what the men on the ship finally did. The Scripture says, "Therefore they cried out to the Lord and said, "We pray, O Lord, please do not let us perish for this man's life, and do not charge us with innocent blood; for You, O Lord, have done as it pleased You." (Verse 14). Notice that this time, they stop invoking their various gods and idols and start invoking the LORD JEHOVAH, the Creator of heaven and earth.

Dear reader, stop running away from God or ignoring Him. The final and permanent solution to your problems, and the ultimate removal of the root of any problem, affliction, or stagnation, will involve you seeking God, the Father of our Lord and Savior, Jesus Christ. He is the eternal Rock. So stop going to straws or consulting mediums, witches, or the dead. Instead, turn to God with all your heart, trusting and standing firm in Him. Furthermore, ask for enough courage to cut off harmful habits and friendships, for: "Evil company corrupts good habits" (1 Corinthians 15:33 NKJV).

Those seemed to be good-hearted men who were suffering and on the verge of misery and death. After all the saga, the men finally "picked up Jonah and threw him into the sea, and the sea ceased from its raging. Then the men feared the Lord exceedingly, and offered a sacrifice to the Lord and took vows" (Jonah 1:15-16 NKJV). We note here two more equally important types of attitude: they picked Jonah up and, in fear of the Lord, offered sacrifices to him and made vows. First, they offered something to the Lord (a seed); that is, they removed the root from their midst and threw it into the sea, and then, they decided that from that day on, they would worship only the Lord. That is why they made vows. You must have a seed. Don't take this lightly because those who have made pacts in the family or at work to harm you will not hesitate to offer as many heads of cattle as it takes on the haystacks and altars of the devil just to see you overthrown and ruined. Them living at the expense of your blood and suffering. Be a vowing man or woman for God. Be a sower. It's funny that the devil's children when making pacts with him through witches, can offer even the hardest sacrifice, while the children of light don't even give offerings or tithes in church.

This shows which group takes spiritual matters more seriously than the other. This is why many believers continuously suffer attacks from covenants and dark spirits because their going to church seems like a joke. How is a covenant made by sacrificing two oxen going to cause the believer only to sleep and wish things well without doing anything for the Lord or reacting to God's love? Scripture says, "And they overcame him by the blood of the Lamb and by the word of their testimony, and they did not love their lives to the death" (Revelation 12:11 NKJV). Even the Archangel Michael and his angels needed the blood of the lamb, that is, of Christ, to overcome and precipitate the devil and his angels (agents of darkness) from heaven to earth. The words of their testimony were accompanied, or rather, based on the blood of Jesus, for there is power in it. Power is enough to destroy all evil.

How to do the prayer of consultation to identify the root of the problem

In Jonah's case, God sent a big fish that swallowed him and carried him to Nineveh for three days to fulfill his ministry.

With the example of Jonah, I don't mean that you should hate certain people. You shouldn't because the Holy Bible encourages us to love our enemies. However, you must distinguish between the enemy and the friend. The Scripture says: "For we do not wrestle against flesh and blood, but against principalities, against powers, against the rulers of the darkness of this age, against spiritual hosts of wickedness in the heavenly places. Therefore take up the whole armor of God, that you may be able to withstand in the evil day, and having done all, to stand" (Ephesians 6:12-13 NKJV). Did you notice the part where it says, "Having done all?" Well, this implies that for victory over the forces of evil to be obtained, you must do something. It's part of what you are learning in this book about prayer. For beyond all the armor that Paul presents to us (Gird your loins with the truth, breastplate of righteousness, shod your feet with the preparation of the gospel of peace, the shield of faith, helmet of salvation, and the sword of the Spirit which is the word of God), he also adds the expression, "Praying with all prayer..." So you are learning about a type of prayer that will help you identify the root of evil in your life: the prayer of consultation.

Perhaps you have done other types of prayer and have not seen results. The issue is not that the prayer doesn't work, but rather, the type of prayer you have done. You must match the type of prayer to the issue to be dealt with or resolved. For example, the doctor isn't going to recommend medicine for a stomach ache, and you go and take medicine for a headache. Notice that both are medicines, but for different pathologies, with different reactions, and each with its dosage. If it doesn't work, review the recommended dosage. Some prayers require their own dosage.

In some cases, you can simply pray, and it will pass. In others, you may have to fast. In the text from Matthew 10, Jesus gave his disciples power and authority to cast out demons and heal the sick, which they successfully did and returned with satisfactory reports. The problem, however, is that they relied on that anointing alone, ignoring the principle of prayer and fasting. Even though Jesus was the Son of God, he fasted and prayed. He would wake up early in the morning, go to a deserted place, and pray there. At night He did the same exercise in the mountains - that is, in quiet and peaceful places, where He spent time with God in prayer. Some brothers think that just by confessing victory, things will work out, but this is not always the case. For example, Elijah is described as the one who declared that for three and a half years, there would be no rain or dew in Israel, which happened. But this view of the one who just spoke/decreed and then left is a simplistic view given in 1 Kings 17.

You could try to do the same thing, and your words wouldn't match. Why? Because you haven't read the whole context of Scripture. You just read 1 Kings 17 and might say, "I decreed, I confessed, I spoke, but nothing happened. This doesn't work." The problem is that you are missing part B of this context - the lack of knowledge. So James adds more light when he tells us that Elijah was a man subject to the same passions as we are, that is, a human being like you and me. However, he prayed, and there was no rain for three and a half years, and he prayed again, and the sky gave rain, and the earth produced. Note that we can identify two verbs used in the same context from the narrator's perspective: "Say" and "Pray." Thus I quote the expressions:

A) 1 Kings 17:1, "And Elijah the Tishbite, of the inhabitants of Gilead, said to Ahab..."

B) James 5:17 "Elijah was a man with a nature like ours, and he **prayed** earnestly..." we then read in verse 18, "And he **prayed** again...."

When you spend time with God in prayer, your spirit is recharged so that your words carry power. Thus, whatever you say will come to pass without fail.

Jesus' disciples were now given power in Matthew 10, which worked until Matthew 16 because, in chapter 17, nine of his disciples had trouble casting out a demon of deafness and dumbness in a young lunatic. At that time, Jesus was on the mountain in prayer with three of his disciples - Peter, James, and John - until he was transfigured in glowing, white glory. Then, when he came down, he cast out the demon with a simple, calmly spoken command: "Deaf and dumb spirit, I command you, come out of him and enter him no more" (Mark 9:25 NKJV).

Matthew narrates, "And Jesus rebuked the demon, and it came out of him (the boy); and the child was cured from that very hour" (Matthew 17:18 NKJV).

The nine disciples asked him apart why they had not been able to cast him out. In their view, they had done everything He had taught them, and they had seen Him do everything, but there was no result. The Master's answer was simple: "However, this kind does not go out except by prayer and fasting" (Verse 21). But, unfortunately, and to their amazement, they didn't fast or pray until then.

I am explaining to you that there are spiritual principles, and you must apply them to see results because they don't fail.

Legality given to the devil to afflict man: how to break it?

We studied in the introduction to this part that Christ defeated the devil on the cross at Calvary; that is a fact. However, he continues to destroy lives, families, and nations, which is also a fact. The question is: where did this power or authority come from, and where did he acquire this destruction weaponry if we read that he was disarmed and Christ triumphed over him on the cross? Well, one must realize that God, while being merciful, is also the righteous God. Have you ever heard the expression "Jehovah Tsidkenu?" This is one of God's attributes and means "the LORD our RIGHTEOUSNESS." He is upright in His ways and judgments. Because of His love, He sent Jesus to die in the sinner's place. Still, if the sinner rejects His love and mercy, he will be judged and thrown into the lake of fire with the devil and his agents of darkness. The devil understands this aspect of God's justice very well and knows how to exploit it well. That's why he could go to God in the Old Testament to accuse human beings of their wrongdoings and demand that they be punished. And God allowed him to do so because of his justice. His justice is the principle of the subsistence of God's throne and God's kingdom. If He were to lose this quality or attribute, He would be unreliable.

Glory that the LORD is trustworthy! Abraham, who was held as God's friend, had the revelation of God's righteousness. Notice his words when he interceded for men "...shall not the Judge of all the earth do right?" (Genesis 18:25b NKJV). It is from this aspect of his justice that he issues righteous judgments. Did you know that on earth, there is no righteous justice? Only God has righteous justice. That is why Paul also testified, "To demonstrate at the present time His righteousness, that He might be just and the justifier of the one who has faith in Jesus" (Romans 3:26 NKJV). This is why the angels in heaven called the devil the accuser of the brethren. Notice this verse: "Then I heard a loud voice saying in heaven, "Now salvation, and strength, and the kingdom of our God, and the power of His Christ have come, for the accuser of our brethren, who accused them before our God day and night, has been cast down" (Revelation 12:10 NKJV).

Note this: although the devil has been defeated, there are things he can still use as a pretext to return recurrently to attack the believer without pity or mercy. However, all this legality of the devil is given to him by man. Since God has given the earth to man, the devil will come in and bite if a man opens the door. This is why Paul sounds the alarm, "Neither give place to the devil" (Ephesians 4:27 KJV). This verse makes it clear that even the believer, born again and filled with the Holy Spirit, can give place to the devil if he is not careful. And when the devil takes over, he will use every opportunity to set up his kingdom, steal, kill, and destroy his family. He may be cast out only after he has done much damage and harm. You must not give him this opportunity to create roots of generational curses in the family.

1. Family covenants based on blood.

If any ancestor in a family made a blood covenant with the devil to get rich, have power, or for any other reason, he literally sold his family to Satan. Covenants don't die, although the people who make them die. Therefore, generations and generations can be born, grow up and live in suffering because of this covenant. This is because every covenant or pact is commenced by blood. That blood makes the devil legal in this family.

Consequently, people face embargoes in their sentimental, professional, financial, and even academic life. In other words, finding oneself with no stable relationships, happy and lasting marriages, job problems, and mental and financial blockages is possible. What is happening? Dark spirits are employed and allocated to this family to monitor them, afflict them, and block their progress. If someone is not saved, they may turn from one witch doctor to the next, looking for a solution to no avail. Even if they are ignorant that this exists, they may try to scientifically identify and solve the root of the problem without success.

When you are born again through faith in Jesus, you are freed from curses and covenants by the blood of Jesus. But you need to proclaim the victory of Jesus' blood over your life so that these things don't bother you. This is because spirits don't die or disappear as they do in the material world. Instead, they stay around, looking for an opportunity to attack.

Solution: Spend time with God in prayer, have a healthy intimacy with the Holy Spirit and live by God's word. Say: "In the holy name of the Lord Jesus Christ, I annul all covenants, reverse all curses in my life and family, and declare that we are free from all interference from these spirits and their spiritual satellite. Starting today, I go off their radar. I will never be traceable, for I dwell in the highest hiding place and the shadow of the almighty restfulness. No plague shall come upon my house. I am seated with Christ in the heavenly places above all principalities and powers and over every force of evil. I am free, I and my house. I lift all generational covenants and curses from my paternal and maternal family in the name of Jesus Christ."

2. Blood covenants that you have made yourself.

If you have ever in your life been led into a hut, or you yourself went to make a pact to protect yourself, get rich or have power, you have opened doors to the devil in your life. What to do? You must:

A. Repent before God, recognize that you have erred, that you have sinned;

B. Confess this sin of spiritual involvement with the kingdom of darkness;

C. Renounce these covenants. Give up all the utensils and elements of darkness that were offered (pots, clothes, oils, statues, idols, rings, canes, etc.) to be burned.

Thus the Scripture testifies: "And many that believed came, and confessed, and shewed their deeds. Many of them also which used curious arts brought their books together, and burned them before all men: and they counted the price of them, and found it fifty thousand pieces of silver" (Acts 19:18-19 NKJV). You can take these things to the church to be burned and be set free.

D. Turn your back on this covenant life and turn entirely to God.

Ask for the blood of Christ to cleanse you from all evil. Then, say this prayer: "Lord God, I have sinned against you, involving myself in covenants with the kingdom of darkness. But now, I repent and return to you. Now, I renounce all works of witchcraft, all involvement and handling of diabolical instruments, and all my connection with the kingdom of darkness. And I accept Jesus Christ as my personal Lord and Savior. May the blood of Christ purify my spirit, conscience, and my body. I declare that I am saved and free in the name of Jesus."

E. From now on, be a person of prayer and live by faith in God's word.

3. Negative words that you have spoken consciously or unconsciously.

Words are spirits, and they don't die. They hang around in the spirit world looking for incubation for their materialization, whether they are good or bad, for good or evil. The only way to undo negative words you have spoken or someone has spoken against you is to speak other words instead of the first ones. Dear reader, did you know where you are today, what you are, and what you have are the fruits of words that haunt you in the spirit world? Starting today, take words seriously. In the spiritual arena, words are objects. Jesus said, "For by your words you will be justified, and by your words you will be condemned" (Matthew 12:37 NKJV). Whatever good you want to see in your life, proclaim and prophesy it over yourself. This is why we are encouraged to study and meditate on God's word (Psalms 1:1-3; Joshua 1:8).

I remember a sister for whom I had prayed years ago. When she was still a little girl, an elderly man passed by her parent's house, who lived in the same area, and would always tell her: "You are my wife," in a joking tone. Years later, he died, and a demon in the form of a husband of the night entered her and possessed her. She was never happy sentimentally. Now she was an adult living at home in a common-law marriage; she was still unhappy. I was evangelizing from house to house at the time and stopped by their house. She still remembered everything she had heard from the older man. Still, she wasn't concerned about it because there were no connecting elements between what the older man said and what she had come to live with since she didn't know spiritual things.

The demon manifested when I prayed for her, saying he was her husband and that she couldn't be happy. I cast him out, and she was set free. She accepted Jesus as Lord and Savior, and her life and her husband's life changed completely. Her husband, who couldn't get a job because of this spirit, got a job and began to prosper. What happened? Was it the older man's spirit that entered her and possessed her? No. But the devil used the words of that older man and the connection he had with the family to introduce a demon into her life legally. Had her mother been saved and mature in spiritual things and the knowledge of God's word, she would have nullified those words and saved the girl. Glory that it was time to pray for her.

Blessed reader, be careful with your words. Paul said, "Let the word of Christ dwell in you richly in all wisdom, teaching and admonishing one another in psalms and hymns and spiritual songs, singing with grace in your hearts to the Lord. And whatever you do in word or deed, do all in the name of the Lord Jesus, giving thanks to God the Father through Him" (Colossians 3:16-17 NKJV). Protect your life and your destiny through words. The text in James 3:5 NKJV says, "Even so the tongue is a little member and boasts great things. See how great a forest a little fire kindles." The health of your life depends on the health of your heart and tongue.

4. Constant fear and/or worry.

"For the thing I greatly feared has come upon me, and what I dreaded has happened to me. I am not at ease, nor am I quiet; I have no rest, for trouble comes" (Job 3:25-26 NKJV).

Such was the mentality and heart of the most highly protected, blessed, prosperous man. God had put such a fence around him and his family that, for ages, the devil had been trying to destroy him in every possible way, but without success. Job, his family, and his farm enjoyed prosperity, health, and happiness. However, Job made a grave mistake: he was always worried and afraid. By living in that state, he broke a spiritual principle according to which: "He who digs a pit will fall into it, and whoever breaks through a wall will be bitten by a serpent" (Ecclesiastes 10:8 NKJV). Satan is regarded as the dragon or the ancient serpent (Revelation 12:9). The serpent has always been there, looking for an occasion to accuse Job before God and to attack him. It wasn't God who tempted Job. It was he himself who, because of constant worry and fear, broke through the wall of protection that God had put up for him. This caused the devil to go to God in heaven to accuse Job and ask for access to him. For this and other reasons, the Bible urges us not to be afraid and not to worry or fret about anything.

Dear reader, trust in God, spend time in praise and worship, and avoid letting worry and fear invade your heart.

5. Behavioral misconduct and disobedience to God's instructions.

This can also be one of the roots that allow the devil to launch attacks against your life legally, even when you are in Christ. Hymenaeus and Alexander were delivered to Satan by Paul because they were blaspheming against God's way. A man or woman who starts his or her ministry well but strays from God's way because of glory, fame, and ambition can open doors for the devil to attack you legally. For example, suppose he lives in sexual immorality, leaving his wife or husband, and gets involved with people outside his home or marriage. In that case, he can open doors of dangerous attacks on his life, ministry, and family. David had the same problem when he became involved with Bathsheba and, for a moment, lost the kingdom. His son Absalom usurped the throne and made his wives and concubines, bringing shame and vexation to Israel and the house of David.

Solution: genuine repentance and pleading the mercies of God. In Psalms 51, we read, "Have mercy upon me, O God, according to Your lovingkindness; according to the multitude of Your tender mercies, blot out my transgressions. Wash me thoroughly from my iniquity, and cleanse me from my sin. For I acknowledge my transgressions, and my sin is always before me. Against You, You only, have I sinned, and done this evil in Your sight—that You may be found just when You speak, and blameless when You judge[...] make me to hear joy and gladness, that the bones You have broken may rejoice." (Psalms 51:1-4, 8 NKJV).

How to proceed with a repentance that brings restoration:

A. Be genuine. Coming out deeply from your broken heart;

B. Objectively confess your sin. Telling God the mistake you made with your own mouth,

C. Decide to turn your back on this sin and the habits that accompany it.

If your repentance follows this pattern, you will be forgiven, washed, and cleansed. And God will give you the joy of salvation again (1 John 1:9). Moreover, the Scripture says, " In mercy and truth atonement is provided for iniquity; and by the fear of the Lord one departs from evil" (Proverbs 16:6 NKJV).

6. Exacerbated love of money.

Money is essential for God's work and bringing sustenance to our families. However, it shouldn't be the reason we do what we do. You shouldn't love money more than God and people. Don't let the love of money lead you astray from God's way. Many make covenants because of the pursuit of fame, power, and money. They love the pleasures of this world rather than their own souls. Therefore, they sell their souls for eternity in the lake of fire for the sake of temporary pleasures. The love of money, pride, and sexual immorality can open doors for the devil to bring destruction.

7. Pride/Sovereignty.

On one of the occasions when David was already known as a champion, was king of all Israel, and had everything from gold, silver, and thundering victories that the Lord had given him, pride entered his heart. So the Scripture says, "Now Satan stood up against Israel, and moved David to number Israel" (1 Chronicles 21:1 NKJV). Did you notice the expression "moved?" Well, this is one of the devil's tricks. He seeks the weakness of man, of the believer, and exploits it very well. He moved David to number the people as a sign of pride as if he owned them all. The Scripture says, "And God was displeased with this thing; therefore He struck Israel" (Verse 7). In one day, seventy thousand men died in Israel because of a plague, a disease. The covering they had was taken away.

Despite all this, David repented of this evil and offered peaceful sacrifices to the Lord. In this situation, you must ask God for forgiveness, but at the same time, come up with an offering that costs you something and offer it to the altar of the Lord in the Church. A man named Ornan decided to give David the field where he was to make the sacrifice to the Lord. But David said, "No, but I will buy it for its price; for I will not take that which is yours to offer to the Lord, lest I offer a burnt offering without cost" (Verse 24). He did so, and the plague stopped.

The basis for consultation prayer in the identification of the root of evil

Understand this: the devil is and will always be the root cause of man's suffering. Or better put, he will be the enforcer of oppression and evil upon man. So what we want here is to identify the door through which he has entered so that he is cast out. The door closed, so we no longer have this legally recurring presence and attacks. Satan has been defeated and no longer has any legality over the believer. First, however, we want to identify what made it legal for him to enter: how did he enter, from where, and who opened the door for him in the family?

There are two foundations:

1. The one that you yourself open the doors to.

This one usually concerns something the believer must have done that gave way to the devil. Identify it, deal with it, and the problem is solved.

Now, from David, we learn a model of how to pray the prayer of consultation. First, observe David's words: "Search me, O God, and know my heart; try me, and know my anxieties; and see if there is any wicked way in me, and lead me in the way everlasting" (Psalms 139:23-24 NKJV).

This is the basis for making the prayer of consultation in identifying the root of a recurring problem if you feel that you must have done something that opened doors to the devil. Ask God to probe your heart. If there is any unconfessed sin, quickly confess it before God, who is just and faithful to forgive you and cleanse you from all iniquity. Yes, He can cleanse you. The key is genuine repentance.

Declare these words: "All the idle and negative words fighting against my glorious destiny that I have uttered with my mouth be done away with now. In their place, I declare I am prosperous and free, in the name of Jesus."

2. The door that others have opened, through which the devil has gained access to you.

This, for instance, can be the fruit of friendship associations, blood ties, or affinity ties that have opened doors to the devil. Suppose you were born into a family with covenants; you didn't make them. Still, having been born into that family, you may suffer their influence if you don't identify and revoke them. Don't forget that the devil comes because someone legally invited him through sacrileges and/or covenants. Or even because unconsciously, when still a baby, you were dedicated to demons without knowing it, or you were given things consecrated to demons that you didn't know about but which from then until now have caused you some embarrassment and imbroglio.

As a born-again, Spirit-filled believer, you are responsible for doing something. That is why the Scripture says, "Therefore submit to God. Resist the devil and he will flee from you" (James 4:7 NKJV). It is you who must resist the devil, and you have no other alternative unless you flee. The Scripture doesn't say, "Cry, wail, or scream, and the devil will flee from you," but it says, "Resist." How to resist?

Looking at Jesus' temptation in the wilderness, we see Him using the expressions "It is written" and "It is said." Therefore, you must do the following:

1. Identify the root cause of the problem.

Notice this Scripture: "Now there was a famine in the days of David for three years, year after year; and David inquired of the Lord. And the Lord answered, "It is because of Saul and his bloodthirsty house, because he killed the Gibeonites" (2 Samuel 21:1 NKJV).

At this point, there was a famine in Israel, and David, analyzing his conduct and words, knew that he hadn't done anything contrary to the Word of the Lord. He praised, worshipped, and prayed but still, the problem persisted. So he decided to make a prayer of inquiry or consultation. He inquired of the Lord, went to God, the source of all things, and consulted just as a patient goes to the doctor to find out what ails him. The doctor has the appropriate tools to make a diagnosis or examination. Note that the examination or diagnosis is preliminary before the doctor prescribes medication. David knew that God was his physician and the physician of the nation of Israel. Therefore, he didn't consult God but the Lord. In response, God told him the root of the problem; behold, David was not the cause. It was his predecessor because he shed innocent blood and broke his covenant with the Gibeonites. When Joshua was fighting against the Philistines in defense of the Gibeonites, God had stopped the sun and the moon to give victory to Israel (Joshua 10:6-17). David asked the Gibeonites what they wanted to be done, and they asked for the heads of Saul's sons.

When David solved this root, the problem ended, and there was abundant food in Israel.

To identify the root, you should pray, "Father, in the name of Jesus, I surrender to you today. I present this situation to you (mention it); reveal to me what is behind it." You can do this in fasting prayer, and God will answer. It may be through a dream, a word, a voice in your heart, or circumstances. Be attentive to God's answer.

2. Apply the blood of Jesus on it.

Once the root of the problem has been identified, apply the blood of Jesus to it. The Holy Bible says that the blood of Jesus speaks better things than the blood of Abel. So attests the text in Hebrews 12:24 NKJV: "to Jesus the Mediator of the new covenant, and to the blood of sprinkling that speaks better things than that of Abel."

Notice that the blood of Jesus speaks. If it speaks, it means it has a voice. Spiritually, you are covered by the blood of Christ. The Spirit of Jesus' blood covers and protects you. Through this blood, the price was fully paid for you and me to be definitively free from sin and the devil's influence. In fact, the blood of Christ was the very last to be shed on the strongholds of hell, and we are members of the body of Christ, his church. We have been given authority so that the gates of hell will not prevail against us. However, you want those spirits and their problems to disappear for good forever.

You are in the red sea, the place of baptism and separation between the oppressor and the oppressed, between Pharaoh and the Hebrews, between the devil and you and your family. As I write these lines, I feel the anointing of God descending on you, dear reader, breaking every covenant and removing all evil from your life. From today on, your life will never be the same. Receive light and grace and victory now.

Before the Red Sea, Moses said to the children of Israel, "Do not be afraid. Stand still, and see the salvation of the Lord, which He will accomplish for you today. For the Egyptians whom you see today, you shall see again no more forever. The Lord will fight for you, and you shall hold your peace" (Exodus 14:13-14 NKJV).

As a servant of God, I declare the same thing about your life: "The oppression and problems you had been suffering all your life;

those sentimental, professional, financial, and academic embargoes you will no longer have and will never see again forever." Receive your deliverance now.

The red sea symbolically represents the blood of Jesus, it starts the deliverance process and separates the believer from the world and the devil and sin to start living by the word and dependent on the Spirit of God and His provision.

Apply the blood of Christ now; say, "Blood of Jesus, by the Eternal Spirit, speak over my life and family from this day forward. By the blood of Christ, I completely reverse all covenants made and curses spoken against my family and me. Therefore, let all voices contrary to my progress, stability, health, and prosperity be silenced in the name of Jesus. And I declare that I am victorious and off their radar from this day forward."

3. Be formed in the word of God and confess it continually.

The Scripture says, "Stand fast therefore in the liberty by which Christ has made us free, and do not be entangled again with a yoke of bondage" (Galatians 5:1 NKJV). Covenants and curses work like a yoke; they keep people's lives tied up. You are free from the yoke of bondage now. Free as a bird that was in a cage, and from today on, you will fly as an eagle. I declare that everything about you begins to blossom.

Restoration and restitution. Confess with your mouth: "In the name of Jesus, I have conquered, I am free, I am prosperous. There is progress in my life and life and health in my house." Steady your heart in God's Word and fight your good fight of faith; make progress through God's Word, and confess it. Seek God's promises and declare them over your life and family. Cling only to the Word of God.

4. Claim restitution.

5. **Say this with me:** "Everything that had been stolen from me, all the glories, I get them back now, in the name of Jesus. I receive the opportunities to prosper in the name of Jesus. I have restored joy and

peace today, and my potential is activated. From this day forward, I will live in the best of grace, in fertile land, and to the fullest of my potential. I am free in my spirit, mind, and body from all interference of the evil one, in the name of Jesus." I declare everything you want to happen in your life.

Exercise

1. Summarize in three lines what you have learned in this chapter;

2. Identify the root of any problem in your life;

3. Identify the root of any problem in your life.

Chapter VII
The Prayer of Intercession

"So I sought for a man among them who would make a wall, and stand in the gap before Me on behalf of the land, that I should not destroy it; but I found no one" (Ezekiel 22:30 NKJV).

The scripture mentioned above faithfully summarizes an intercessor's need and role. Note the words "make a wall," "stand in the gap," and "before me." An intercessor is someone who stands in the gap on behalf of someone and serves as a wall of protection before an authority to plead on his behalf; or before an enemy to protect against him. In both cases, the intercessor puts himself in the middle as a wall of protection or as a kind of lawyer practicing advocacy on behalf of others. Therefore, the intercessor establishes a connection between the two parties, God and men, but on behalf of God. It's interesting to note that the figure of the intercessor is recommended and sought after by God Himself to stand before Him in prayer on behalf of others. God endows the intercessor with qualities that make him inclined to be interested in the good of others and not just in his own things or interests. The intercessor uses prayer as a tool in the battle against evil, injustice, and diabolical oppression of people and, together with God, reinforces that God's will be done on earth as it is in heaven. Moreover, even when the people stray from the ways of the Lord, he intercedes for them, crying out for mercy so that God's wrath will abate and he will not let the scourge fall on his people.

The fact that God Himself profiles intercessors and looks for them shows how much He loves humanity and doesn't want anyone to be lost but for all to come to the path of salvation.

Intercession extends God's mercies over humanity and nullifies the devil's evil plans against it. Therefore, an intercessor is a spiritual warrior who relies on his faith in God and, through prayer, intercedes for the good of others. Consequently, intercession is a continuous work before the Lord. Note that none of the types of prayer we have studied so far creates an office for the person praying, except the prayer of praise and worship and the prayer of intercession. For example, the prayer of praise creates a ministry for the person praying; he is a minister of praise before God and for God. Don't confuse the minister of praise to God and in front of the people in the church. This has another status, for he can be a psalmist. The prayer of worship makes the person who prays a worshipper; this is an office before God and for God. Similarly, the prayer of intercession makes the believer who prays an intercessor. This office serves as a link between heaven and earth in the sense that the spiritual man or woman who intercedes takes the affairs of earth and delivers them to heaven so that God can act for the common good.

What makes intercessory prayer different from petitionary prayer is that in intercessory prayer, we don't pray for ourselves but for others. The fundamental principle of intercessory prayer is this: to pray to God for the interest and good of others, not for our own. This is why intercession is a spiritual service with few candidates because many focus on their own interests. "Why should I spend a long time praying on behalf of others when I also have my own issues to disclose to God?" - Someone may ask. The answer is simple: because others' is your good as well. Intercessory prayer shows our love for people and is a way to practice the Lord's commandment when he said, "You shall love your neighbor as yourself." There is no better way to show a lasting love for people than to pray for them, even when they don't deserve it. This is why Jesus said, "You are the salt of the earth; but if the salt loses its flavor, how shall it be seasoned? It is then good for nothing but to be thrown out and trampled underfoot by men" (Matthew 5:13 NKJV).

At the time, Jesus used salt as an example. This precious ingredient served many purposes that are irreplaceable even today. For example, salt serves to give flavor to food. Can you imagine a good feijoada or beef or chicken stew without salt? It would have no flavor. Salt makes the biggest difference, which is why it's a necessary ingredient in food preparation. All the other ingredients find expression, and their presence in food is heightened when salt is present. In addition, salt serves to preserve food in places where you don't have refrigerators or freezers. It serves as a preservative so that food doesn't rot. Using the allegory of salt, Jesus gave the Church an important message: we are why this world is not destroyed. We are why the devil has failed to destroy or decimate humanity completely. Why? Because some men and women spend time with and before God, interceding on behalf of humanity. And because He is the one who raised the intercessors, hears their prayers, answers their cases, and responds to them positively and actively.

Therefore, the intercessor is clothed with authority through his faith in God to undo the devil's works whenever he designs plans to thwart men's happiness on earth. Jesus said, "And unless those days were shortened, no flesh would be saved; but for the elect's sake those days will be shortened" (Matthew 24:22 NKJV). What days? Days of the great tribulation. The fact is that God works with the intercessors to preserve humanity, peace, harmony, and man's well-being. He gave the earth to man and needed man to intercede on its behalf.

Jesus Christ - humanity's greatest intercessor

Jesus Christ was and still is humanity's greatest Intercessor. His compassion for humanity and His love for souls make Him an Advocate for us. Therefore, He is our Redeemer. The text from 1 John 2:1 NKJV says, "My little children, these things I write to you, so that you may not sin. And if anyone sins, we have an Advocate with the Father, Jesus Christ the righteous." Jesus' life is an intercession for us. He died vicariously in our place so that we might live through Him. He presented his blood to the Father as the price of the eternal sacrifice he made on behalf of humanity. We are protected, washed, and sanctified by His blood. He sits with the Father, representing us as our Advocate.

The devil can no longer accuse us. Jesus made a very profound intercessory prayer that, even though it was made two thousand years ago, still involves, protects, and blesses us today. Look at his words: "I have given them Your word; and the world has hated them because they are not of the world, just as I am not of the world. I do not pray that You should take them out of the world, but that You should keep them from the evil one" (John 17:14-15 NKJV). Jesus prayed that the Father would deliver us from evil. Every day, the evil that the devil had planned for us doesn't happen because Jesus' words cover us like an insurance policy. You may think, "But where did Jesus pray for me?" See verse 20: "I do not pray for these alone, but also for those who will believe in me through their word." This part includes you and me. Glory to God! Praise God for Jesus, our Intercessor, Advocate, and Savior.

Looking at the Scriptures, we find several intercessors who excelled in this ministry. For example, Abraham interceded with God on behalf of the cities of Sodom and Gomorrah. Thus the Scripture says, "And Abraham came near and said, "Would You also destroy the righteous with the wicked? Suppose there were fifty righteous within the city; would You also destroy the place and not spare it for the fifty righteous that were in it? Far be it from You to do such a thing as this, to slay the righteous with the wicked, so that the righteous should be as the wicked; far be it from You! Shall not the Judge of all the earth do right?" (Genesis 18:23-25 NKJV). In the following verse, the Lord answered, "If I find in Sodom fifty righteous within the city, then I will spare all the place for their sakes" (verse 26). So Abraham stood in the gap in intercession until he came down to the number ten. But there were not even ten righteous persons. So God sent two angels to save Lot, his family, and everyone in his house.

God's judgment had come, and the two cities would be burned, but that wouldn't happen until Lot, and his family left. What restrained these angels from burning these cities right away? Abraham's prayer - his intercession. Lot had no idea what was happening because everything seemed like a typical day when people went to work, got married, ate and drank, did business, and had their lives going on as usual. They didn't know that danger and destruction were near. They practiced abomination before God, having inhuman, unnatural relationships. Only Lot and his two obedient daughters were saved, and the ambitious wife looked back and became a salt statue that was later burned by fire along with all the inhabitants of the two cities. Lot was saved through Abraham's intercessory ministry.

Dear reader, did you know that your family can be protected and even prosper without knowing that it is thanks to your tireless and continuous intercessory prayers for them? It's true. Abraham was an intercessor.

The other example of an intercessor was Moses. The people had rebelled and strayed from the ways of the Lord, the true God. They were worshiping idols, thus making themselves abominable before Him. God wanted to destroy them immediately, but Moses interceded for them until God changed His mind on the matter.

These were men who walked close to God and had access to the throne of heaven to intercede until God changed His mind concerning some matters and plans on earth. This just shows how powerful intercessory prayer is. These men found favor before God and interceded until his wrath abated. The Lord said to Moses, "I have seen this people, and indeed it is a stiff-necked people! Now therefore, let Me alone, that My wrath may burn hot against them and I may consume them. And I will make of you a great nation" (Exodus 32:9-10 NKJV). Moses' response was a prayer of intercession on behalf of the people before God. Thus the Scripture says, "Then Moses pleaded with the Lord his God, and said: "Lord, why does Your wrath burn hot against Your people whom You have brought out of the land of Egypt with great power and with a mighty hand? Why should the Egyptians speak, and say, 'He brought them out to harm them, to kill them in the mountains, and to consume them from the face of the earth'? Turn from Your fierce wrath, and relent from this harm to Your people. Remember Abraham, Isaac, and Israel, Your servants, to whom You swore by Your own self, and said to them, 'I will multiply your descendants as the stars of heaven; and all this land that I have spoken of I give to your descendants, and they shall inherit it forever" (Exodus 32:11-13 NKJV). Notice God's reaction: "So the Lord relented from the harm which He said He would do to His people" (verse 14).

God gives intercessors a special grace to get plans already laid out in the spiritual arena and about to take place in the physical world, to be changed completely.

Moses was also a great intercessor for his people. Notice that God had said the same thing to him as to Abraham, that he would make him a great nation: "And I will make you a great nation" (Genesis 12:2a). We read earlier, when the Lord said to Moses, "... and I will make of you a great nation" (Exodus 32:10b NKJV). Had he not been a person with love for the people, he would have accepted being made a great nation. Still, he preferred the good of the people to being a great nation himself. This is what the world needs today; selfless leaders who strive for the good of their people, stripped of greed, avarice, and selfish ambitions. Leaders who serve the people and not those who serve themselves. Leaders who create an environment where all thrive and not where many are imprisoned, threatened, or harmed. Leaders who are righteous and upright. Moses proved to be a great intercessor who used his closeness to God to plead for the good of his people. He stood at the source of inexhaustible resources and used them for the good of the people when he had a chance to get rid of the people and have his name engraved on the wall of fame.

It was this love that made him leave the palaces of Pharaoh and the lust of the magnificent Egyptian empire; to suffer with God's people for an eternal and glorious city - for eternal life. He wanted to please God and denied being called the son of Pharaoh's daughter. The use of this expression "son of Pharaoh's daughter" (Hebrews 11:24) is a gentle expression, not to say, "prince of Egypt and grandson of Pharaoh, being in the line of succession to the throne - the crown." All that mattered to him was to please the God of his parents, Abraham, Isaac, and Israel, and to gain eternal life. Eternity with God was more important than a brief moment of pleasure. He was a great intercessor.

Time would be short for me to list other intercessors who even individually changed the course of events. For example, in the case of Daniel, after reading Jeremiah's prophecy that Israel would be captive in Babylon for seventy years, he would return to his land of Israel. Did he notice that the promise wasn't fulfilled because there was a prince of darkness, the prince of Persia, who barred the people's liberation and controlled the kingdom and the oppressive government responsible for the imprisonment of God's people? Therefore, as an individual, he set out to fast for twenty-one days and seek the Lord's face for the sake of the people. Here is an excerpt from his words of prayer: "Now therefore, our God, hear the prayer of Your servant, and his supplications, and for the Lord's sake cause Your face to shine on Your sanctuary, which is desolate. O my God, incline Your ear and hear; open Your eyes and see our desolations, and the city which is called by Your name; for we do not present our supplications before You because of our righteous deeds, but because of Your great mercies. O Lord, hear! O Lord, forgive! O Lord, listen and act! Do not delay for Your own sake, my God, for Your city and Your people are called by Your name" (Daniel 9:17-19 NKJV). God responded and sent the Archangel Gabriel to give him the good news. In addition, Archangel Michael was also sent to fight on behalf of the nation of Israel to be delivered from slavery in answer to Daniel's prayer - a great intercessor.

These were all men like you and me, who had love for their people, fear, and reverence for their God and wanted His purposes to be fulfilled in their people.

Characteristics of the intercessors

1. They study the nature and attributes of God.

We have seen in the scriptures how much Moses and the others appealed to God's mercies and the fact that He is very long-suffering and compassionate. Of course, this isn't to say that the intercessor has the power to command God. Still, as a servant advocate, he pleads for his people, appealing to God's mercies. That's why Abraham called God "The Judge of all the earth." He knew who God was just by his actions.

2. Intercessors know the promises of God and use them in their prayers for God's intervention in favor of men.

This characteristic distinguishes the intercessor from those who only pray for other people. The intercessor must study and meditate on God's word to know his will and promises and to stand on God's words as one who reminds God of what he has said and asks him to fulfill his word. This is why Moses, in his intercession, invoked the fact that the Lord was the God who had made promises to Abraham, Isaac, and Israel and that God shouldn't let those promises fall because of his faithfulness; that he should keep his glory and not allow himself to be ridiculed by the Egyptians thinking that he was unable to preserve his people or unfaithful to his promises. Knowing God's word is important because God has exalted it above his name. He honors his word, and none of his promises will fall short. This is why Jesus said heaven and earth will pass away, but his words will not pass away (Matthew 24:35).

3. Intercessors are moved by love for people.

This is one of the most remarkable characteristics of an intercessor. He must love people. How can you develop a love for people? Simple: one of the first steps is to start taking an interest in the well-being of others, in their ease and prosperity. When you celebrate the success of others, you will attract success for yourself. We live in a world full of falsehood, hatred, and envy, where many don't want to see the success of others and are bothered by their brilliance. Unfortunately, this kind of behavior is creeping into churches where when a brother or sister witnesses a blessing or blessings on an ongoing basis, some feel hatred and even curse that person. They say they serve and worship God, who is love, but they don't have God's love in their hearts; therefore, they don't know God. The Holy Bible says that the love of God has been poured into our hearts by the Holy Spirit that God gave us (Romans 5:5). Practice God's love. Be happy when others witness glories and celebrate the success of others. Don't be envious or have feelings of hatred for others. Be like God, your father - God is love. Love must be lived out and demonstrated through words and actions, not just words.

4. Intercessors are moved by just causes.

These are causes that move the intercessor. For example, he doesn't take comfort in injustice; he wants to stop the devil's works. The Scripture says, "For this purpose the Son of God was manifested, that He might destroy the works of the devil" (1 John 3:8b NKJV). Suppose Jesus came to undo the devil's works, and He was the visible image of the invisible God. In that case, we, too, have a mission to destroy the works of the devil in the life of our community, district, city, state, nation, or family. We should pray that all the devil's plans will be canceled, plans of accidents, witchcraft, death, and other evils and vicissitudes.

5. Intercessors have fellowship with God.

6. Intercessors trust God and look to Him as the ultimate solution to all problems. That is why they lead people to the knowledge of God.

7. Intercessors are responsible and sensitive.

An intercessor must be sensitive to the suffering of others. He must not be cold, stingy, or mean. Being sensitive makes him easily moved by the cry of the wronged and helps him activate the anointing and connect to the Spirit very easily and quickly.

8. Intercessors are champions. They don't fight for themselves but for others and win in their favor.

9. Intercessors are persistent and persevering. They don't give up easily; they continue to pray until something happens and the situation changes.

10. Combative readiness.

Intercessors always stand in the gap on behalf of people and live connected with God at all times in their spirit. They may be studying, working, or cooking, but they carry with them the awareness of God, of his presence and power.

11. Intercessors are vigilant.

Jesus said, "Watch and pray lest you enter into temptation" (Matthew 26:41 NKJV). Paul exhorts us to watch in the spirit in prayer with all supplication for all the saints "Praying always with all prayer and supplication in the Spirit, being watchful to this end with all perseverance and supplication for all the saints" (Ephesians 6:18 NKJV). The devil prowls around like a roaring lion, seeking whom he may devour. He wants human flesh and to lead souls to hell. Since his attacks are sudden and quick and he is very cunning, you must always be alert and vigilant in the spirit as an intercessor. It's expected, for example, that God shows you in a vision or a dream of something wrong that the devil is planning; or gives you a word of knowledge in your spirit. What to do? Pray incessantly until you cancel that evil: "Father, in the name of Jesus, I stand in the breach for this brother, for this sister, and declare that the evil planned by the devil be canceled." Understand this: lack of vigilance and frequent prayer can take a heavy toll on you because the devil never stops planning his attacks; he likes to strike when you are relaxed. Job's sons were partying when the gale came and destroyed the place where they were, and they would all die. Be vigilant in prayer and cool down in this ministry. So much could have been avoided, and much tragedy could not have happened if Christians weren't so distracted by the cares of this world. Dear intercessor, don't let your guard down. Pray without ceasing.

Principles of intercessory prayer

It differs from the prayer of faith, where you cannot repeat the same request.

1. In intercessory prayer, there is room for repetition. You can keep asking for the same thing and pray until you receive it or until the situation improves, changes, and/or there is a change.

2. In the prayer of intercession, state your request based on God's promises or the knowledge of His will for the situation you are presenting. Invoke instances in the Bible where God has intervened in a person or situation identical to the case you are presenting. Believing and praying that what was done yesterday for others in that situation that had no solution, he can do today as well. If it's a case of injustice, invoke God's justice. If it's a case where the people you are praying for don't know the word of God, but you want them to come to the Lord, invoke the mercies of God.

3. In the prayer of intercession, invoke God's attributes, His qualities. For example, invoke God's power if you pray for a seriously ill family member with no medical hope. When praying, remember that God is all-powerful and nothing is impossible for him. Believe in that power that can reverse any situation.

4. Pray waiting on the Lord, trusting in his mercies and power. As Daniel said, "Incline your ear, O my God, and hear; open your eyes and look upon our desolation, and upon the city which is called by your name; for we do not present our supplications before you on account of our righteousness, but on account of your many mercies."

5. When praying, pour out your soul before the Lord.

This kind of prayer requires that you pray from your heart and not from your mind. So, in some situations, you should have to fast and pray. Daniel Fasted. Jesus said, "However, this kind does not go out except by prayer and fasting" (Matthew 17:21 NKJV). Some situations are so persistent that nothing has changed even after you have prayed. In this situation, the devil wants to test your perseverance and faith in God; he wants to test your patience, attacking and counter-attacking until you give up or lose faith. This is why Jesus asked, "Nevertheless, when the Son of Man comes, will He really find faith on the earth?" (Luke 18:8 NKJV). God will do justice. Some situations require fasting and continuous prayer.

6. Perseverance: In intercession, prayer shouldn't be superficial.

You must persevere until there is change. When Peter was imprisoned and was about to be killed by Herod, the Bible says that the church continually prayed for him to God (Acts 12:5). They probably prayed once as a prayer point for Peter's release, but it seemed that he remained imprisoned. So they decided to pray continuously until an angel of the Lord entered the prison, shone the light, touched Peter, and the shackles fell off for God. He got Peter out of jail. This was so delicate that Peter didn't even know if he would get out of there alive. So he thought what was interceding to him was a vision, not a reality. Even when Peter came to Miss Rode and she, recognizing him by his voice, claimed it was Peter, they thought it was a ghost or an angel of his. This shows how complicated the situation was that there was no other humanly thought out way to get Peter out of that maximum security jail. However, he was released because the church prayed continuously. Intercessory prayer requires persistence and perseverance; to pray continually until there is change. The church only stopped praying when Peter came. You stop intercessory prayer for a specific matter or someone when it is settled. And when resolved, make it a point of thanksgiving and pray a prayer of thanksgiving.

Present the matter clearly to God. Say to Him, "Father, this is the matter I want to resolve, and I commit it to you. This is the person I would like you to touch. Touch it, Father, in the name of Jesus. Intervene because I trust you and have no other way out but the Lord."

Our call to intercede

The text from Jeremiah 29:7 NKJV says, "And seek the peace of the city where I have caused you to be carried away captive, and pray to the Lord for it; for in its peace you will have peace."

God calls us to seek peace, that is, the well-being of our city, family, or country. To this end, we must pray and intercede. The way to seek this peace is through intercessory prayer.

Dear reader, you have been called to intercede. This is why Jesus said that we are the light of the world and the salt of the earth. Light brightens the night so that people do not walk in darkness. Light shows and points the way so that people don't lose their direction. Light takes away confusion and frustration. Salt preserves and protects. Suppose you invest in this ministry of always praying on behalf of others. In that case, God will entrust you to change the destinies of people, families and communities, and even nations. All he seeks is an intercessor.

In Acts 5, the apostles were arrested, and the church did nothing. Then, finally, the angel of the Lord came to deliver them and sent them to the temple to preach (Acts 5:17-21). They continued in this state of spiritual babies without assuming their sovereign responsibility to pray. They thought that everything would always be like this.

They trusted in the anointing the apostles carried and didn't know that the anointing wasn't greater than the Giver, God. This is a warning to ministers of the gospel: the anointing that God gives you is to minister to the people, whether to heal and deliver or preach and teach. First, however, you must trust God and pray always. Your trust must be in the Lord and not just in the fact that you have been anointed.

James was arrested in Acts 12, and the church didn't pray. Herod had him killed. How? He was a highly anointed man, healing the sick and casting out demons. Simple: it was the anointing of the Spirit doing this, enabling him for this ministry. But it needed to be covered by continuous prayer, and the church didn't do it. However, when Peter is arrested, the church wakes up to their responsibility to pray and intercede; they respond to his call to intercession. So the Scripture says,

"Peter was therefore kept in prison, but constant prayer was offered to God for him by the church" (Acts 12:5 NKJV).

The reaction from heaven was immediate. Suddenly, an angel of the Lord descended into the jail and brought Peter out. He touched his side, and the shackles fell off. Peter was saved and delivered from the enemy plans of Herod. Why? Because the church took responsibility: they prayed.

Where was the angel all the time that James was in prison until he was killed? In heaven. Why wasn't he released? Because the church didn't pray. And why was Peter released and freed from Herod's macabre plans? Because the church prayed.

I ask you, dear reader: if Jesus Christ is the same yesterday, and today, and forever, where is that angel now? Well, he is in heaven with Jesus, ready to be released to heal the family members for whom you want to intercede, to open the doors for the deliverance of your family for life, health, marriages, prosperity, and peace. For evil covenants to be canceled and for plans of death, misery, and destruction to be canceled. What should you do now? Intercede.

Remember: "So I sought for a man among them who would make a wall, and stand in the gap before Me on behalf of the land, that I should not destroy it; but I found no on" (Ezekiel 22:30 NKJV).

Be that man today. Be that woman who will cover the wall and stand in the gap. Suppose you practice the principles you have learned today. In that case, you will surely see the glory of God because Jesus Christ is the same yesterday, and today, and forever. Don't give up or weaken yourself. Instead, recognize God's power and call upon Him in prayer for this situation.

Exercise

Write here three prayer points for which you would like to see or have God's intervention:

1.

2.

3.

Write down the names of 3 people you wanted God to heal, deliver, or bless:

1.

2.

3.

Now pray using the name of Jesus. Pray with faith. Fight the good fight of faith. Then, after you see changes, turn these points into items of thanksgiving and praise for what God has done for you.

Chapter VIII
The Concordance Prayer

"Again I say to you that if two of you agree on earth concerning anything that they ask, it will be done for them by My Father in heaven" (Matthew 18:19 NKJV).

The prayer of concordance is one in which at least two people or more come into understanding and mutual faith about a specific matter they want to ask God for or want to be resolved. The principle behind this type of prayer is agreement. This is one of the most powerful types of prayer. In the spiritual arena, you can change any situation and alter any kind of event. However, this is the type of prayer the devil attacks the most because of human ambition, selfishness, and pride; it's difficult to have two people spiritually and psychologically in agreement asking God for something with one purpose and heart intention. Yet, he knows the countless advantages that unity and agreement bring to the lives of human beings.

Studying the Scriptures, we can observe that great things can be done and victories achieved when two or more people come together to pray with interconnected minds and hearts.

In the text from Deuteronomy 32:30 NKJV, we read, "How could one chase a thousand, and two put ten thousand to flight, unless their Rock had sold them, and the Lord had surrendered them?" Notice that one may chase a thousand, but two need not even chase; just by being united, they put ten thousand to flight? This just overlines unity's power when all have the same goal. We see the same thing in Proverbs 27:17 NKJV: "As iron sharpens iron, so a man sharpens the countenance of his friend." We can notice in this scripture that two irons sharpen each other and thus become sharper and more efficient. In other words, what one can do alone is less effective and efficient than what can be done together.

The story of the tower of Babel is one of the examples of how men who have the same language and are united can do it. They would have reached heaven with their tower project if God had not stopped them (Genesis 11:1-9). How did God stop them? He confused their language, and since they could no longer understand each other, they separated and gave up the project. Their project was terrible in God's eyes because they had to multiply and fill the earth and not concentrate in one place, wanting to be God and go to heaven in their way. However, we see here the potential of what unity and agreement can do.

The prayer of concordance reveals God's plan for marriage: for the union of one man and one woman.

For example, a couple united in the same purpose and intention of heart, without quarreling or conflicting interests, can make their plans, draw their dreams and present these projects to God in prayer. Proceeding this way, they can conquer many things in this life and go further than the couple that quarrels and distrusts each other. The husband doesn't trust his wife and vice versa; they only cohabit in the same house. It's common for them to attend the same church, but even so, they find themselves blocked in life. Why? Because they don't agree with each other. Can you imagine if the wheels of a car clashed: the front wheels pulled the car forward, and the back wheels pulled it backward? This car wouldn't function because the four wheels wouldn't agree about its direction and movement. No driver would be able to drive it. It will just burn fuel and make noise, standing still and immobilized in the same place.

Amos once asked, "Can two walk together, unless they are agreed?" (Amos 3:3 NKJV). Obviously not; their progress depends on the union and agreement between the two. Therefore, before they can unite, they must agree.

The psalmist said, "Behold, how good and how pleasant it is for brethren to dwell together in unity! It is like the precious oil upon the head, running down on the beard, the beard of Aaron, running down on the edge of his garments" (Psalms 133:1-2 NKJV).

Countless verses portray the power of unity and agreement. For example, the church is called the body of Christ on earth. And each of us as believers is part of this body, as members of one another and in need of one another. Jesus has given all his authority on earth to the church. That's why in verse 18 of Matthew 18 NKJV, he said, "Assuredly, I say to you, whatever you bind on earth will be bound in heaven, and whatever you loose on earth will be loosed in heaven."

Principles of sentence concordance

In our opening text, we can glean the principles of the prayer of concordance prescribed by the Lord Jesus Christ. He is the truth and has never lied to anyone. Therefore, everything He says is a reality and works for those who apply spiritual laws. Among several principles, we can note the following.

1. For a concordance prayer to be effective, at least two people must be together. It can be more than two, but two is the minimum required for this kind of prayer. Moreover, agreement here means to agree and be united in the same faith, asking for the same thing. One believes that God is able, and the other believes they unite their faith. Then, in one voice raised to heaven, they pray, and God hears and answers.

2. Two people or more must be on earth. They must have a physical body and be somewhere on earth.

3. After they agree and are together in the same place on earth, they can now ask for anything. Did you notice that Jesus didn't limit what you can ask for; he just said, "Anything you ask the Father"? So, ask God the Father, in the name of Jesus.

This type of prayer can be done by a couple, by an engaged couple, by a group of brothers or sisters in the same family, or by brothers and sisters in the same church. It can also be done by a group of friends. You must agree on what you want and specifically present it to God the Father in the name of Jesus.

The Power of the Concordance Prayer

In the text from Acts 4:29, we read about the first public persecution the apostles of Jesus Christ suffered for preaching the gospel and healing a sick man - a lame man. Their detractors threatened them not to preach or speak in the name of Jesus anymore. Faced with this threat from the religious authorities, the apostles reported the incident to the other disciples who were gathered there. Verse 24 says, "So when they heard that, they raised their voice to God with one accord and said: "Lord, You are God, who made heaven and earth and the sea, and all that is in them." Did you notice that they triggered the first principle? They agreed. The Scripture uses the expression "they raised their voice to God with one accord." From the heavens, God heard a group of disciples prayerfully speaking words out of several mouths united by a common purpose. Several hearts and words converge on a single point of prayer to God.

Verse 31 says, "And when they had prayed, the place where they were assembled together was shaken; and they were all filled with the Holy Spirit, and they spoke the word of God with boldness." Notice here that they triggered principles 2 and 3? Notice the expression, "the place where they were assembled together." It means they were somewhere on earth, gathered for a cause. The Holy Bible says, "They had prayed." This means that they asked for something in common: that God would give them boldness to preach the Good News and that He would stretch out His hand to heal, and that signs and wonders would be done in the name of the Lord Jesus. Supernaturally, God answered their prayer with power, as they were all filled with the Holy Spirit and continued to proclaim the word of God with boldness.

Beloved brother or sister, understand this: there is power in the prayer of concordance because the faith of one strengthens the other. So Paul said to the Christians in Rome, "For I long to see you, that I may impart to you some spiritual gift, so that you may be established—that is, that I may be encouraged together with you by the mutual faith both of you and me" (Romans 1:11-12 NKJV).

When two people come together and agree, mutual faith is born, and everyone is strengthened. Furthermore, anything they ask for will be granted.

Another example is the prayer of the church when Peter was arrested and was about to be killed. The Scripture says, "Peter, therefore, was kept in prison, but the church made continual prayer for him to God." How did they make this prayer? By agreeing to his release by asking the Lord for it. Where were they? Verse 12 says that he went to the house of Mary, the mother of John, whose surname was Mark, where many gathered together and prayed. Glory be to God for his prayer of concordance and immeasurable power. Peter was released from prison because this prayer caused God to send an angel to free him. Everything God heard in heaven from their mouths converged on the same prayer point: Peter must be released by God's power and intervention.

We see in the Old Testament how the people of Israel, united and in agreement together with Joshua, surrounded the fortified walls of Jericho until they fell (Joshua Chapter 6).

Imagine that something terrible is happening: a disease, a tragedy, or an attack; you can invite some close brothers and sisters in Christ and pray. You can fight wars, destruction, and the devil's plans. Also, you can pray about some projects that you want to implement. Jesus said: "This will be done for you by my Father in heaven."

Exercise

1. With your husband, wife, children, or siblings, write down what you want to have and achieve as goals on paper. Let these goals be clear and specific for you or everyone involved in the project.

2. If you are a couple, avoid arguing or fighting over petty things. Instead, agree on what you want to ask for, and forgive each other before you pray.

3. Then, with faith, put these requests to God.

Chapter IX
Prophetic Statements

"And it shall come to pass afterward that I will pour out My Spirit on all flesh; your sons and your daughters shall prophesy..." (Joel 2:28 NKJV).

An utterance is a sequence of words that constitute a sentence and a complete thought. Thus, an utterance is an actual unit of verbal communication. It is a speech or a part of a speech linked to the context in which it is made.

Prophecy is the verbal declaration of God's will concerning people, events, situations, or places. Prophecy can be for the past when it seeks what has happened, for the present when it reveals what is happening, or even for the future when it reveals, pre-announces, or foretells what will happen. For example, God anoints men to be prophets. In the office of the prophet, the man of God can go into the past, come into the present and navigate into the future by the Holy Spirit. Prophets navigate in time by the Spirit, revealing things that have happened in the past, in the present, and what will happen in the future. This is because we live in a time on earth, but in the spiritual arena, time doesn't exist. Therefore, God lives in eternity, and His years are indeterminate. For example, what has already happened in the spiritual world may be the future here on earth because it hasn't yet happened. Isaiah, speaking of the passions of Christ, described what he had seen even before it physically happened. His words are: "Surely He has borne our griefs and carried our sorrows; yet we esteemed Him stricken, smitten by God, and afflicted. But He was wounded for our transgressions, He was bruised for our iniquities; the chastisement for our peace was upon Him, and by His stripes we are healed" (Isaiah 53:4-5 NKJV).

Note the tense used here "carried our sorrows," "was wounded," "was bruised," and "was upon him." He narrates this in the past perfect tense as something that had already happened when naturally, not even Mary, who conceived Christ, had been born yet. In other words, the prophet naturally experienced the glories of a future time from a spiritual perspective. This shows that there are two real worlds: the spiritual and the physical worlds. Words spoken in the spiritual world can change things in the physical world, causing sudden changes. However, they won't be just any words. Just because someone has spoken, even though they already have the power to produce death and life for the one who likes to use language, these words can cause positive changes in the physical phenomena we see and experience. However, they must emanate from the spirit of man - from the depths of his being - inspired by the power of the Spirit. Hence, they are called "Prophetic utterances."

Prophetic utterances are those words that man's spirit picks up in the spirit world when it comes into contact with the Spirit of God. They are like fetuses or embryos in a woman's womb. They are deposits of the Holy Spirit in man's heart and go beyond his mind or imagination. They are not premeditated words but instantaneous words by the Spirit concerning a situation, person, event, or circumstance in which you may find yourself. Your spirit is enlightened and raised to a position of hearing these words deep within your heart. And when they are spoken, declared, or spoken, they cause changes in the circumstances or situation in which you find yourself. They move objects, and times, attract people, open paths, capture and bring blessings from afar to near, and suddenly things change for the better. Victory is granted, and God's light begins to shine.

Many Christians never get to experience this dimension because they have never been taught that this exists or have never bothered to study the Scriptures for themselves and discover these things. Understand this: everything you see can be changed. That hill, those barriers that you see, can all be removed from the path. And you can open your way to constant success and victory, regardless of the contrary situation you see. Furthermore, prophetic utterances can bring with them direction, guidance for your life and business, choices to make, and the right decisions to make. When this happens, it's normal for the Holy Spirit to take possession of your mind. You may have thoughts you know are unnatural, not things you envisioned thinking or speaking. Also, you may find yourself saying things that didn't come to be processed in your mind but came directly out of the spirit into your mouth. The constant and frequent involvement of the prophets and men of God immersed in the Spirit of God made it possible for the Scriptures to be written. The Holy Bible says, "Knowing this first, that no prophecy of Scripture is of any private interpretation, for prophecy never came by the will of man, but holy men of God spoke as they were moved by the Holy Spirit" (2 Peter 1:20-21 NKJV). And what they spoke was recorded as Holy Scripture. In practice, they were possessed by the Holy Spirit, surrendered all their mental and human faculties to the service of God's kingdom, and were inspired to speak words directly from the chambers of God's throne.

Your spirit must be activated and receptive to obtain or grasp these words. These are the occurrences of the encounter between the Holy Spirit and the spirit of man.

Let's see: in the text from Acts, Chapter 19:5-6, we read about the experience of twelve men who had been disciples of John. Something happened when Paul laid his hands on them, and the Holy Spirit descended on them. They also had this experience - prophetic utterances. Luke says, "When they heard this, they were baptized in the name of the Lord Jesus. And when Paul had laid hands on them, the Holy Spirit came upon them, and they spoke with tongues and prophesied." This prophesying doesn't mean that they became prophets but were enabled and inspired to produce prophetic utterances. These utterances render glory to God and magnify Him above all circumstances, situations, and people. Prophetic utterances establish God's will in a given situation. They are powerful because it's as if God Himself is speaking and creating things.

You can create things and call them into existence through prophetic utterances. Scripture states that God calls what is not as though it were. Therefore, prophetic words or utterances can give life where there was not and produce things that did not exist. Scripture attests, "...God, who gives life to the dead and calls those things which do not exist as though they did" (Romans 4:17b NKJV).

For example, with prophetic utterances, you can call employment and doors open for work. In addition, you can decree victory over a particular situation and see it resolved. You can even open doors of prosperity and health through them. At this level, everything you say will happen as if it were God Himself speaking. Here, you will be using the image and likeness of God to act like Him, speaking things, and they happen. This is what we call "the believer's prophetic ministry." It doesn't make him a prophet in the capacity or office of a prophet. Still, it puts him in a position where he gets to eat the fruits of his lips, having and seeing what he has said and enjoying what he has prophesied. This weapon is mighty because, with prophetic utterances, you can nip the evil in the bud, undo the devil's works, annul demonic covenants, and cancel the effect of sorcery and curses; all this just by speaking words inspired and recharged by God. Prophetic decrees are used in spiritual battles against the spiritual hosts of wickedness in heavenly places. Paul said, "And take the helmet of salvation, and the sword of the Spirit, which is the word of God" (Ephesians 6:17 NKJV). These words become a sword in your mouth and, empowered by the Holy Spirit, go on to cut down all evil and destroy all the works of the devil.

Jesus lived in constant communion with the Spirit, so his words came out with power, and whatever he said came to pass. His words caused a fig tree to wither, calmed storms and waves, multiplied bread and fish, and exercised dominion over the spiritual forces of darkness and nature. So it was no accident that early in his ministry, he took hold of the words revealed to Isaiah, "The Spirit of the Lord is upon me..." (Isaiah 61:1 NKJV).

This is why Joel said that in the last days, God would pour out of his Spirit on all flesh, and the sons and daughters would prophesy. We are sons of prophecy; we are the fruit of words. Great men and women are made of words - prophetic words. They change times and circumstances and create an environment that didn't exist before, an environment conducive to their health and prosperity, even in a world where misery and the devil ravage. O glory! If you could understand this and put it into practice, your life would never be the same.

Look at Job 22:27-28 NKJV: "You will make your prayer to Him, He will hear you, and you will pay your vows. You will also declare a thing, and it will be established for you; so light will shine on your ways."

The word "declare," employed here, means "to speak, issue an utterance," meaning you will speak about some business or matter. What you say will stand firm in the spirit, and the light will shine in the physical arena. As a result, you will get what you have said in words given by the Spirit of God. With this tool, you will never be at a disadvantage but always on top, as long as you remain connected to the source of life - to the Spirit of God. This is why verses 29-30 say, "When they cast you down, and you say, 'Exaltation will come!' Then He will save the humble person. He will even deliver one who is not innocent; yes, he will be delivered by the purity of your hands."

Assuming you have lost a job or been demoted, you can prophesy your own promotion and reverse the stitch-up. Suppose the doctor said you are threatened by miscarriage and will lose your pregnancy. In that case, you can say, "In the name of Jesus, I reverse this and declare that my fetus is fine and I will have a healthy delivery."

Many believers have the Holy Spirit, but their lives are not changed because they have never taken advantage of the Spirit's ministry. They have Him dormant and inactive in them. But He came to enable and empower us to live a supernaturally natural life. So you can have what you say as long as you say it in faith and under the inspiration of the Holy Spirit.

How to obtain prophetic statements and enact them?

First of all, prepare your spirit. Don't let anything disturb you. Remember the words of Jesus, "Peace I leave with you, My peace I give to you; not as the world gives do I give to you. Let not your heart be troubled, neither let it be afraid" (John 14:27b NKJV). Your heart should be at peace and relaxed, and your mind should also be calm and baring all contrary thoughts. God speaks in the peace of our spirit.

Secondly: activate your spirit. Activating your spirit is like turning on a light switch and the bulb lighting up; if you turn it off, the bulb goes out. Between the light of God's glory in your life and the frustration due to darkness is your spirit - your inner man. If he is consciously connected to the Spirit of God, he will see the glory of God as Stephen saw the glory of God when others saw only blue or cloudy skies. If your spirit is disconnected from the spiritual world, from God, you will see in the flesh and be frustrated. This is why Paul exhorted us to set our minds on the things above and not on the things on the earth (Colossians 3:1-2). Likewise, Isaiah directed, "You will keep him in perfect peace, whose mind is stayed on You, because he trusts in You" (Isaiah 26:3 NKJV). Activating your spirit is like turning on or running an electric current generator; it only produces the electric current when it's on, then the lamps come on, and the rest of the stereo and appliances start working. Many have the Generator - the Holy Spirit, but it's turned off, inactive.

How to activate your spirit

Well, practice the prayers of praise and worship. Also, practice the prayers of thanksgiving. I have already taught this in previous chapters, so you must do a little revision. Understand that the prophetic utterances are fruit, that is, they are the culmination of the spiritual activities produced by the prayer of praise and worship by the prayer of thanksgiving. God wants us to praise and worship him because when praise goes up, glory comes down. And that enables man's spirit to hear God's voice. For example, God is talking to you now. He's saying something right now, but you're probably not hearing it because your spirit is not activated. So to catch those words, you must spend time with God in praise and worship.

In the book of 2 Kings 3:15, Elisha is asked to give direction to the kings of Israel and Judah about the decision they wanted to make: to go into battle because they would win; or not to go because the Lord would deliver them into the hands of their enemies. Elisha was a prophet; he was hearing from God. However, he wasn't always listening to God. He needed to activate his spirit to open his spiritual antennae to pick up God's signal, hear his word, and decode the message. He needed to activate his spirit to get the prophetic utterances. He couldn't speak from his mind. His spirit had its own way of activating itself that always worked for him. That's why he said, "But now bring me a musician." Then it happened, when the musician played, that the hand of the Lord came upon him. And he said, "Thus says the Lord: 'Make this valley full of ditches.' For thus says the Lord: 'You shall not see wind, nor shall you see rain; yet that valley shall be filled with water, so that you, your cattle, and your animals may drink." He went ahead and gave them clear instructions on how to face or approach the battle; he gave them strategies. And they succeeded. Where were those words that Elisha spoke? In the spirit, He needed to connect his spirit to hear, receive, and enunciate them to materialize. They don't fail because they come from the Spirit.

Third:

You can spend time with God's word in your mind and your heart, meditating on it. And God will give the spoken words.

Fourth:

Praying in tongues can also help you activate the spirit and catch the prophetic utterances. We have learned about praying in tongues, and I advise you to review the chapter.

My advice to you is this: wait on the Lord with an open heart and have a pad and a ballpoint pen to write or a tape recorder to record what God will say to you because these words are essential. They come from the throne of God, and once they are established through your mouth, they will come to pass.

Well, now it's time to put what you have learned into practice.

May God bless you.

Conclusion
Final notes to remember

In this book, we have substantially dealt with the concept of prayer, its importance to the believer, and how to pray correctly to obtain results. In addition, we have studied the types of prayer and the principles that govern them so that they are effective and productive. So, having read this work divided into four parts, I hope its revelations have blessed you. It contains this great privilege God has granted to man: the privilege of praying. And with it comes one of the most incredible powers - the power to effect change in adverse circumstances, alter the course of events, and strengthen the fulfillment of God's will on earth. As Jesus taught, "Your kingdom come. Your will be done on earth as it is in heaven" (Matthew 6:10 NKJV).

Prayer makes this possible, for whenever man prays, heaven reacts. Therefore, prayer is fundamental and indispensable in the believer's life, for it contributes to his spiritual growth and helps him maintain and develop his communion with God.

From Part I - The Concept of Prayer

In part I, we understood that prayer is communion with God, that is, communication with God. However, beyond this laconic and general definition, I explained that to pray is to give God legal permission to intervene in the affairs of the earth. This puts prayer in a crucial position. Think about it: how could man, created in the image and likeness of God, being on earth, in a material, sensory and visible world, be able to talk to God, who is Spirit, who created the whole universe, without prayer being that channel of connection? This is why I explained that just as an embryo is connected to its mother's placenta through the navel, from which it is sustained, prayer is likewise man's spiritual navel that always connects him to God on earth. In Matthew 18:19 NKJV, Jesus stated, "Again I say to you that if two of you agree on earth concerning anything that they ask, it will be done for them by My Father in heaven."

Did you notice the expression "on earth?" This means that while we are on earth, we need to always make contact with our home country - the kingdom of heaven. The kingdom that makes us ambassadors for Christ, representing his interests here on earth. That is why God has given man dominion over all the earth. No spirit devoid of a physical body has legality on earth unless it comes and acts in partnership or covenant with a human being (who has a physical body). Therefore, God made a covenant - a pact- with the children of Israel that Moses mediated based on the blood of sheep and lambs. Later, for these last days, the same God sent his only begotten Son, Jesus Christ, who made a new covenant based on his own blood to restore the broken fellowship between God and man because of sin.

For this reason, the name of Jesus has been given to us to use in prayer and spiritual battles. Furthermore, we have been given this name so that we may live through it. As the Scripture says, "And whatever you do in deed or word, do all in the name of the Lord Jesus" (Colossians 3:17 NKJV).

The earth belongs to the Lord, but He has given it to man. Therefore, even demons operate based on blood covenants made by men - giving them the legality to destroy families and homes, disrupt social order, and torment human lives. Nevertheless, we have power over the devil and his demons through the blood and name of Jesus Christ (Revelation 12:11).

Because the earth has been given to man, spiritual intervention by the kingdom of heaven will require prayer. Thus, when you pray through this procedure, you give God the legal right to intervene in the affairs of the earth, for without prayer, God will not intervene. We see this in Acts 12 when James is arrested and later killed by the edge of the sword. The Church knew that he was a man of God, anointed, and one of the spiritual leaders and pillars of the early Church. However, they were still spiritual babies and had not yet understood prayer's need, responsibility, and importance. They expected God to do something without them giving Him legal permission. Unfortunately, there was no heavenly intervention, and James was killed, to the delight of the detractors of the Church. Satan went one step further and had the apostle Peter, James' ministerial colleague, arrested and put under the same conditions: he locked him up in prison, bound with chains, and garrisoned by about sixteen armed soldiers. He expected to present him to the Jews the next day to be killed.

The news of this dreadful Herodian plan reached the ears of the Church, who, from a human point of view, could do nothing, for Herod was a king, and his word was a sentence. However, they remembered that they had a heavenly Father, a God about whom they had seized, and a mighty name called Jesus. So they awakened to their sovereign responsibility to pray. So they gathered at the house of a woman by the name of Mary, the mother of John Mark, and prayed without ceasing. God heard the prayer, released just one angel who brought light into the prison, touched Peter on the side, and the chains fell off for him. Then the angel of the Lord brought him out of prison, and the iron gate of the prison also opened by itself. What happened? Peter was released, and King Herod was killed by the same angel who had released Peter. What drew the ministry of this angel to come down to Peter's rescue? The Prayer of the Church. The same angel was with Jesus in heaven but wasn't released when James was arrested because the Church didn't pray.

To this day, there are angels of God: angels of healing, angels of deliverance, angels of prosperity, and the angels of protection that can be released to help humans, deliver our family members, open doors of prosperity, and rescue us in dead-end situations. All this when we pray. We can therefore claim that prayer moves the heavens and the armies of God to patrol the earth, protect, heal and deliver humans when they pray. As an example, we find in the Bible instances where angels bring food to humans, as in the case of Elijah; provision of water - as in the case of Hagar when the Lord opened her eyes to see the well in the desert; promotion - as in the case of Jacob when the angel of the Lord changed his name to Israel. In addition, we have examples of protection, as in the case of Lot, and deliverance, as in Peter.

Angels fought against enemy armies in defense of Israel when King Hezekiah and the prophet Isaiah prayed. In the ministry of Jesus, they healed many people just on the command of a word of command from the mouth of the Lord. The Scriptures reveal instances when angels brought judgment and delivered justice against tyrannical kings, as in the case of Herod, or when an angel of the Lord prevented Balaam, the prophet, from cursing God's people - the people of Israel. Angels stopped the mouths of lions, as in the case of Daniel, and rescued many people. This ministry of angels can be released to you, dear reader, and any member of the body of Christ and citizen of the kingdom of heaven when you pray. This is why prayer is indispensable.

From Part II - The Importance of Prayer

In part II, we saw the importance of prayer and its benefits for humanity on earth. There are two main notes that I would like the reader to retain in this part:

First:

The importance of prayer goes beyond the visible material things and benefits that God can give when we pray. The most significant importance of prayer lies in its impact on man's spirit. Something happens in our spirit whenever we pray that is more important than what we can physically receive. In prayer, there is contact between the Holy Spirit and the spirit of man. In this contact, there is a transfer of power and glory. We are recharged in our spirit with power, and that anointing passes into our mind and body. We become entirely submerged in the power and glory of God as if a ball of light covered us on all sides. Because of this, anything we touch is blessed and what we say happens. Through hands, we transfer power, and through words, we create things. This is why Jesus said, "And these signs will follow those who believe: In My name they will cast out demons; they will speak with new tongues; they will take up serpents; and if they drink anything deadly, it will by no means hurt them; they will lay hands on the sick, and they will recover" (Mark 16:17-18 NKJV). Did you notice that He didn't say that they "shall pray for the sick and they shall recover," but that they "will lay hands on the sick and they will recover?" Why just lay hands on them? Because the believer, the disciple of Jesus Christ, is a carrier of God's glory, this glory and anointing is activated when we pray. Therefore, as a Christian, it's vital that you spend qualitative and quantitative time with God in prayer. This was the greatest secret of Jesus Christ - communion with the Father. He would wake up early when it was still dark, go to a deserted place and pray there. And when he left that place of prayer, he would cast out demons and heal the sick in the twinkling of an eye because of his glory.

Therefore, prayer serves as a spiritual recharging process for the minister of the gospel and the believer in general. One must always refuel oneself like the fuel tank of a car that is going to travel long distances.

Second:

The several benefits of prayer make it an indispensable principle in the life of humans on earth. For example, prayer prevents the devil from decimating all humanity on the face of the earth. Of the numerous latent benefits of prayer, here are some to retain:

1. Prayer strengthens our communion with God;

2. Prayer increases our spiritual sensitivity;

3. Prayer helps cancel out evil in the spiritual arena;

4. Prayer reinforces God's will on earth and helps fulfill his promises and prophecies.

From Part III - Principles for effective prayer in the New Testament

In part III, I explained all about the principles of prayer and how to pray to receive answers from God. We concluded that God desires that we pray, and it's his will that we receive what we ask of him. First, however, we must pray according to his will. To pray according to his will is to pray according to the prescription of his word, and it doesn't fail, for God has exalted it above his name. And what does God's word prescribe to us about how to pray? Well, we must realize our need for God - we need Him. There is no way to pray without this need, this thirst and hunger for God because we depend on Him. To do this, we have to pray from our hearts. Prayer must not come from the mind but from the heart. Already God looks at the heart: it depends on Him for everything and trusts Him.

Moreover, in the New Testament, we are recommended to pray in the name of Jesus Christ. He Himself said: "Most assuredly, I say to you, whatever you ask the Father in My name He will give you" (John 16:23 NKJV). Jesus gives us this total assurance that by praying and using his name, "In the name of Jesus," the request will be stamped and authenticated for a postponement to the believer. Allied with this, we must pray to the Father, for God is our Father by virtue of our faith in Jesus Christ. So you pray, "Father, in the name of Jesus..." Pray in faith, expecting answers. When you pray, forgive if you have hurt someone. And after you have prayed, give thanks as if you have received what you asked for.

From Part IV – Types of Prayer

In part IV, I taught about the types of prayer you can use to help yourself in any situation in life. For every moment of your life and stage, there is an appropriate type of prayer, whether to ask, give thanks, praise, and worship, or pray on behalf of others. We learn all this to activate your spirit so that you hear God's voice. For example, we learn about the prayer of petition and its principles. The prayer of thanksgiving, the prayer of faith, the prayer of praise and worship, the prayer in tongues, intercessory prayer, the prayer of consultation, and the prayer of concordance.

In the prayer of petition, as the name implies, we ask for anything, even to supply our needs. However, you need to be objective and specific in what you are asking for and do it following God's word. You need to ask in faith and then give thanks. By giving thanks, what you have asked for becomes yours and materializes.

The fundamental principle in the prayer of faith is to believe that God has heard you and answered you whenever you pray. Therefore, you must not repeat the same thing over and over again. On the contrary, you must stand on God's word like Mount Zion and be steadfast. This is because God answers to faith and not to tears.

In the prayer of thanksgiving, we exalt God's deeds in our lives, specifying in detail what He has done for us and why we thank Him.

In the prayer of praise and worship, the principle is that we want to exalt God's attributes and qualities above people, events, and circumstances. God is the center of everything, omnipotent, omniscient, invincible, and unchanging. Therefore, praise leads to worship, and worship leads to surrender to the Lord. In this way, we become immersed in Him and filled with the Holy Spirit, pleasing Him in everything.

In the prayer in tongues, We speak with God and give signs to the angelic spirit world using spiritual tongues, given by the Holy Spirit to believers who have been born again in Christ. They are the tongues of the new creation. With them, we pray, ask, praise, and magnify God. Furthermore, when we pray in tongues, we are edified and recharged in our spirit. Furthermore, this is how we can ask for everything we want without our minds interfering in the process, limiting the scope of what we should touch in prayer. This is why Paul said, "For if I pray in a tongue, my spirit prays, but my understanding is unfruitful" (1 Corinthians 14:14 NKJV).

Looking at the cost-benefits between praying with our mind from the intelligible language we understand and praying with the spirit (praying in tongues), the best order is: pray with the spirit first and then pray with the understanding; sing with the spirit and then sing with the understanding (verse 15). Paul used this order so much that he even stated, "I thank my God I speak with tongues more than you all" (verse 18). For this reason, he was always anointed so that even his handkerchiefs and aprons absorbed the anointing emanating from him, healed the sick, and cast out demons. Therefore, it is essential to pray in tongues because it is the best way to have the spirit pray in a sanctified language - the language of angels, the language of the new creation.

In addition, we learn about the **prayer of consultation.** This is where the petitioner wants to seek or know God's direction on some matter in which he must make a decision or choice. Here we seek God's will and guidance on what direction to take so we will succeed in what we want to undertake. Consultation prayer can also be done to make an inquiry in the spirit, that is, a probing to see what doors were opened that gave the devil the legality to continue to attack your life or afflict your family, even after Jesus defeated him on Calvary's Cross two thousand years ago. So we want here to identify the door through which he has entered or has entered so that he is cast out. The door closed, so we no longer have these recurring presences and attacks.

We also learn about **intercessory prayer**. In this kind of prayer, the goal is to pray on behalf of other people for God's intervention for their own good; that's why it is called intercession. Intercession is one of the noblest ministries because it puts the intercessor in the breach as a point and channel of blessings for others. The fundamental principle for this prayer is that the intercessor must have a love for people, faith in God, and be moved by just causes and compassion for the suffering and afflicted.

Finally, **a prayer of concordance** is one in which at least two people enter into understanding and mutual faith about a specific matter they want to ask God for or want to be resolved. The principle behind this type of prayer is agreement. This is one of the most powerful types of prayer. You can change any situation and alter any kind of event in the spiritual arena. However, for the prayer of agreement to be effective, at least two people must be gathered together.

This is the kind of prayer with which two or more believers can change adverse circumstances on earth, making a positive and glorious impact, and at the same time, destroy the works of the devil. Looking at the world, for example, we see and hear about the destructions, cries, and sorrows caused by the devil on individuals, families, and nations. However, if only two or more brothers united in the same faith, being on earth and praying in agreement, the devil's plans would always be foiled.

Spend time with God
The prophetic statements

One of the most excellent benefits of spending time with God in prayer is that your spirit - your inner man will become sensitive to the things of the Spirit of God, to the spirit world. Prayer increases our spiritual sensitivity and helps to materialize God's plans on earth. It helps cancel out evil in the spiritual arena. So when you pray, your spirit comes into contact with the Spirit of God, and there is a transfer of energy, life, power, and glory. And as an essential benefit also, you can receive prophetic utterances. Prophetic utterances are words your spirit will pick up, like an antenna picks up signals or magnetic waves. Light will shine on your paths as you pick up these words of God's Spirit and utter them or enunciate them. Victory happens, and evil is defeated. With these prophetic decrees, you can create your desired future through words. Words are charged and imbued with power that, when spoken, whatever you say comes to pass in the physical world.

Having learned all these concepts, principles, and types of prayer, it is time to put them to work. Prayer is work. Now, put your faith into practice and start praying; your life will never be the same.

I hope you have been incredibly blessed by the teachings and revelations you have received in this book. Pray always. Pray when all seems not well, and pray when all is well. Pray at all times. Jesus said, "Watch and pray lest you enter into temptation" (Matthew 26:41 NKJV). A slip in prayer can cost you dearly because the devil doesn't like hot believers and prayer increases your spiritual fire. Don't let the flame of God's fire in you go out. Activate the gift of God that is in your life by praying. Remember: whatever we want from God, we ask for it in prayer, and whatever we have, we keep it through prayer. It's indispensable for our lives while we are in this world. Therefore, prayer is a spiritual umbilical cord for the believer. God wants to hear your prayers and answer them. Pray now.

May the grace of the Lord Jesus Christ be with your spirit.

About the author

Onório Cutane

He is an apostle, teacher, and prophet with an apostolic-prophetic calling. He is a humble servant of God with a dynamic ministry of teaching, healing, and deliverance that has helped many people to be delivered from the power of darkness and converted to the kingdom of light and love.

Thousands of people have been blessed and now experience a victorious life through the anointed word he teaches. Founder and president of the Nations for Christ Ministries Church, the apostle is a writer, songwriter, and televangelist. He has conducted massive evangelistic crusades called "Heavenly Atmosphere" that have carried the manifested presence of the Holy Spirit wherever he ministers. Apostle Onório Cutane's mandate is to expand the kingdom of Heaven and prepare the Church for the second coming of Jesus.

In late 2019, Apostle Onório Cutane pioneered one of the first Evangelical television stations in Mozambique. It's called "KINGDOM TV," and it has been bringing the Good News of the kingdom of God and the power of God to many in Mozambique.

Apostle Onório's ministry is international, with churches in Africa, Europe, Brazil, and the United States.

He is the author of the best-seller "The Model Father," which has brought Divine healing to many.

Dedication

To my Lord and Savior, Jesus Christ, in whose name we have access to God the Father. I'm grateful for the grace to serve him.

To God's children worldwide, who pray day and night, seeking God's intervention and justice in their afflictions. May this book be helpful to you in your journey with God here on earth.

Specifically to you, dear reader, who purchased and read this book. May it help strengthen your communion with God and live victoriously. May you use it well.

Acknowledgments

To God the Father for his eternal and unconditional love for me and the call to the ministry;

To the precious Holy Spirit for the revelations and for being my ever-present helper, without whom this book would not have been a reality;

To the beloved Cutane family, for their continuous and unconditional support.

To my children, Prince and Esther, for always entertaining me; may oil never be lacking on their heads.

Other Books by apostle Onório Cutane

1.   **Do Not Break the Wall:** Secrets to Living under Divine Protection

2.   **God's Medicine:** How to Receive and Maintain Divine Healing

3.   **Grace to Reign:** Principles to Living in God's Grace and Reigning in Life

4.   **The Lordship of Jesus and the Kingdom of Heaven**: How to Live above the circumstances of the world

5.   **The Good Fight of Faith:** How to Fight and win: secrets of constant victories in spiritual battles

6.   **The Revelation of Jesus Christ:** Who is Jesus Christ? Identity, Mission, and Mandate

7.   **The Four Basic Ministries of the Believer:** Secrets to greatness in the kingdom of God

8.   **The Model Father:** 11 essential responsibilities of a father

9.   **The Spiritual World:** Understanding how Spiritual Forces dictate the Life of Humans on Earth

10.   **The Four Essential Habits of the new Creation in Christ:** How to program your spirit for the glorious life

Readers's Testimonials

SHARE YOUR TESTIMONY WITH US!

1.   If you have been blessed through the teachings in this book and would like to share your testimony with us, write to us at: testemunho@ogcpublications.com

2.   If you want to know more about Apostle Onório Cutane's literary works, visit our digital bookstore to access more works by Apostle Onório Cutane through: www.ogcpublications.com

3.   If you want to know more about the ministry of Apostle Onório Cutane, go to: www.onoriocutane.org

4.   Watch the online services and the lives of the ministrations and teaching and prayer sessions of the man of God, Apostle Onório Cutane, through: www.kingdom24.tv

Thank you for purchasing and reading this book.

www.ingramcontent.com/pod-product-compliance
Lightning Source LLC
Chambersburg PA
CBHW051141120626
46547CB00012B/892